ROUTLEDGE LIBRARY EDITIONS: WILLIAM BLAKE

Volume 8

WILLIAM BLAKE'S EPIC

WILLIAM BLAKE'S EPIC
Imagination Unbound

JOANNE WITKE

LONDON AND NEW YORK

First published in 1986 by Croom Helm Ltd

This edition first published in 2016
by Routledge
2 Park Square, Milton Park, Abingdon, Oxon OX14 4RN

and by Routledge
711 Third Avenue, New York, NY 10017

Routledge is an imprint of the Taylor & Francis Group, an informa business

© 1986 Joanne Witke

All rights reserved. No part of this book may be reprinted or reproduced or utilised in any form or by any electronic, mechanical, or other means, now known or hereafter invented, including photocopying and recording, or in any information storage or retrieval system, without permission in writing from the publishers.

Trademark notice: Product or corporate names may be trademarks or registered trademarks, and are used only for identification and explanation without intent to infringe.

British Library Cataloguing in Publication Data
A catalogue record for this book is available from the British Library

ISBN: 978-1-138-93813-7 (Set)
ISBN: 978-1-315-67509-1 (Set) (ebk)
ISBN: 978-1-138-93920-2 (Volume 8) (hbk)
ISBN: 978-1-138-93929-5 (Volume 8) (pbk)
ISBN: 978-1-315-67510-7 (Volume 8) (ebk)

Publisher's Note
The publisher has gone to great lengths to ensure the quality of this reprint but points out that some imperfections in the original copies may be apparent.

Disclaimer
The publisher has made every effort to trace copyright holders and would welcome correspondence from those they have been unable to trace.

WILLIAM BLAKE'S EPIC: Imagination Unbound

Joanne Witke

Ph.D., 1974
English Language and Literature
University of California
Berkeley,
California, U.S.A.

CROOM HELM
London & Sydney

© 1986 Joanne Witke
Croom Helm Ltd, Provident House, Burrell Row,
Beckenham, Kent BR3 1AT
Croom Helm Australia Pty Ltd, Suite 4, 6th Floor,
64-76 Kippax Street, Surry Hills, NSW 2010, Australia

British Library Cataloguing in Publication Data

Witke, Joanne
   William Blake's epic: imagination unbound.
   1. Blake, William, *1757-1827*. Jerusalem
   I. Title
   821'.7   PR4144.J43
   ISBN 0-7099-3658-3

Printed and bound in Great Britain by
Mackays of Chatham Ltd

CONTENTS

LIST OF ILLUSTRATIONS v

PREFATORY NOTE vii

PART ONE	PROLOGUE: PLATO, BERKELEY, AND BLAKE	1
PART TWO	BLAKE AS ARTIST	17
PART THREE	ATTACKS UPON JERUSALEM	35
PART FOUR	THE SATANIC TRIUMVIRATE	59
PART FIVE	DEFENDERS OF JERUSALEM	77
PART SIX	ENCOUNTERS WITH THE ENEMY	99
PART SEVEN	GRIM WAR CONTINUES	139
PART EIGHT	JERUSALEM RESTORED	177
PART NINE	EPILOGUE	217

INDEX 225

*In memory of
Sir Geoffrey Keynes
A man of the greatest skill
in restoring the body
of Blake's writings*

LIST OF ILLUSTRATIONS

1. *The Meeting of a Family in Heaven*   51
2. *Jerusalem* 25   57
3. *Jerusalem* 26   69
4. *Jerusalem* 1   78
5. *Jerusalem* 6   79
6. *Jerusalem* 28   101
7. *Jerusalem* 32   109
8. *Jerusalem* 46   131
9. *Jerusalem* 50   136
10. *Jerusalem* 51   137
11. *Jerusalem* 53   141
12. *Jerusalem* 57   148
13. *Jerusalem* 63   156
14. *Jerusalem* 69   166
15. *Jerusalem* 75   174
16. *Jerusalem* 76   176
17. *Jerusalem* 78   181
18. *Jerusalem* 81   187
19. *Jerusalem* 97   208
20. *Jerusalem* 99   213
21. *Jerusalem* 100   215

PREFATORY NOTE

Blake's defense of the human imagination and his epic *Jerusalem* are one and the same. To elucidate the aesthetic meaning, this critical study takes as its point of reference the poem's stated purpose, to "Create a System." The problem to be solved here is fundamentally philosophical though the formal categories are literary. Further, because the creation of this system is coterminous with epic action, the philosophical substance of *Jerusalem* is inextricably bound to its structure: an adequate discussion of one necessarily entails the other. Hence the present inquiry has a threefold objective: discover *Jerusalem*'s philosophical nucleus, simultaneously show how this poem works as an epic, and, not least important, reveal the principles underlying Blake's art.

So that readers may readily follow the sequence of events involved in creating the new system, the argument will proceed serially by plate, according to the pagination of copy D,[1] and topologically within each plate, delineating the philosophical facts contextually, explicating them in terms of the poem's imagery and narrative, and then relating these facts to biblical parallels and literary allusions. It is not the intent, however, to deal with all the ideas, images and allusions Blake introduces to elaborate the critical situation he presents in this epic. Since he views the contemporary crisis and its solution analogically, he

---

[1] Of the five extant copies of *Jerusalem* and two different arrangements of plates (A,C,F and D,E), "Copy D is... the later of the two," G.E. Bentley, Jr., *William Blake's Writings,* 2 vols. (Oxford, 1978), vol.1, p.735. David V. Erdman, *Poetry and Prose of William Blake* (New York, 1970), observes the earlier order. Essentially, the difference involves a block of four plates in Chapter 2: see Part Six, n.8 of the present study.

enters into many areas of human activity and alludes to a wide range of works, both ancient and modern. Thus the present study in no way implies that it exhausts the meanings of *Jerusalem*, or that it says everything which needs to be said about it as a poem. Nor does this study deal with political and psychological issues, already extensively explored by critics.[2] To avoid complicating an already complex subject, works, allusions and issues not directly related to the poem's philosophical import and general structure will not be discussed or perhaps not even indicated except where such additional information clarifies the point under consideration. The attention throughout is directed primarily towards explicating the philosophical principles of a system the protagonist announces he must create, how, and why he creates it.

As it is not the province of this study to explain all the imagery or discuss all theoretical perspectives, or recapitulate all interpretive commentaries, so it is not the function to criticize the philosophical systems Blake rejects or accepts. Rather, the main design is to show how he conceives, modifies and incorporates certain principles and their consequences to fashion an epic wherein he opposes the prevailing aesthetic system and constructs his own system defining the nature of art and the creative process. Professor Thomas Frosh has expressed the need of "a fuller account than anyone has yet supplied of Blake... who asked us to enter into his images and who also had to create a system to avoid enslavement" [SIR (Winter 1977), p.127]. It is hoped the present work in some measure answers that need by revealing the philosophical principles of Blake's system, allowing us to enter more fully into his images at a fundamental level in the context of his times.

The illustrations are reproduced by kind permission of the Houghton Library, Harvard University, and The Huntington Library. For unfailing encouragement and support I am indebted to my sister Jean Kyle.

Joanne Witke

Olympia, Washington

---

[2] E.g., David V. Erdman, *Blake: Prophet Against Empire* (Princeton, 1969); Harold Bloom, *Blake's Apocalypse* (New York, 1965); Thomas R. Frosh, *The Awakening of Albion: The Renovation of the Body in the Poetry of William Blake* (Ithaca, 1974).

PART ONE

PROLOGUE

At the end of his journey in *The Marriage of Heaven and Hell,* the poet remarks to his guide: "All that we saw was owing to your metaphysics."[1] In this passage William Blake conveys an important fact: there is a definite relationship between one's interpretation of events and the philosophy one accepts. This is the situation also in the arts if the artist is more than a craftsman in some applied art. How a poet, a painter, or any artist conceives his subject and how he communicates it depend on the metaphysical and epistemological principles of the system he embraces.[2] Although poems, paintings, and other artifacts do not bear their entire justification on these principles, nonetheless, every serious artist adopts, often implicitly, some general conceptions upon which his individual works rest. To reveal the assumptions ineluctably woven into an artist's imaginative productions so that a wide audience may understand and thus take pleasure in them is in large part the responsibility of philosophic critics.

We know that Blake was well read in philosophy. He mentions Paracelsus and Behmen (Boehme); he comments, often at length, upon the doctrines of Pythagoras, Plato, Aristotle, Epicurus, Bacon, Newton, Locke, and Swedenborg. On the basis of Platonic elements occurring in Blake's thought, Platonism has been extensively applied

---

[1] Blake, *Complete Writings,* ed. Geoffrey Keynes (Oxford, 1971), p.156. All quotations follow exactly the spelling and punctuation of this edition

[2] In "Blake and the Artistic Machine: An essay in Decorum and Technology," (PMLA, vol. 92, nr. 5, October 1977), pp.903-927, Morris Eaves discusses the technological developments in the practice of art; he expands these ideas in *William Blake's Theory of Art* (Princeton, 1982), which he draws out from "Blake's idea of artistic line," p.10.

by critics to his works and has served as the major philosophical frame for them.[3] But Blake's concept of form integral to his imaginative creations does not fit into Plato's philosophy. Though Plato and Blake both hold that reality consists in forms, Plato's forms differ radically from Blake's in substance and in manner of knowing them. Reasoning is the leading principle of Plato's philosophy; his forms therefore are rationalist in character. Sensory experience, on the other hand, is fundamental to Blake's forms; they thus have a distinct empirical stamp. Since the philosophy neither of Plato nor of the other thinkers named above can adequately account for Blake's sensory particulars or his creative imagination, we need to look to another source.

We have evidence that Blake annotated Berkeley's *Siris*. A copy of it containing marginal notes in Blake's hand is extant.[4] These annotations, which also contain allusions to other works by Berkeley, bespeak a broad philosophical connection between Blake and Berkeley.[5]

To avoid some common misconceptions about *Siris* and hence to clarify the relationship not only between Blake and Plato but also between Berkeley and Plato, and ultimately between Berkeley and Blake, let us ask, what exactly is *Siris*?[6] Berkeley himself provides the answer: *Siris* is a chain of philosophical reflections on a "dry subject

---

[3] See especially George Mills Harper, *The Neoplatonism of William Blake* (University of North Carolina, 1961), and Kathleen Raine, *Blake and Tradition*, 2 vols. (Princeton, 1968).

[4] This volume was in Lord Rothschild's library, which now has been turned over to King's College, Cambridge (G.E. Bentley, Jr., letter 27 Nov. 1982). Allusions in the annotations confirm Sir Geoffrey Keynes' statement that Blake also read other works by Berkeley: "Blake's Library," TLS, 6 Nov. 1959. Keynes dates the annotations 1818-20. An earlier date, however, seems highly probable inasmuch as many of the images and ideas in *Siris* plainly appear in Blake's *Jerusalem* (1804-20). In addition, his metaphysical principle stated in Berkeleian terms is apparent in a letter of 1799 to Dr. Trusler: see Pt. Two. David V. Erdman, *The Poetry and Prose of William Blake* (Doubleday, 1970), does not speculate on the date of these annotations.

[5] Some critics have noted this connection, e.g., Northrop Frye, *Fearful Symmetry* (Boston, 1967): "we should expect Blake to be influenced by Berkeley," p. 14; but none has furnished evidence for it.

[6] In his "Introduction to *Siris*," Professor Jessop discusses the origin and nature of some misinterpretations of this curious work: *The Works of George Berkeley*, ed. A.A. Luce and T.E. Jessop, vol. 5 (London, 1953), pp.3-23. References to *Siris* followed by paragraph number are from this text.

varied by digressions, traced through remote inferences, and carried into ancient times, whose hoary maxims, scattered in this essay, are not proposed as principles, but barely as hints to awaken and exercise the inquisitive reader."[7] Specifically, the subject is metaphysics, an intellectually difficult and abstruse but a vitally important and much debated topic in the aftermath of Newtonian science. In his "rude essay" of 1744 Berkeley proceeds by "insensible transitions" and conjectures, accumulating some venerable authorities to strengthen his metaphysical doctrine,[8] which he systematically laid out in his treatise *The Principles of Human Knowledge* published in 1710. Reflecting now upon some ancient thinkers both Greek and Egyptian, Berkeley believes they justify his supposition of an eternal spirit or infinite mind as the universal efficient cause in opposition to the Newtonian theory of material causality. He contends that when philosophers of antiquity posited a nature permeated with occult forces—such as animal spirits, invisible fires, or inexorable fates—and abstracted their gods accordingly, they, unlike modern natural philosophers, still attributed order, harmony and unity to a mind. Even the Stoics, who worshiped a corporeal deity, "did not, at bottom, dissent from the forementioned doctrine; inasmuch as they supposed the world to be an animal consisting of soul or mind, as well as body."[9] To them, nature without a governing mind operating by blind chance would be inexplicable. Berkeley even surmises that the chief philosophers and wise men of antiquity had "some glimmering of a divine tradition."[10]

Berkeley's tenderness towards thinkers who relate the structure of the universe to a mind should not, however, be construed as a repudiation of empiricism and sensory particulars in favor of rationalism and abstract ideas. Though eager for classical support, he is circumspect and selective. Of the ancient philosophies Berkeley considers, he treats guardedly, if he mentions at all, those parts, often fundamental, that differ from his own philosophy. He elicits primarily items congenial to his own doctrine of the mind. Everywhere he proceeds cautiously as we can see from his recurrent use of the word *seem*: for example, in §311, dealing with the self-subsistence of

---

[7] Berkeley, *Siris*.350.
[8] Berkeley, *Siris*.297.
[9] Berkeley, *Siris*.323.
[10] Berkeley, *Siris*.301.

physical objects, "it doth not seem to have been admitted either by Plato or Aristotle.... It must, nevertheless, be owned with regard to Aristotle, that even in his Metaphysics there are some expressions that seem to favour the absolute existence of corporeal things.... These passages would seem to imply a distinct and absolute existence of the objects of sense." And again, in §313 referring to the Peripatetics' doctrine of latent first principles in the mind, he conjectures, "This seems to illustrate the manner in which Socrates, Plato, and their followers, conceived innate notions." Berkeley's intellectual journey into antiquity is extensive, yet throughout his speculations he stands firmly by the empirical system he constructed in the *Principles*. The aphorisms in *Siris* embody all the results of his earlier insights.[11]

Certainly, in view of his purposes he presents ancient rationalists positively, and sometimes with praise, but never without qualification: no, not even Plato, whom Berkeley admired all his life. In his interpretation of Plato's philosophy he follows closely the commentary of Proclus, an early Christian philosopher, whom he mentions several times.[12] Even the Platonist Alexander Fraser notes that in some sections of *Siris* "there is more than is found in Plato."[13] Blake's annotations indicate some of these differences: for example, see his assertions quoted on pages 9 and 11. To assume that either Berkeley or Blake accepted or rejected every aspect of Platonism would be equally ludicrous. Both men appreciated Plato's genius; accepted some of his opinions; utilized some of his philosophic and poetic imagery (Berkeley even imitated Plato's literary style and form of the dialogue); and both embraced Christianity, which contains Platonic elements. But philosophically neither was ever a Platonist.

According to Plato, forms or ideas are concepts intuited by reason and developed through dialectical argument without reference to sensory objects. Things, whether they pertain to politics, ethics, or art ideally have a determinative essence, which he insists reason alone

---

[11] This agrees with Professor Jessop's reading of *Siris, op.cit.* (supra n.5), pp.12-13: "Every general doctrine, and virtually every particular doctrine, of his *Principles* is reaffirmed in *Siris*.... the Berkeleian philosophy [is] the same at the end as at the beginning."

[12] Proclus (411-485) conceived the relation of God to the world as essentially a free, creative act.

[13] *The Works of George Berkeley*, 4 vols., ed. Alexander Campbell Fraser (Oxford, 1901) vol.III, p.289, n.2.

can educe. The method he repeatedly dramatizes in the *Dialogues* involves considering a number of hypothetical instances, placing them in a general class, then through question and answer abstracting from them certain qualities and comparing these in order to demonstrate a universal characteristic which defines the object at issue. Forms are thus absolutes embodied in abstract ideas; visible things are understood only through their logical relation to these ideas. This theory Plato substantiates in *Parmenides*: "ideas are, as it were, patterns fixed in nature, and other things are like them, and resemblances of them" but not identical to them.[14] In *Timaeus* he elaborates this distinction: "reality" does not belong to things "that we perceive through the body"; it belongs to "self-existent ideas unperceived by sense and apprehended only by the mind;... but mind is the attribute of the gods and of very few men."[15]

No such dualism exists in Berkeley. He does not separate things from ideas, nor mind from intellect, and hence does not confine knowledge to a select few. His distinction is between ideas and mind, not between appearance and reality, not between sensible objects and ideas. Ideas *are* physical objects, which are real; and our knowledge of them is certain "as we see and perceive them"; they are "passive without any thing active."[16] Whereas Plato's ideas constitute a realm of self-existent entities, for Berkeley "that anything should exist in itself or absolutely is absurd."[17] He does not deny intellectual categories or purely mental activities: "Some, perhaps, may think the truth to be this—that there are properly no ideas, or passive objects, in the mind but what are derived from sense: but that there are also besides these her own acts or operations: such are notions."[18] These, however, like ideas, are passive and mind dependent. He is not merely saying that knowledge of the physical world and concepts are intellectual acts; rather, he maintains that the very *existence* of the world and everything in it is "inexplicable... otherwise than by recourse to a mind or spiritual agent."[19]

---

[14] *The Dialogues of Plato*, 2 vols., tr. B. Jowett (Random House, 1937), vol.II, p.93.
[15] *Ibid.*, p.32.
[16] Berkeley, *Siris*.292.
[17] Berkeley, *Siris*.311. This statement is directed at Lockeans, but it also contains a telling difference between Berkeley's and Plato's theory of ideas.
[18] Berkeley, *Siris*.308.
[19] Berkeley, *Siris*.237.

These statements presuppose and are compatible with the *Principles*, where he defines his concept of idea and of mind: "ideas" are qualities "actually imprinted on the senses;... as several of these [qualities] are observed to accompany each other, they come to be marked by one name, and so to be reputed as one thing." He continues:

> But besides all that endless variety of ideas or objects of knowledge, there is likewise something which knows or perceives them, and exercises divers operations, as willing, imagining, remembering about them. This perceiving, active being is what I call *mind, spirit, soul* or *my self*. By which words I do not denote any one of my ideas, but a thing entirely distinct from them, wherein they exist, or, which is the same thing, whereby they are perceived; for the existence of an idea consists in being perceived.[20]

By *spirit* Berkeley means a knowing mind which perceives ideas: spirit, mind and self are in reflexive relation with each other. By *idea* he means "any *sensory* object, and therefore any corporeal object, whether perceived, remembered, or imagined";[21] imagination is a form of perception. He makes only a psychological, not an ontological, distinction among ideas; they vary in vivacity and constancy, but not in their nature: every idea is something particular, something visible. Consequently, sense experience is a necessary condition for ideas, not because, as in Locke, they derive from sensible objects, but because ideas *are* sensory objects. The common sense realism that runs throughout Berkeley's philosophizing is absent from Plato's *Dialogues*. Plato's ideas transcend sensible objects; Berkeley's do not. A fundamental presupposition in the latter's thought is the essential identity of reality and sense experience.

An analogous isomorphism underlies Blake's concept of form. At *Siris* §310, where Berkeley looks to Aristotle for validation and infers from Themistius' commentary on *De Anima* "that all things are in the soul," Blake remarks, "This is my Opinion, but Forms must be

---

[20] Berkeley, vol.2, *Principles of Human Knowledge,* ed. T.E. Jessop (London, 1949), §1-2.

[21] *Ibid.,* "Editor's Introduction," p.8.

apprehended by Sense or the Eye of Imagination."[22] Forms are sensory objects perceived by the imagination, which is consubstantial with spirit, for imagination is "the Divine Body in Every Man." Further, because he regards sensory experience and life itself the effects of spirit, Blake writes, "The Four Senses are the Four Faces of Man & the Four Rivers of the Water of Life"; forms imply sensation and it in turn implies human life, a perceiving spirit. Blake nowhere makes a Platonic distinction between things perceived by sense and those perceived by mind, which he uses interchangeably with imagination; they constitute a single act. The reality of every thing is "Its Imaginative Form," its perceivable sensory qualities. Blake's forms, therefore, differ from Plato's in substance and ground; they are perceived immediately by imagination through the senses, not through a dialectical process of ratiocination.

Plato, Berkeley, and Blake all emphasize the essentialness of mind with respect to reality. Berkeley agrees with Plato that to perceive "the true principle of unity, identity, and existence," we must look beyond corporeal objects to the mind.[23] And at *Siris*.309, Blake adds : "The Natural Body is an Obstruction to the Soul or Spiritual Body."[24] But Plato's concept of mind differs from Berkeley's and Blake's notion. In Plato's system the mind is primarily a clarifying and classifying instrument, performing contemplative and logical functions. Through rumination, analysis, and abstract reasoning the mind discerns relations among pure qualities, connects them, orders them into ideal objects, and thereby comprehends natural phenomena but does not bring them into existence. In contrast, Berkeley and Blake move away from these Platonic absolutes and towards the dynamic concept of empiricism. They regard mind as a power that not only understands but also *creates* the objects of experience: they equate mind and spiritual substance, which Blake calls *spiritual body*. Berkeley states: "all phenomena are in the soul or mind," which is "the power or force that acts, moves, enlivens."[25] Blake characterizes this power as "The All in Man," the substance

---

[22] Quotations in this paragraph are from Blake, "Annotations to Berkeley," pp.773-775.
[23] Berkeley, *Siris*.294.
[24] Blake, "Annotations to Berkeley," p.775.
[25] Berkeley, *Siris*.251,322.

that makes possible his existence without which there can be neither perception nor reasoning.[26] The Blakean and Berkeleian mind is more than the Platonic faculty of intellectually grasping meanings; as creative substance and principle of life, it is fundamentally existential, whereas the Platonic *nous* is essentially rational insight without reference to sense impressions. According to Berkeley and Blake the mind's main function is to perceive the sensible world, rather than to reason abstractly about it. The relation between mind and natural phenomena for them is a *causal* one; for Plato, a *logical* one.

This difference is reflected in their theory of knowledge. Plato teaches that knowledge is a kind of remembering and reasoning, which he pictures gracefully in the myth of *Phaedrus* and illustrates pointedly through geometrical figures in *Meno*. The process of knowing involves rousing by reminiscence and elucidating by reason certain forms laid up in the mind, necessarily separate from the world of generation. By deduction from these unchanging forms or true objects of knowledge we arrive at the nature and meaning of the ever-changing world of visible particulars. Science therefore is a system of explicit and logically connected ideals or archetypes. The philosopher-scientist proceeds by dialectics to the principle of the One, to a coherent and unified body of abstract ideas. In this objective Newton's and Locke's view of knowledge resembles Platonism; however, it must be remembered that Plato's system rests entirely on *a priori* principles, whereas philosophies of the former have an *a posteriori* basis. Blake takes this fact into account, most notably in *The Song of Los*. There (perhaps drawing upon *Siris*.298 for names of Greek philosophers but making a point different from Berkeley's) he traces the source of Newton's and Locke's abstractionism: "To Trismegistus, Palamabron gave an abstract Law:/ To Pythagoras, Socrates & Plato./... Till a Philosophy of Five Senses was complete./ Urizen wept & gave it into the hands of Newton & Locke" (3:18-19, 4:16-17).[27] The principle of abstraction in Greek philosophy

---

[26] Blake, "Annotations to Berkeley," p.773.

[27] Newton belonged to the Society of Cambridge Platonists. His view of the world is Platonic in its theological extensions, which he, however, did not make. But some Deists, such as his friend and disciple Samuel Clarke, carried out a Platonic metaphysics using constructions and axioms of geometry as similes to clarify theological concepts. The comparison between Platonism and Deism is a gross simplification, yet there are similarities between them inasmuch as both hold that the

has come down through the ages to Newton and Locke; upon this principle they have abstracted qualities from sensory objects and built a world of material causality.

Though Berkeley developed his philosophy specifically in opposition to Newton's and Locke's doctrine of abstract ideas, nonetheless, the Berkeleian concrete sensuous world displaying the perfections of an eternal spirit stands in striking contrast to Plato's ideal abstract world as well; it persists throughout *Siris* despite the repeated enlistment of Plato for metaphysical support. Again seeking corroboration for his view, Berkeley writes: "As the natural connexion of signs with the things signified is regular and constant, it forms a sort of rational discourse and is therefore the immediate effect of an intelligent cause. This is agreeable to the philosophy of Plato, and other ancients."[28] Indeed Plato insists that intellect and reason control knowledge of the physical world; but he does not characterize the sensory world as either constant or rational. Always he ascribes these properties to abstract ideas, not to natural phenomena: the order of nature is understood solely in relation to a reasoned system of abstract ideas. For Berkeley, on the other hand, the physical world as the creation of an intelligent Being is orderly, rational, and hence knowable through direct experience. Sensory forms are self-evident perceptions of what truly exists. He does not differentiate either between perception and reality or between sensing and knowing: "the phenomena of nature, which strikes on the senses and are understood by the mind, form not only a magnificent spectacle, but also a most coherent, entertaining, and instructive Discourse." So, whereas a Platonist constructs general ideas to deduce knowledge of particulars, a Berkeleian observes facts and records the connections he actually sees in nature. For him shadows are Lockean abstractions, not sensory particulars as for Plato.

In all of this, Blake agrees with Berkeley and disagrees with Plato: "Knowledge is not by deduction, but Immediate by Perception or Sense at once."[29] Knowing and sensing are simultaneous events

---

sensible world is mathematically ordered. It is not my concern here, however, to explore the important differences either between them or between Plato, Newton and Locke, but, as Blake saw, for these three philosophers reality is beyond perceived objects. "Five Senses" refer to Aristotle's analytical philosophy.

[28] Quotations in this paragraph are from Berkeley, *Siris*.254.
[29] Blake, "Annotations to Berkeley," p.774.

because we have no other knowledge of the world than our perceptions. Blake sees reality within the world itself; Plato conceives reality in terms of categories and regards the sensible world relationally. In *Timaeus* we are told "the body of the world is harmonized by proportion";[30] conformably, the reality of a thing is proportionate to the absolute qualities it possesses according to fixed ideas; science is a study of these absolutes. But Blake rejects relative proportion as a determinant of the world's particulars; he objects to Plato's use of ideas in a generative sense; to him it suggests they have creative powers. At *Siris*.303, where Berkeley defends sensory apprehension of harmony and proportion, Blake adds: "Harmony [and] Proportion are Qualities & Not Things.... Every Thing has its own Harmony & Proportion."[31] In his view reality is not an abstract system of absolute entities which the actual world imitates in varying degrees. Rather, the reality of everything is determined by its actual qualities: sensible objects having their own identity, their own structural relations, constitute the real world. He does not dispute the Platonic notion of a governing mind in knowledge; but he joins reality to perceived particulars. His system, like Berkeley's, is a whole mechanism of cause and effect: Plato's system rests on the relational principle of the one and many, bifurcated into a world of reality and appearances.

Although Berkeley remarks that Plato's concept of the One contains more piety than the naturalists' theory of God as a remote original cause, nevertheless, he does not accept Plato's notion of "God as abstracted or distinct from the natural world."[32] The Platonic One—the beautiful, the just, the good—is an abstract idea that imparts value to the world; it is not a creator of the world in Berkeley's sense of the One. Harmony, justice, and virtue are, according to Berkeley, attributes of a really living spirit, and not merely aesthetic and ethical characteristics attached to the mathematical concept of unity. While he accepts the Platonic view that the world is one and that order and harmony of the universe proceed from a divine intellect, Berkeley insists upon the immediacy of God with respect to sensory objects. The world is conjoined to God by way of a creative

---

[30] Plato, Vol.II, p.15.
[31] Blake, "Annotations to Berkeley," p.774.
[32] Berkeley, *Siris*.300.

and perpetually acting spirit, but not in the manner of an animal united to its soul as put forward in *Timaeus*. In Berkeley's opinion "to conceive God to be the sentient soul of an animal is altogether unworthy and absurd"; He is neither an abstract idea denoting unity symbolized by the number *one* nor the soul of the world in analogy with an animal; rather, God is "pure mind or intellect," but as substance He is causally related to the natural world.[33] Since this is a uniquely Christian notion, it differs drastically from a pagan notion of God, yet for the same reason it is not a problematic difference for Berkeley between himself and Plato. Berkeley elaborates his theory of divinity because it is critical to his arguments against Newton and Locke, the primary objective in *Siris*.

God as a constantly operative power is central also to Blake's view of the world. Alongside Platonism, Blake rejects all systems and cultures that posit an abstract god. Reacting to views expressed in *Siris*.300 concerning the Egyptians, Blake writes: "They also consider'd God as abstracted or distinct from the Imaginative World, but Jesus, as also Abraham & David, consider'd God as a Man in the Spiritual or Imaginative Vision."[34] In other words, God is the eternal spirit which actively creates our objects of experience, not merely a symbol of order and unity dissociated from human perceptions. Again at §307 where Berkeley discusses Aristotle's abstract approach to theology, Blake retorts: "God is not a Mathematical Diagram."[35] These words convey more than a propensity for the concrete: they make a metaphysical statement. Neither Plato's, nor the Egyptians', nor Aristotle's abstract deity is a creative substance in either Berkeley's or Blake's sense.

Though Plato refers order to intellect, he ascribes life to natural processes. But notwithstanding what Plato himself presents in *Timaeus*, Berkeley cannot accept a plastic nature. Here, then, is another metaphysical point of difference between them. Berkeley introduces generation because it, like the notion of God, bears directly on his quarrel with Newton and Locke; but this subject with respect to Plato, whom Berkeley is using to reinforce his causal principle, presents a delicate situation. For that reason he refers here to Plato

---

[33] *Ibid.*, 289.
[34] Blake, "Annotations to Berkeley," p.774.
[35] *Ibid.*

only indirectly: "Some Platonics, indeed, regard life as the act of nature, in like manner as intellection is of the mind or intellect. As the First Intellect acts by understanding, so nature according to them acts or generates by living. But life is the act of the soul."[36] In contrast to Platonists, Berkeley consistently holds that life seminally and ever depends on a spiritual agent: "Life and Immortality were brought to light by the Gospel."[37]

Now hear what Blake says at *Siris*.302: "Plato did not bring Life & Immortality to Light. Jesus only did this."[38] Christ in his divine human personality is essentially related to Blake's concept of God as spirit and man as spirit incarnate. The animating force of life is spirit, which is the principle of eternity as well. Since spirit is the source of existence, natural processes are subordinate to it. The disagreement concerning the cause of existence between Plato, on the one hand, and Blake and Berkeley, on the other hand, arises from their disparate metaphysical assumption, which extends to their concept of man. Plato assumes mathematical proportion orders reality, of which the world is a copy; thus he postulates reason as man's essential quality. Berkeley and Blake believe reality resides in the sensory world having its existence in a spiritual agent; hence they posit spirit to be man's essence. Reason orders, but, in the words of Berkeley, "spirit... quickens and inspires"; he equates this divine creative principle with "personality," a concept entirely foreign to Plato.[39] Blake identifies this divine principle in man as imagination. Because Plato turns to the contemplation of an abstract One and away from the creativity of individuated spirits, Blake ends his commentary aphoristically with a historically inaccurate but philosophically informative personal statement: "What Jesus came to Remove was the Heathen or Platonic Philosophy, which blinds the Eye of Imagination, The Real Man."[40]

---

[36] Berkeley, *Siris*.278.

[37] Berkeley, *Sermon* IX, "For the Propagation of the Gospel" (pub. in London 1731 and reprinted 1752), vol.7 (London, 1955), p.116. Cf. the opening words of *Sermon* VIII, "On Eternal Life": "Christ came from heaven on this very message from God to man, to bring life and immortality to light," p.106.

[38] Blake, "Annotations to Berkeley," p.774.

[39] Berkeley, *Siris*.362; 346.

[40] Blake, "Annotations to Berkeley," p.775; his aversion to Plato's philosophy does not extend to systems *per se*. Harper claims "it was surely Plato's emphasis on system that led at last to Blake's distrust of him," *op.cit.* (supra n.5), p.vii. This im-

Following Berkeley into the depths of his introspections and Blake to the end of his annotations, we have discovered metaphysical and epistemological differences between their views and Plato's. While his emphasis on the centrality of mind in knowledge is congenial to Berkeley's and to Blake's cardinal principle, their theories about the nature of mind and what it sees, and hence about the nature of forms and how we come to know them, differ from Plato's. Berkeley assigns absolute essence to mind, and Blake more particularly to imagination; both attach ideas to sensory particulars, real qualities perceivable directly through experience by all men in this world. Plato does the opposite: he assigns absolutes to ideas and removes them to a supersensible world where disembodied philosophical souls, circling about in chariots, gain insight into abstract forms and store them in the mind for recall as a means to understanding the physical world. The sensible world for a Platonist is ever an imperfect imitation of fixed abstract ideas existing in a rationalized world mathematically ordered. Consequently, the Platonic world is inaccessible to the senses and must be apprehended through reason, whereas sensory experience is both a necessary and a sufficient condition for knowing the Berkeleian and the Blakean world.

Although Berkeley's chain of reflections leads him to the friendly camp of Plato along with other rationalists in Western Philosophy and to places beyond, the first and last links are securely fastened to his *Principles*: during his sojourn to thinkers of ancient times, Berkeley remains an empiricist. By appealing to general accumulated wisdom, he hopes to vindicate his causal principle and expunge forever the false doctrine of naturalists. His main intent in *Siris* is to show that some of the greatest thinkers of antiquity, preeminently Plato, set divinity in the celestial regions and hence were not atheists, as he contends modern naturalists are since they locate the universal power in matter. That the ancients were pagans, not atheists, becomes a refrain in *Siris*.

Generally agreeing with this sentiment, Blake charges Plato with heathenism, not with atheism. Nonetheless, Blake cannot accept a ra-

---

plies that Blake for a time accepted Platonism. But as G.E. Bentley, Jr., reports, "There are no statements of allegiance to Plato, or to the classics in Blake's writing, and there are many denunciations" ("Blake Scholars and Critics," *University of Toronto Quarterly* [Spring 1970], p.93). In other contexts, Blake makes three favorable references to Plato: e.g., see Pt. Two.

tionalist system. Though his "Visionary forms"[41] suggest Platonic ideas, they have an experiential content wholly absent from Plato's abstract forms.

Thoroughly committed to perceived particulars, Blake has a settled dislike for all rationalist and mathematical philosophies. So neither his forms nor his symbols derive from Pythagoreanism either.[42] Besides his protracted attack in *Jerusalem* upon mathematic and abstract treatment of the world, of religion, morality, and art, Blake directs his satirical remarks in *An Island in the Moon* specifically against Pythagoreans. Their world view is glaringly opposite to Blake's: they regard the universe quantitatively; Blake sees it qualitatively. According to Pythagoreans, since numbers are the ground of things, reality belongs to mathematical forms, which the empirical world copies. All life is an unfolding of numerical relations derived from the One, which occupies first position in the system of numbers. Because they believe that mathematical relations determine the true form of everything, Pythagoreans, like Platonists, elevate reason to a commanding place and correspondingly relegate sensory particulars to an inferior level. To Blake, however, a world made up of mathematical forms united in an abstract deity is repugnant. For him, as for Berkeley, the book of nature is written in objects, not in numbers.

Neopythagoreans give a mystic direction to the ancient philosophical doctrine, yet, like Neoplatonists, they retain its rationalist, dualistic, hierarchical, and abstract features. Philosophies having any such properties are anathema to Blake. His 'mysticism,' or more precisely his notion of prophetic wisdom, like his number-symbolism, is in biblical rather than in Neopythagorean tradition.[43] In the former, revelation is fixed by historical authority as a well-ordered

---

[41] Blake, *Jerusalem* 98:28. The meaning of this phrase will be discussed at length in Pt. Eight.

[42] E.g., see Harper's "The Divine Tetrad in Blake's *Jerusalem*," *William Blake, Essays for S. Foster Damon,* ed. A.H. Rosenfeld (Providence: Brown University Press, 1969) pp.235-255. Although numbers in this prophetic poem function symbolically, their significance comes from Christian doctrines rather than from Pythagorean cosmology.

[43] Blake's letter 22 Nov. 1802 to Butts: "I still & shall to Eternity Embrace Christianity and Adore him who is the Express image of God.... I have Conquer'd, and shall still Go on Conquering."

succession of communications, usually pertaining to political and ethical affairs, imparted by God to prophets; in the latter, revelation, more often called *enlightenment*, is a purely intellectual process whereby an individual frees himself from the sensory world and rises to a supersensuous realm to contemplate true Being in the abstract. For Blake there is no Pythagorean or Platonic imprisonment of the body since sensory experience constitutes existence. Everywhere he remains in touch with the experiential world, even during his most 'visionary' moments, in fact especially then, as subsequent pages will show.[44]

---

[44] The analytical discussion above does not exhaust all the differences either between Plato's and Berkeley's philosophy or between Plato's and Blake's system; it emphasizes fundamental differences between Plato and Berkeley along with Blake, and at the same time points to similarities between Berkeley and Blake, all with a view towards understanding the system created in *Jerusalem*.

PART TWO

BLAKE AS ARTIST

Blake's antipathy to Platonic philosophy is related to his work not only as poet but also as artist, a profession in which he received formal training. In Plato's system art is imitative, sometimes purveying false ideas but always twice removed from the reality of abstract ideas. Painting Plato rejects on metaphysical grounds, and poetry because it appeals to the passions instead of reason and on that account can be dangerous to society. Blake, on the other hand, has a high estimate of all art. He regards it objective and true, having equal place with other kinds of knowledge, and hence a means of improving and enriching society, not harming it. In his view, art is founded on the same grounds as all knowledge, namely on the perceived particulars, the real world. Blake could not therefore accept the rationalist and abstract principles on which Plato's philosophy depends and from which his views on art derive.

Abstraction in the system of art prevailing in his day is precisely what Blake objects to and vigorously condemns at great length because it impinges immediately upon his work. Although his contemporaries admired his early poems for their fineness of technique, originality of rhythm, and freshness of thought, they dismissed his late poems, now called *prophetic books*, as oddities lacking both a literary form and a philosophic center. His paintings and engravings fared much worse. Critics treated them as if they were products of madness, of manic, not mantic, origin: "the wild effusions of a distempered brain," one critic called them.[1] Why? Because Blake's

---

[1] G.E. Bentley, Jr., *Blake Records* (Oxford, 1969), p.216.

creations did not conform either in subject or in style to the art in vogue.

Its canons descended from Newtonian physics founded on a mathematical science of mechanics and on abstract reasoning applied to the phenomena of nature. As is well known, Locke constructed a comprehensive philosophy upon the new science. How it became the ruling philosophy of art, however, is not well known. Newton had by reasoning from mathematical principles described forces by which particles are moved. Subsequently, Locke denominated these forces *substances*, placed them within particles, and thus extended Newtonian physics into a materialist metaphysics. In his *Essay Concerning Human Understanding* he rejects innate ideas and argues that all legitimate ideas originate from external forces in nature, which impress themselves on the initially "empty cabinet" of the mind "either through the senses by outward objects, or by its own operations when it reflects on them.... All those sublime thoughts which tower above the clouds, and reach as high as heaven itself, take their rise and footing here."[2] In the reception of sense impressions, which Locke also calls *simple ideas*, "the understanding is merely passive; and whether or no it will have these beginnings... is not in its own powers." Whenever "we would proceed beyond these simple ideas... we fall presently into darkness."

Simple ideas do not, however, constitute knowledge; rather, they provide its materials and, according to Locke, its only materials. Once the mind is stored with these temporally and logically prior ideas, reason must perform certain operations upon them before we attain to knowledge. From a well-supplied memory, reason at pleasure abstracts simple ideas and methodically compares them; then, drawing on these comparisons, reason selects general sensory qualities and compounds them into abstract ideas. These are the real objects of knowledge. Indeed, the agreement or disagreement of ideas abstracted from nature is the essence of demonstration, that fertile method of reasoning Newton skillfully used in science to prove the truth of his general theory. If we wish to enlarge our knowledge in other areas of human interest, Locke insists we must submit to the authority of

---

[2] John Locke, *An Essay Concerning Human Understanding* (Dover, 1959) 2 vols., vol. 1, bk.I, ch.i, §15; bk.II.i.24-25; ch.xxiii.32.

reason, "that faculty whereby man is supposed to be distinguished from beasts."[3]

Locke's exaggerated regard for reason leads him to limit divine revelation and scorn enthusiasm, which he associates with religious fanaticism. No experience of outward sense or inward perception can be accepted as evidence of revelation if it is *"contrary to, and inconsistent with, the clear and self-evident dictates of reason."*[4] Whatever we can know of spirits must, of course, be obtained from revelation; and whatever God reveals is certainly true. But, Locke adds, "whether it be a *divine* revelation or no, reason must judge." When God makes someone a prophet, He does not deprive that person of right judgment. Whatsoever credit we give to any illumination or proposition more than it receives from the principles and proofs of reason is, Locke asserts, owing to "enthusiasm." This "wrong principle" of knowledge is founded neither on reason nor on divine revelation; it rises "from the conceits of a warmed or overweening brain." Because immediate revelation is a much easier way than the tedious labor of strict reasoning to establish opinions and regulate conduct, Locke contends that some men pretend to revelation and persuade themselves they are under the peculiar guidance of heaven. But on rational examination, these men will find "this light they are so dazzled with is nothing but an *ignis fatuus*." Before we can accept any inspiration as divine or a proposition which we take to be thus inspired, it must conform to reason's principles, the "natural way" of knowledge. "Reason," Locke concludes, "*must be our last judge and guide in everything.*"

Locke's *Essay* captivated England and almost instantly became its authoritative philosophy; in the ten-year period following its publication, there were four editions of this work. The popularity of this philosophy had not diminished a century later when Sir Joshua Reynolds, president of the Royal Academy, where Blake was a student, introduced Locke's principles into art and disseminated them through the *Discourses*. Addressing himself to advanced students, Reynolds gives them the proper orientation to their profession: "every man's life must be employed in collecting materials for the exercise of

---

[3] Locke, vol.2, bk.IV, ch.xvii, §1.

[4] Quotations in this paragraph are from Locke, vol.2, bk.IV, ch.xviii, §10 and ch.xix, §8,7,10,14.

genius. Invention, strictly speaking, is little more than a new combination of those images which have been previously gathered and deposited in the memory.... mere enthusiasm will carry you but a little way."[5] The artist's stimulus, like everyone else's, whatever his interest, comes from a fund of ideas laboriously acquired from nature; and his craft, like all intellectual arts, hangs on a fixed body of rules, which every serious artist must learn and obey.

Having laid the Lockean cornerstone, in his next lecture reproducing almost verbatim Locke's disparagement of divine revelation Reynolds makes divine inspiration a subject of jest. He warns students about the futility and dangers of looking to heaven for inspiration and guidance. On hearing that painters and sculptors receive their perfection from heaven, "a student by such praise may have his attention roused, and a desire excited;... yet it is possible that what has been said to excite, may only serve to deter him. He examines his own mind, and perceives there nothing of that divine inspiration, with which, he is told, so many others have been favoured."[6] Reiterating his naturalist position, in a subsequent lecture Reynolds unmistakably again echoes Locke: "The mind is but a barren soil.... Nature is, and must be the fountain which alone is inexhaustible; and from which all excellencies must originally flow."[7]

When he expatiates on the subject of taste and genius, Reynolds develops the foundational part of his aesthetics, embodying exactly Locke's methodology and ideal of abstract ideas:

> we may truly say, that they [taste and genius] always operate in proportion to our attention in observing the works of nature, to our skill in selecting, and to our care in digesting, methodizing, and comparing our observations.... This long laborious comparison should be the first study of the painter, who aims at the greatest style. By this means, he acquires a just idea of beautiful forms; ...from their general figures, he makes out an abstract idea of their forms more perfect than any one original.... This idea of the perfect state of nature, which the Artist calls the

---

[5] Sir Joshua Reynolds, *Discourses on Art*, ed. Robert R. Wark (Collier, 1966), Disc. Two, pp.31-34.
[6] Reynolds, Disc. Three, pp.44-45.
[7] Reynolds, Disc. Six, pp.90-92.

Ideal Beauty, is the great leading principle, by which works of genius are conducted.[8]

Effective artistic expression is a product of observing nature under the dominion of established rules. Like Locke, Reynolds rejects innate ideas; ideas come from repeated experience and close comparison of objects from which the artist abstracts general characteristics. Superlative genius is but the "perfection of this science of abstract form": in this the whole beauty and grandeur of art consists.[9]

Reynolds constantly reminds aspiring artists they must aim at the general effect, avoid all details, and sacrifice particulars, however excellent and expressive in themselves. Particularities in a work "are always so many blemishes."[10] Everywhere he pronounces a high encomium upon artists who leave out particulars and attend to the whole. Of English painters he cites Wilson and Gainsborough as staunch generalizing types, whose talents and acquirements, especially those of the latter, he greatly admires. These men studiously observed nature, compared its forms, abstracted qualities from them, and articulated objects in a general way. Reynolds tells his students they may acquire an eminence equal to these artists by steadfastly following the same procedures.

There is no easy method of becoming a good artist. One of the most dangerous errors, in Reynolds' opinion, is to believe that everything is done by so-called genius, "supposed to be a power of producing excellencies, which are out of the reach of the rules of art."[11] A painter must of necessity be "an imitator" not only "of the works of nature" but also "of the works of other painters." Genius, no less than "originality of invention," is "the child of imitation."

---

[8] Reynolds, Disc. Three, pp.45-46. There is a trace of Platonism here in that he sees beauty as an ideal abstract form; but his forms, because they are Lockean, have an *a posteriori* origin: a Platonist starts with an *a priori* form of absolute beauty and imitates it; an artist of Reynolds' school starts with sense impressions and puts a select few of them together into an abstract form.

[9] Reynolds, Disc. Ten, p.157.

[10] Reynolds, Disc. Six, p.93.

[11] Quotations in this paragraph are from Reynolds, Disc. Six, p.87. Strains of neoclassicism appear in Reynolds' insistence of habitual imitation, continued study of ancient monuments, and necessity of rules resulting from his determined diminution of native genius; his leading principles, however, are firmly tied to natural philosophy.

To interpret literally the metaphorical or poetical statements about inspiration and genius is absurd. And again Reynolds interjects Locke's opinion: of course, it is much easier for students, who frequently are terrified at the toil required to become a skillful artist, to claim "inspiration from heaven" or native genius. Reynolds never tires of reminding his listeners that great works are produced under the direction of rules.

But in denying divine inspiration and unfettered individual expression and in emphasizing the necessity of imitation and rules, he does not wish to reduce art to a manual occupation:

> As our art is not a divine *gift,* so neither is it a mechanical *trade.* Its foundations are laid in solid science:... it works under the direction of principle.... It is the sense of nature or truth which ought more particularly to be cultivated by the professors of art;... and we may add, that the acquisition of this knowledge requires as much circumspection and sagacity, as is necessary to attain those truths which are more capable of demonstration. Reason must ultimately determine our choice on every occasion.[12]

The method that in science leads to nature's secrets leads also to truth in art. Science and art "have inalterable and fixed foundations in nature, and are therefore equally investigated by reason, and known by study." Inventions that "shrink from reason" are "more like the dreams of a distempered brain than the exalted enthusiasm of a sound and true genius. In the midst of the highest flights of fancy or imagination, reason ought to preside from first to last."[13]

Astonishing how closely Reynolds not only patterns his theory upon Locke's philosophy but even uses Locke's words and tone, as critics were later to use those of Reynolds. Throughout the *Discourses* Locke's principles uphold and mediate Reynolds' statements. Just as Locke made nature the origin and scientific method the means of knowledge, so Reynolds makes them the standards of art, which level-headed critics and artists alike must heed. Just as Locke brought religion before the bar of reason, so Reynolds does the same with art. He disparages divine revelation and scorns enthusiasm as Locke had

---

[12] Quotations in this paragraph are from Reynolds' Disc. Seven, pp.105-126.
[13] Cf. the critic's words quoted above.

done. Yet Reynolds never mentions Locke by name. Notwithstanding, the makeup of Reynolds' aesthetics and its limitations were transparent to Blake. At Discourse Eight he summarizes his observations and makes plain his feelings about this book, which undermined his creative powers and struck painfully at his art.

> Burke's Treatise on the Sublime & Beautiful is founded on the Opinions of Newton & Locke; on this Treatise Reynolds has grounded many of his assertions in all his Discourses. I read Burke's Treatise when very Young; at the same time I read Locke on Human Understanding & Bacon's Advancement of Learning; on Every one of these Books I wrote my Opinions, & on looking them over find that my Notes on Reynolds in this Book are exactly Similar. I felt the Same Contempt & Abhorrence then that I do now. They mock Inspiration & Vision.[14]

Blake does not deny the importance of perseverance, of select reading, and studying great works. He abhors Reynolds' theory because it is based on false philosophical principles. He agrees with Reynolds that art, like science, turns on experience and conveys truth;[15] but he disagrees on the source of our experience, on the form of reality, and on the means of attaining to knowledge of true forms. Blake is convinced that all things are effects of imagination, the human spirit. Experience, ideas and forms come directly from this

---

[14] Blake, "Annotations to Reynolds," pp.476-477. Blake owned all three volumes of the second edition of *Discourses*, but his marginalia are written in the first volume only. In his introduction to this edition, Edmond Malone relates that Reynolds enjoyed a life-long friendship with Burke, to whom he submitted for examination some of the early discourses but does not acknowledge his debt to Burke. Characteristically, Reynolds rarely identifies his sources; he refers to Bacon only in qualifying terms to strengthen the force of rules in art. Blake's copies of Burke's *Treatise* and Locke's *Essay* are not extant.

[15] Blake also agrees with Reynolds on minor points of execution, such as disposition of drapery, firmness of outline, and precision of representation, but for Reynolds these techniques always refer to abstract ideas; and sometimes, not often, he agrees with Reynolds' critical judgment about painters, Poussin for example. But mostly, Blake exuberantly agrees with the exceptions Reynolds makes to his own principles: for instance, sometimes "we must depart from nature" for the sake of the intended effect of a work (Disc. Eight, p.143), whereon Blake notes, "These are Excellent Remarks on Proportional Colour" ("Annotations to Reynolds," p.479).

creative source; execution depends on individual genius. Whereas Reynolds regards art an invention having its origin in nature observed according to fixed rules, Blake maintains that artists' inspirations come from within, from spirit and hence are divine. Countering Reynolds' denial of divine inspiration, his ridicule of poets waiting for the call of inspiration, and his reduction of visionary art to a situation "viewed indistinctly as through a mist," Blake (reminiscent of Berkeley in *Siris*) cites venerable authorities to support his own opinion: "The Ancients did not mean to Impose when they affirm'd their belief in Vision & Revelation. Plato was in Earnest:... [He] believ'd that God did Visit Man Really.... How very anxious Reynolds is to Disprove & Contemn Spiritual Perception!"[16]

Blake makes clear his difference with Reynolds is owing to metaphysics, not to terminology:

> It is not in Terms that Reynolds & I disagree. Two Contrary Opinions can never by any Language be made alike. I say, Taste & Genius are Not Teachable or Acquirable, but are born with us. Reynolds says the Contrary.[17]

Indeed, Reynolds assumes taste, "a power of distinguishing right from wrong," and genius, a method rationally carried out, are learned through rules formulated by Locke (Discourse Seven). But for Blake taste is determined solely by the artist according to his particular purpose; and genius is nothing other than spirit or self, at once man's personality and source of his acts, be they perceptions of the world or creations of art. Reacting to Reynolds' caution against

---

[16] Blake, "Annotations to Reynolds," p.473. Undoubtedly, he here is referring to the *Phaedrus*, where Socrates enumerates several kinds of madness; among these are the divine gifts of prophecy and poetry: possessed by the muses, prophets and poets are seized by a madness, an "inspiring frenzy" that "awakens lyrical and all other numbers" (Plato, vol.I, p.249). Blake, however, cannot on philosophical grounds accept the notion that inspiration is a madness. Hence in his *Note-Book*, obviously referring to this same passage, he writes: "Plato has made Socrates say that Poets & Prophets do not know or Understand what they write or Utter.... Plato confutes himself" because he assigns opposite characteristics to them, namely divine wisdom and madness: if they are taken out of their senses, how can they be wise? if they are wise, then they are not mad ("A Vision of the Last Judgment," p.605).

[17] Blake, "Annotations to Reynolds," p.474. Paul B. Armstrong applies this fact to criticism in "The Conflict of Interpretations and the Limits of Pluralism," PMLA (May 1983).

supposed powers of native genius and against the vacuity of mere enthusiasm, Blake exclaims: "Meer Enthusiasm is the All in All!"—enthusiasm in an ontological sense that implies a belief in spirit as the power underlying all human actions and existents in the universe.[18]

From this belief it follows that sensory experience is a spiritual act; consequently, Blake maintains that objects as we perceive them define the real world. In this view of reality he is at odds with Reynolds, who makes a Lockean division between sense impressions and general ideas: the latter represent things as they truly are; the former are but materials we must examine to extract a general character of things. Therefore it is Reynolds' presiding principle that every art is built upon general nature. But Blake adds, "What is General Nature? is there Such a Thing? what is General Knowledge? Strictly Speaking All Knowledge is Particular."[19] He does not concur with Reynolds' praise of Gainsborough's generalizing powers; instead, he believes that in reducing things to general figures Gainsborough fails to elevate his grand subjects. To Reynolds' repeated reminder that the artist must invent upon the general principle, Blake exasperatedly retorts: "General Principles Again! Unless You Consult Particulars You Cannot even Know or See... any Thing." He utterly rejects Reynolds' dictum of leaving out particulars and retaining only the general: "Singular & Particular Detail is the Foundation of the Sublime," by which Blake means ultimate reality.[20] Reynolds calls tending to particulars the "insipid manner," and contrasts it with the "*grand style*," which attends to the general effect. With equal insistence Blake claims the grandeur of art consists in particularized qualities because that is the way objects exist in the world. So while he agrees with Reynolds that art is iconic of reality, he disagrees on what constitutes reality and hence on what constitutes great art.

This metaphysical difference between them is clearly reflected in their definition of form and how we come to know true forms.

---

[18] Blake, "Annotations to Reynolds, p.456.

[19] Quotations in this paragraph are from Blake's "Annotations to Reynolds," p.459 and p.456; and from Reynolds' Disc. One, p.20 and Disc. Four, p.55.

[20] Reynolds has an entirely different concept; he counts "obscurity" as one part of the sublime (Disc. Seven, p.107).

Reynolds, in accordance with Locke's epistemology, holds that through exercise of reason the artist improves upon the originals of nature by determining general forms and then expressing them in abstract ideas.[21] This perfection by reason conveys true forms and ideal beauty for which every artist should strive. Blake questions this theory in its entirety. "What has Reasoning to do with the Art of Painting?" he asks.[22] Painters' forms are given in perception without the intervention of reason. The same applies to poets' forms: "All Forms are Perfect in the Poet's Mind, but these are not Abstracted or Compounded from Nature, but are from Imagination."[23] Though Reynolds allows imagination a role in art, he does not consider it a source of inspiration; art is ever rooted in nature, and form is always a problem to be solved by reason. For Blake, on the other hand, form is a particularized object perceived by his imagination and executed according to his distinctive sensibilities.

It is not surprising that Blake rebels against an aesthetics which dismisses his spiritual perceptions and constrains his powers of expression. Referring specifically to Discourse Four and Five, wherein Reynolds elaborates and applies his principles, Blake resolutely voices his refusal to comply with these prescriptions: "Let him who will, follow such advice. I will not."[24] In line with Locke's unperceivable corporeal substances, Reynolds counsels artists to capture the hidden essence of things, generalize and represent it abstractly. Blake disdainfully calls them "Pretended Copiers of Nature" because neither general nor abstract shapes and colors are its true forms.[25] While Reynolds' followers, such as Constable and Gainsborough, judiciously cultivated the sense of nature in compliance with rules of reason, abstracting and compounding ideas to paint idealized

---

[21] Though he agrees with Plato that abstract ideas represent reality, Reynolds does not reify them; he accepts neither Plato's *a priori* system nor his view of painting as an imitation of reality: see Disc. Thirteen, pp.203-204.

[22] Blake, "Annotations to Reynolds," p.458.

[23] *Ibid.*, p.459. Reynolds associates imagination with indistinct expressions; these are permissible in poetry but not in painting. Referring to imagination in relation to an observer, Reynolds declares that "leaving any thing to the imagination opposes a very fixed and indispensable rule in our art" because an observer's "imagination supplies more than the painter himself, probably, could produce" (Disc. Eight, p.145).

[24] Blake, "Annotations to Reynolds," p.461.

[25] Blake [Public Address], from the *Note-Book,* p.594-595.

landscapes, seascapes, or portraits of socially prominent personages, Blake continued to receive his inspiration and visions directly from the creative power of imagination, depicted singular events relating to man as a spiritual being, and rendered his objects with the most scrupulous adherence to individualized detail. Blake was thoroughly imbued with principles diametrical to Reynolds' Lockean doctrines.[26]

It was in reaction to Locke that Berkeley developed his philosophy in the *Principles*; he replaced material forces with spiritual powers, abstract reasoning with sensory experience, and abstract general ideas with particular ideas, introducing a new causal principle and a new concept of knowledge. Whereas Locke maintained that ideas are effects of powers resulting from primary qualities within physical objects, Berkeley argues that "the various sensations or ideas imprinted on the sense ... cannot exist otherwise than in a mind perceiving them.... Their *esse* is *percipi*.[27] The existence of sensible objects, like thoughts and passions, is identical with their being perceived. The world is forever being created in the mind of perceivers. Contrary to Locke's opinion, there is no "natural efficient cause, distinct from a *mind* or *spirit*." Berkeley uses the term *spirit* interchangeably with mind, signifying "one simple undivided active being." It is "perfectly unintelligible," he asserts, to attribute an existence to any part of the universe "independent of a spirit," a principle he reaffirms in *Siris*.237. He brings everything within the range and orbit of the mind: "all the choir of heaven and furniture of the earth, in a word all those bodies which compose the mighty frame of the world, have not any subsistence without a mind." Moreover, sensory impressions are real qualities of things. In *Siris* he draws up

---

[26] Neither an exhaustive analysis of Reynolds' aesthetics nor a complete comparison between it and Blake's view of art is intended; that would not only require a book in itself but also take us too far afield. The concern here is to show that Reynolds founded his theory of art on the principles of natural philosophy, which Blake does not accept.

[27] This is one of Berkeley's most puzzling statements, which philosophers discuss right up to the present day. I take this proposition to mean that reality is a perceivable event, although I am aware this phrase itself entails further philosophical questions. These, however, are outside the scope of my present investigation. For a penetrating analysis of Berkeley's dictum, see Benson Mates' article, "Berkeley was Right," *University of California Publications in Philosophy* (Berkeley, 1957) vol.29, pp.158-174. Quotations in this paragraph are from Berkeley, *Principles*.3, 107, 27, 6, 88.

an army of ancients to battle natural powers; in the *Principles* he relies on his own experience and insights to attack abstract reasoning. Locke distrusted the senses; he believed that we see only appearances; that our ideas are merely secondary qualities of originals or external things; and that abstract reasoning infers their real qualities. He therefore assigned a higher ontological status to abstract ideas than to perceived particulars. But Berkeley contends it is "a manifest contradiction that any sensible object should be immediately perceived by sight or touch, and at the same time have no existence in Nature, since the very existence of an unthinking being consists in *being perceived.*"

All things in their own nature are particular. Their qualities are mixed, several in the same object; hence we cannot "abstract one from another, or conceive separately those qualities which it is impossible should exist so separated."[28] Although Locke supposed the capacity to abstract discriminates man from brutes, Berkeley with a touch of Socratic irony says he fears that he along with a great many other beings who pass for men must be reckoned among the brutes, for no man can perform abstractions in the Lockean manner. Berkeley admits he can by either dividing or compounding represent to himself a partial idea of those things he has already perceived. But whatever he conceives "must have some particular shape and colour" as well as size. Similarly, whatever quality he pictures must be particularized. Somewhat indignantly he concludes: "for any one to pretend to a notion of entity or existence *abstracted* from *spirit* or *idea*, from perception and being perceived, is... trifling with words."

Berkeley makes certain his readers see he is not only quarrelling at a word; his disagreement with Locke is metaphysical.[29] Whereas the latter posited a corporeal substance, which impresses ideas upon a passive mind, Berkeley on experiential grounds asserts "there is not any other substance than *spirit*." To this end he defines fully what he means by it: "that which perceives ideas, and wills, and reasons about them. What I am my self." He thus reverses Locke: ideas are "entirely passive" and have their existence only in being perceived; "whereas a soul or spirit is an active being, whose existence consists

---

[28] *Ibid.*, Introd.10; 81.
[29] *Ibid.*, §7; 139.

in... perceiving ideas and thinking." This metaphysical difference between Locke and Berkeley obtains also between Reynolds and Blake.

Berkeley undercuts Locke's metaphysics by countering the rules of reason on which it rests: "To discern the agreements or disagreements there are between my ideas, to see what ideas are included in any compound idea, and what not, there is nothing more requisite, than an attentive perception of what passes in my own understanding."[30] It seemed to him that if we cannot trust perceived particulars, the whole system of knowledge collapses; reason cannot affirm an entity beyond the facts of experience. Rather than "reducing each particular phenomenon to general rules"—which Newton had done in science, Locke in philosophy, and Reynolds later would do in art—Berkeley suggests we "should propose to our selves nobler views, such as to recreate and exalt the mind, with a prospect to the beauty, order, extent, and variety of natural things; hence, by proper inferences to enlarge our notions of the grandeur, wisdom, and beneficence of the Creator." And later in *Siris*.308-309, referring to Locke's reduction of innate ideas to an arbitrary mixture of abstract qualities, he characterizes ideas of beauty and goodness as notions we have by inward feeling.[31]

These sentiments accord with Blake's approach to art. Instead of depicting abstract ideas of general qualities, he recreated beauty as he felt it and diversity of forms as he perceived them. He was not merely indulging his own tastes and mental powers or exploring recondite subjects; rather, he was expressing the inseparable link between the human spirit and world of experience. He firmly believed that in portraying his perceptions he was presenting an objective reality and thus avoiding the indefiniteness of abstract reasoning, which naturalist and generalizing painters of Reynolds' school were displaying in their works. He was therefore irritated with Dr. Trusler, who rejected a commissioned painting on a moral subject because he found the representation abstruse. In his reply of 23 August 1799 to Trusler, Blake remarks: "What is Grand is necessarily obscure to Weak

---

[30] *Ibid.,* Introd.22; 109. It should be clear that Berkeley does not condemn either reasoning or abstraction; nor does he deny the usefulness of certain categorical notions such as comparisons, differences, identities. His objection pertains to Locke's peculiar doctrine of abstraction; he contends it is a misuse of reason.

[31] These differ from Platonic self-existent qualities: see the previous section.

men."[32] And in the same letter, responding to Trusler's complaint that the painting "seems to be in the other world or the World of Spirits" rather than in "This World" of nature,[33] Blake emphatically states, "I see Every thing I paint in This World.... To me This World is all One continued Vision of Fancy or Imagination." Because Blake equates imagination with spirit, he expands the range of experience beyond nature. To him there is no anomaly between the two worlds; to him this world is an aesthetic and creative experience of the human spirit.

But most of the nation's art connoisseurs, critics, and painters along with the general populace uncritically subscribed to Reynolds' Lockean theory. They either did not accept or perhaps did not understand a philosophy that causally connects the world to an active spirit. To confirmed Lockeans, spirit and this world seemed incommensurate; to them spirit was some tenuous rarefied phenomenon of the upper air remote from our experience, or some supernatural thing floating about in the lofty borders of heaven. Consequently, critics and artists applied Reynolds criteria and, usually under a cloak of anonymity, rejected without hesitation Blake's works. For example, an unnamed reviewer of *The British Critic* (September 1796) referred to Blake's Leonora designs as "imaginary beings, which neither can nor ought to exist."[34] A few months later (January 1797) a contemporary artist, John Hoppner, imitator of Reynolds and portrait painter of famous ladies, publicly declared that Blake's drawings for Edward Young's *Night Thoughts* "were like the conceits of a drunken fellow or madman."[35] Others sank to the occasion.

These savage attacks were evidence of how completely Lockean doctrines and censures had taken over art. The critics were formidable

---

[32] Blake, *The Letters*, p.793. Cf. Berkeley, *Siris.* 366: commenting on things divine, he writes that what Plato "speaketh of the super-celestial region, and the Divinity resident therein, is of a strain not to be relished or comprehended by vulgar minds." In his letter Blake also cites Plato among the wise ancients who considered most effective "what is not too Explicit... because it rouzes the faculties to act." However, the reason Blake gives for ambiguity in moral instruction does not, at least to my knowledge, occur in Plato's writings: Plato worries about irrational action; rational acts he encourages.

[33] Bentley, pp.60-61.

[34] Bentley, p.55, 58.

[35] Cf. Locke's words quoted earlier.

adversaries; yet Blake would not submit to a system that not only bound his creative powers and violated his concept of excellence in art but also contradicted his view of the world and conflicted with his moral values. His convictions were strong. He persevered in his own genius, determined to exhibit his imaginative visions; but critics were relentless in their derision. Progressively, he was forced to depend on the patronage of a few individuals. In September 1800 he accepted Hayley's offer of employment and moved to Felpham, where Blake thought he could carry on his "beloved Arts."[36] Soon, however, he discovered that Hayley too regarded Reynolds' views as authoritative. Mentally distressed at being confined to mere imitation at the expense of his divinely bestowed talent to portray "Great things" of the spirit, Blake makes known his anguish to a friend: the assigned work at Felpham is "carrying me over Mountains & Valleys, which are not Real, in a Land of Abstraction, where Spectres of the Dead wander." And he asks, "who shall deliver me from this Spirit of Abstraction & Improvidence?"[37]

Berkeley had attempted the delivery of philosophy by repeatedly attacking abstract reasoning and its improvident product. He was the first to see and openly announce that Locke's doctrine of matter seriously undermined both knowledge and religion; in his opinion this doctrine has been "the main pillar and support of *scepticism,* so likewise upon the same foundation have been raised all the impious schemes of *atheism.*"[38] As early as 1710 he put forth arguments he believed would be proof against assaults on the efficacy of spirit. Without company of others he continued to combat the general passion for corpuscular philosophy. Despite his efforts, enthusiasm for this philosophy increased. Yet Berkeley did not despair; this watchman of spirit never gave up his philosophic defense. In his last published essay he observes that a "lapsed state of human kind" was not unknown to philosophers of the past, and that mankind was uplifted from this fallen state: "Theology and philosophy gently unbind the ligaments that chain the soul down to earth, and assist her flight towards the sovereign Good."[39] To this end he worked

---

[36] Blake, *The Letters,* "To Thomas Butts 10 January 1802," p.812.
[37] *Ibid.,* 11 September 1801," p.809.
[38] Berkeley, *Principles.* 92.
[39] Berkeley, *Siris.* 302.

unceasingly, confident that the time would come when the present age too would "recover and raise" itself from its "low condition."

The spiritual recovery Berkeley envisioned, however, did not occur in his lifetime. No amount of physical or mental exertion on his part could withstand the immense power natural philosophers had placed in their methodological machinery and masses of matter, reinforced by the help of such prestigious institutions as the Royal Academy. Even before the end of the century Blake was feeling the oppressive effects. At Felpham, the restrictions imposed upon his work made his life intolerable. With a "heart ... full of futurity," he left there in 1803 and returned to London, where he suffered renewed attacks.[40] An anonymous critic, patently using Reynolds' standards and terms, writes: "the mind is shocked at the outrage done to nature and probability"; arguing *ad hominem*, this same critic judges Blake's illustrations to Blair's *Grave* as "beyond the 'verge of legitimate invention'... absurd effusions ... the offspring of a morbid fancy" *(Antijacobin Review* 1808).[41]

To Blake this slanderous criticism demonstrated clearly that art had become an appendage of natural philosophy. For over twelve years his imaginative designs were ridiculed as hyperbolic and his notions of visionary art mocked as mad. He could no longer in silence bear the continued assaults on his works, or as he called them, his *acts of the spirit*. At the beginning of his annotations to the *Discourses*, Blake writes: "Having spent the Vigour of my Youth & Genius under the Opression of Sr. Joshua & his Gang of Cunning Hired Knaves Without Employment & as much as could possibly be Without Bread, The Reader must Expect to Read in all my Remarks on these Books Nothing but Indignation & Resentment." His experience at Felpham vividly revealed the need to liberate art from its control by Royal Academicians. Now, the time of redemption surely had come. Having prepared for it in *Milton* (1804-1808) by authenticating himself as the nation's bard divinely inspired, Blake carries out this redemptive struggle. In a letter to a friend Blake relates that despite the restraints put upon his creative energies at Felpham his spiritual life did not cease, nor his visions forsake him:

---

[40] Blake, *The Letters*, "To Thomas Butts 25 April 1803," p.823.
[41] Bentley, pp.204-207.

"...none can know the Spiritual Acts of my three years' Slumber on the banks of the Ocean, unless he has seen them in the Spirit, or unless he should read My long Poem descriptive of those Acts: for I have in these three years composed an immense number of verses on One Grand Theme, Similar to Homer's *Iliad* or Milton's *Paradise Lost*, The Persons & Machinery intirely new to the Inhabitants of Earth (some of the Persons Excepted)."[42]

This long poem is *Jerusalem*, an epic counterpart of the *Discourses*.[43] In its literal sense, Blake's epic embodies a conflict between two systems of art involving two views of the world, between Reynolds' system grounded on rules that chain the soul and fetter the artist to earth, and Blake's system founded on spiritual power, which unbinds the imagination and breaks all fetters. The narrative and rhythm of the poem flow from the clash between the principles and consequences of these opposing systems—all wondrously wrought with Blake's art. Through action, dialogue, and illustration Blake presents a critical event vitally affecting art and mankind. His intense emotional involvement in this historical event is explained by the devastating attacks upon his art.[44]

---

[42] Blake, *The Letters*, "To Thomas Butts 25 April 1803," p.823.

[43] Blake makes a similar statement to the one quoted above in *Jerusalem* 3:1; and at 12:58 he makes explicit the implied comparison of his vision to Ezekiel's. David V. Erdman believes the above passage "fits *Milton* better than *Vala* or *Jerusalem*," *The Poetry and Prose of William Blake* (New York, 1970), p.727.

[44] These facts should deter critics from regarding *Jerusalem* as only a personal struggle within Blake's own psyche. The calamities to which he bore witness lasted longer than the Trojan war.

PART THREE

ATTACKS UPON JERUSALEM

Blake fits the attacks on divine inspiration and individual genius into a general war on spirit, allegorically representing it as Albion's cruel war against Jerusalem. At the generic level *Jerusalem* belongs to epic, but not classical epic. Although Blake compares his epic to *The Illiad* and *Paradise Lost*[1] and uses some classical epic techniques, he chooses the four-part structure of the Gospel to frame his narrative, not only lending it increased authenticity, sublimity and pathos but also investing his poem with apocalyptic significance.[2] His choice of form

---

[1] Like these, *Jerusalem* dramatizes a flaw in human judgment; but the war is conducted neither with bronze sword nor with cannon in heaven; the warfare is verbal and takes place on earth. Because Milton conceives his subject (England's political turmoil as a rebellion against reason) mythologically as a fall, allusions to his epic are numerous in *Jerusalem* though the cause of the nation's low condition and the solution differ radically.

[2] Cf. Stuart Curran's essay, "*The Structures of* Jerusalem," *Blake's Sublime Allegory,* eds. Stuart Curran and Joseph Anthony Wittreich, Jr., (University of Wisconsin, 1974), pp.329-346: Curran believes the model for *Jerusalem* is Milton's "Paradise Regained: the antithesis of Christ and Satan"; he postulates seven structures, totaling 53 parts, which he relates to The Book of Revelation, moving "through seven visions, stressing their general character in multiples of fourteen"; he sees "no narrative progression whatsoever." Hazard Adams, "Blake, *Jerusalem,* and Symbolic Form," (*Blake Studies,* 1975), pp.143-166, states that its structure "is its form...a structure that is about itself" (p.156). Minna Doskow, *William Blake's Jerusalem: Structure and Meaning in Poetry and Picture* (Fairleigh Dickinson, 1982), characterizes the poem as Albion's "states of consciousness" involving 3 errors and argues a thematic moral structure; "Time is transcended as one action is consecutively revealed": the "religious," "philosophic," and "affective errors" are outlined in Ch. 1 and individually explored in Ch. 2, 3 and 4 resp., pp.15-20. Morton Paley, *The Continuing City,* William Blake's *Jerusalem* (Oxford, 1983), interprets it as "Sexual Myth," attributing Albion's fall to "a primordial sexual encounter," and reads the poem as "a non-narrative visionary work," p.167 and 285.

assumes a parallel between the events of Palestine during the first century and England in the eighteenth century. Blake's knowledge of the Bible and its pertinence to the on-going life of man lies behind this assumption. A general statement by Berkeley, who also had a high sense of biblical history, makes explicit the connection between fallen nations in the past and those in the present: "captivities, distresses, and desolations" of Israel were turned and its people shown compassion upon their return to God. In view of this, he asks, "why may we not in reason hope for something analogous? . . . It cannot be denied that there was a great Analogy between the Jewish institutions, and the Doctrines of the Gospel."[3] Blake epically pursues and particularizes the analogy in his inspired fourfold poem recounting the fall of a nation and its salvation.[4] Though its dramatic personae include figures from biblical history, though the Gospel form carries some of the epic's meaning, and though Christian myth interpenetrates its four-dimensional space-time, *Jerusalem* is not a retelling of the Gospel's story. Blake never forgets the events he narrates belong uniquely to his time and intimately to his experiences as artist. To give his aesthetic argument greater force, he subsumes it under the more general biblical analogy.

Because *Jerusalem*, like the Gospel, in form and content manifests the eternal spirit, in his address "To the Public" Blake invokes "Jesus our Lord, who is the God *of Fire* and Lord *of Love*, to whom the Ancients look'd and saw his day afar off." This invocation alludes to the Old Testament and to *Siris*, for it may be recalled Berkeley speculates that even heathens anticipated the God of the New Testament. In fact the intonation of *Siris* is that belief in matter as the universal power is atheistic and goes against *all* tradition.

The phrase 'Lord *of Love*' plainly refers to spirit revealed in the New Testament. But in what sense is the Lord a God *of Fire* in the context of natural philosophy? In this we have help from Berkeley. He developed this notion at great length in evident opposition to Newton's hypothesis of a corporeal agent (a pervasive aether) as the cause of gravitation. Though Berkeley agrees that attraction is the effect of "some active subtle substance," he calls it *fire* or *vital spirit*

---

[3] Berkeley, "Propagation of the Gospel," vol.7, p.125.
[4] The Gospel-form is argued in my essay "*Jerusalem*: A Synoptic Poem," *Comparative Literature* (Summer 1970), pp.265-278.

and argues that this substance is "the first natural mover."[5] A celestial fire is God's medium for animating the whole and ordering its several parts. Further, as the divine fire in nature is the instrumental cause of vegetation and motion, so the "animal spirit in man is the instrumental or physical cause both of sense and motion ... in the several parts of his body, whether voluntary or natural." This "pure spirit or invisible fire" everywhere present "is the general source of life, spirit, and strength." All this is contained in Blake's epithet and his accompanying statement as he continues his parallels between past and present: "We who dwell on Earth can do nothing of ourselves; every thing is conducted by Spirits, no less than Digestion or Sleep." Keeping to his literary model, Blake correlates and at the same time expands this statement with a comparable saying in the First Gospel:

Ἐδόθη μοι πᾶσα ἐξουσία ἐν οὐρανῷ και ἐπὶ γῆς.

In sum, spirit is the vital principle in man, the cause of all his motions, be they voluntary or involuntary, and the sole power in heaven and on earth.

Natural philosophers' exclusion of this power had far-reaching consequences, for, as Berkeley notes, a nation's "religion, manners, and civil government" ever take "some bias from its philosophy."[6] Natural philosophy draws after it atheistical concerns centering on self-interest; and history shows that nations are "undone" or "flourish" depending on whether men pursue their own interests or those of their country.[7] Hence, in Berkeley's opinion, England was running headlong into ruin, for natural religion and morality have most contributed to the nation's downfall.

Blake sees England going to final ruin because its art is chained to natural philosophy. Reynolds was proud of this connection; he fulfilled the promise of his first lecture "to discountenance that false and vulgar opinion, that rules are the fetters of genius."[8] Later, in a speech delivered at the opening of the Royal Academy, he makes

---

[5] Berkeley, *Siris*.147,152-157,212. Among the ancients, he finds corroboration for his notions in the thought of Heraclitus, for whom "an ever-living fire" expresses the process of change and world movement in ever-recurrent forms (*Siris*.175).

[6] Berkeley, *Siris*.331.

[7] Berkeley, "An Essay Towards Preventing the Ruin of Great Britain," vol.6 (1953), pp.69-85.

[8] Quotations are from Reynolds, Disc. One, p. 21; Disc. Nine, pp.150-151.

imperious claims for his theory. He points to the collateral relations between art, human nature and society: it is "necessary to the security of society, that the mind should be elevated to the idea of general beauty, and the contemplation of general truth." By implication his theory benefits England. He has purified art of its original sensual tendencies by subjecting it to the rules established by natural philosophy: like science and knowledge, art through sense "must make its way to reason," which "abstracts the thoughts from sensual gratification," thereby advancing the "dignity of our nature" and the intellectual "excellence" of a nation. Let every artist remember "that he deserves just so much encouragement in the state as he... contributes in his sphere to the general purpose and perfection of society."

Blake alludes to these speeches in his introductory address:

> Poetry Fetter'd Fetters the Human Race. Nations are Destroy'd or Flourish in proportion as Their Poetry, Painting and Music are Destroy'd or Flourish! The Primeval State of Man was Wisdom, Art and Science.[9]

He certainly concurs with Reynolds that the relationship between art, science, humankind and nations is close; he makes an ever greater claim: art and science are vital to a nation's future. But he thoroughly disagrees with Reynolds' view of art as a gradual scientific progress to discover the general. Blake makes art autonomous, placing it among man's first noble intellectual pursuits, connate with his origins. His pronouncements, however, contain more than a desire to ensure the nation's glory. It would be oversimplifying a complex situation to assume Blake was acting only in the national interest. To be sure, he recognized the significance of art for a country's cultural development and its immortal embodiment. But he also had deep personal motives for offering the nation a new theory of art. Its principles are directly related to an unfettered practise of his art, as they were to the preservation of Berkeley's theological commitment. Though *Jerusalem*'s scope comprehends Berkeley's and the nation's interests, Blake writes not as philosopher or moralist; he writes as artist and poet.

---

[9] Similar assertions appear in Blake's "Annotations to Reynolds": "The Foundation of Empire is Art & Science. Remove them or Degrade them, & Empire is No More.... Art is First in Intellectuals & Ought to be First in Nations," pp.445-446.

The poem proper begins with an announcement of the general theme in a solemn Miltonic tone:

Of the Sleep of Ulro! and the passage through
Eternal Death! and of the awaking to Eternal Life.

A lofty subject. Blake qualifies himself as a truth-telling poet, divinely inspired. He hears the Savior "dictating the words of this mild song," which accounts also for the poem's episodic quality, repetitions, and loose narration characteristic of oral epic and the Gospel. Albion, projected as a father, suffers from a "soul's disease." Why? He has closed his eyes to spiritual perception and accepted rules of science as the foundations of art, which is the source of eternal life. Until Albion awakens from the sleep of *Ulro,* Blake's derivative from *rules,* he invites eternal death: death communicates itself from Reynolds' system to the whole nation. The poet hears the Savior pleading with Albion to open his eyes to truth, assuring him, "I am not a God afar off." As spirit, God resides in Albion's bosom, and Albion in Him: they are "One." But Albion refuses the solicitations of divine love because he believes spirit is a "Phantom of the over heated brain!"—an allusion to Reynolds, who refers to divine inspiration as a "phantom" and inventions which neglect reason the products of a fevered brain.[10] Because spirit and its effects have not been mathematically demonstrated, Albion, repudiating his Emanation, retorts: "Jerusalem is not! her daughters are indefinite." Emanation is an apocalyptic idiom for the nearness or immanence of the eternal spirit's power. Jerusalem is a particularization of that power as well as a symbol of peace.[11] As manifestation of spirit, she is conjointly the source of Albion's illustrative accomplishments in art and his well-being: they are Jerusalem's "daughters." Albion denies this: "My mountains are my own"—mountains are traditionally associated with temples and places of worship. Convinced that all power comes from matter, he resolves to deify it, set everything on its solid foundation, impose his system upon the whole world, and claim

---

[10] Reynolds, Disc. Six, p.87.
[11] Etymologically, *Jerusalem* means *the habitation of peace;* Rev. 21 describes Jerusalem as a bride and a great city. For a historical repertory of the idea of Jerusalem developed by writers, see Paley, *The Continuing City,* pp.136-166.

it for his own: "Humanity shall be no more, but war & princedom & victory!" [4:1-32][12]

Albion is a victim of natural philosophy. Through wrong judgments and false opinions, he has fallen into that "low situation" Berkeley, reversing Locke, describes as a "region of darkness and dreams."[13] Its sleepers wildly fancy that natural phenomena are explicable on mechanical principles alone; so they posit "such phantoms as corporeal forces;" or they infer a divine intellect as the remote original cause that created the world and set it a-going by itself. Even ancient philosophers in their logical systems of the world attributed the origin and order of generation to "an eternal necessary emanation." Berkeley insists on more: "We cannot make even one single step in accounting for the phenomena without admitting the immediate presence and immediate action of an incorporeal Agent, who connects, moves, and disposes all things." Yet natural philosophers "suppose him at a great distance off"; by "an aversion of thought, a wilful shutting of the eyes," they escape seeing divine traces of wisdom in nature; their self-sufficient but unknown corporeal substance introduces "so many sceptical and impious notions, such an incredible number of disputes," throwing knowledge, religion and peace into confusion.[14]

Thirty years later Berkeley observes the situation has worsened: "corpuscularian and mechanical philosophy" is no longer confined to "inquisitive persons," no longer a theoretical question; it has taken a fast hold on the greater part of mankind; it has become a cultural catastrophe.[15] How did this happen? He notes with regret that "when it entered the seminaries of learning as a necessary accomplishment, and most important part of education," it indisposed men "for spiritual, moral, and intellectual matters." Consequently, fifty years after the advent of natural philosophy, knowledge remains confounded, atheism gains ground, immorality abounds, and controversies multiply. Paradoxically, education is leading men to an abyss of darkness and destruction.

---

[12] Numbers in brackets at the end of a paragraph refer to *Jerusalem's* plate and line, and apply to quotations within that paragraph.

[13] Berkeley, *Siris*.340,293,362,237: phantoms are unperceived ideas; hence in §293 he objects not to perceptions of imagination but rather to *grafting* these acts of the mind *as if* they were effects of external forces.

[14] Berkeley *Principles*.150;154;96.

[15] Berkeley, *Siris*.331.

A half century later Blake sees all this and more, which he vividly conveys through familiar symbols associated with the nation's established places of learning: "The banks of the Thames are clouded! the ancient porches of Albion are/Darken'd! they are drawn thro' unbounded space, scatter'd upon/The Void in incoherent despair!" His great universities and the Royal Academy teach that all power comes from impenetrable particles in motion, thereby obscuring knowledge in mists and dispersing everything into unfathomable chasms below the earth and infinite spaces above it. "Cambridge & Oxford & London" are mechanically "driven among the starry Wheels, rent away and dissipated." As the forces of matter advance against spirit, "Albion's mountains run with blood" and "cries of war" reverberate in Ulro. [5:1-6]

The same situation exists on the continent. There, mechanical philosophers have set their machines in motion, involving every nation in cruelties, war and destruction. Turning to the "Universities of Europe," the poet beholds

...the Loom of Locke, whose Woof rages dire,
Wash'd by the Water-wheels of Newton: black the cloth
In heavy wreathes folds over every Nation: cruel Works
Of many Wheels I view wheel without wheel, with cogs tyrannic
Moving by compulsion each other, not as those in Eden, which,
Wheel within Wheel, in freedom revolve in harmony & peace.
[15:14-20]

Because Locke's philosophy now controls Albion's art, the poet weeps "Upon the Emanations of Albion's Sons, the Daughters of Albion,/ Names anciently remember'd, but now contemn'd as fictions/ Although in every bosom they control our Vegetative powers." Among his daughters with whom we empathize are *Cordella, Gonorill, Ragan, Gwendolen,* and *Sabrina,* legendary figures of Albion's past recreated and particularized in works of art by his celebrated poets Shakespeare and Milton. In these compressed lines [5:37-44] directed against Reynolds, Blake conveys with respect to poetry, sentiments Berkeley expresses about abstract morality. He speculates the present age would not find itself in such a lamentable state if at least ancient philosophy were not neglected in the universities. It would be of great benefit to our land if men "would imbibe the notions" of celebrated ancients.[16] They did not regard "goodness, beauty, virtue and suchlike" as "figments of the mind, nor mere mixed modes, nor yet abstract ideas in the modern sense, but the most real beings."

For the origin of these intellectual difficulties which lead to the aesthetic conflict Blake presents, we may again refer to Berkeley, who traces it to "the opinion that the mind hath a power of framing *abstract ideas*" of things and recounts in great detail how this opinion became a doctrine.[17] Having observed that space, time, and motion are common to all things, Newton abstracted these quantities, which he considered absolute or true and distinguished them from relative or apparent, "which distinction," Berkeley says, "doth suppose those quantities to have an existence without the mind: and that they are ordinarily conceived with relation to sensible things, to which nevertheless in their own nature, they have no relation at all." Indeed in *Principia* Newton explains that instead of these absolutes, "we use relative ones... in common affairs; but in philosophical disquisitions, we ought to abstract from our senses, and consider things themselves, distinct from what are only sensible measures of them."[18] Locke made this dictum central to his philosophy, distinguishing between apparent or secondary and true or primary qualities, which the mind singles out for abstract ideas.

To Berkeley the most abstract and incomprehensible of these ideas is *matter*. Natural philosophers say that extension, solidity, and motion in general are modes of matter. They describe it as "an inert, senseless, unknown substance; which is a definition entirely made up of negatives"; matter, as they conceive it, is in fact "a *non-entity*."[19] From a strictly empiricist perspective material substance has no meaning. Those "absolute magnitudes and figures" supposed to be in things are "a vain supposition" based on a false principle of reasoning. The ancients saw this; they taught that matter is "neither

---

[16] Berkeley, *Siris*.332,335.

[17] Berkeley, *Principles*.Introd.6,110.

[18] Sir Isaac Newton, *Principia,* trans. Andrew Motte, ed. Florian Cajori (1934, rpt. Berkeley; University of California, 1971), p.8.

[19] Berkeley, *Principles*.68; *Siris*.304,306. Would the latest speculations about quarks, leptons and other unseen particles support Berkeley's criticism of unknown matter? They certainly would have furnished Blake with materials to create more imagery.

an object of understanding nor of sense"; it is made out by a "certain spurious way of reasoning." Objects of this *logismo notho* have "nothing positive, being only a mere privation, as silence or darkness."

Because Locke's philosophy is the citadel of Reynolds' system, these ideas figure prominently in Blake's narrative; he creates them as images, building upon philosophic points, extending their significance and deepening our emotional response. Non-entity, incoherence, chaos, darkness, the void, and related imagery pervade *Jerusalem*. The strife in art has the same cause as the controversies in other domains:

> Abstract Philosophy warring in enmity against Imagination
> (Which is the Divine Body of the Lord Jesus). [5:58-59]

Abstract reasoning, which sinuously weaves through the text, is the matrix of the war in art; imagination is the matrix of the poem's creativity. In equating imagination and spirit, Blake gives full scope and validity to imagination as the source of all ideas, thus giving universality to art—to the artist's inspiration and his work—thereby avoiding the subjectivity of art as self-expression. He does not conflate the personality of the artist and his craft, as did numerous critics.

As usual, he communicates his ideas through distinct names of characters as well as through their actions and through denominated places. The *Spectre* personifies spurious reasoning, which selects qualities from the perceived world to form a supposed real world of abstract ideas. This is the meaning of the "Void outside of Existence" engraved above the archway on the frontispiece. Because natural philosophers have replaced spiritual power and humanity with an abstract idea of material forces, we read further that Albion's "Sublime & Pathos become Two Rocks fix'd in the Earth;/His reason, his Spectrous Power, covers them above." As will be seen, pathos and the sublime have a metaphysical content. At 5:51-53 Blake adds biblical symbolism to portray opaque matter and absolute space: "A pillar of smoke writhing afar into Non-Entity, redounding/Till the cloud reaches afar outstretched among the Starry Wheels/Which revolve heavily in the mighty Void." Since abstract reasoning has far-reaching ramifications, the Spectre's character will be developed fully as the narrative unfolds, detailing the harmful effects for art.[20]

In emotive language he describes the abstracting process, showing how Albion's sons turn it into a moral doctrine to keep themselves in power:

> They take the Two Contraries which are call'd Qualities, with which
> Every Substance is clothed: they name them Good & Evil;
> From them they make an Abstract, which is a Negation
> Not only of the Substance from which it is derived,
> A murderer of its own Body, but also a murderer
> Of every Divine Member: it is the Reasoning Power,
> An Abstract objecting power that Negatives every thing.
> This is the Spectre of Man, the Holy Reasoning Power,
> And in its Holiness is closed the Abomination of Desolation.
> [10:8-16]

Philosophically, they arbitrarily distinguish between primary and secondary qualities, naming the former *true* or *absolute* and the latter merely *apparent* or *sensory*. The primary qualities they generalize to form an abstract idea of material substance, which not only negates particulars and spiritual substance, wherein all qualities have their existence, but also murders human beings, whose very life is this divine substance. Blake recognizes the practical and theoretical value of reason but rejects it as the essential faculty of man and over-ruling principle of human perceptions and choices; the function of reason is to order perceptions, not to indulge in object making.[21] It is important to distinguish rationality or reasonable behavior and reasoning according to formal rules of logic for induction, deduction, and abstraction. Blake opposes reason in its spectrous power, not reason *per se*. It is the naturalists' use of abstraction to which he and Berkeley object. Modern naturalists are much like materialists of antiquity, who in their attempt to account for the various forms in nature by an underlying substance destroyed the very cause of motion

---

[20] In *Alciphron*, "The First Dialogue," §4, Berkeley uses the term *spectre* to characterize abstractions by deists, charging them with "spectres of their own raising."

[21] On Albion's awakening, reason is ordered to its proper place (pl.95); only the Druid Spectre is annihilated (pl.98).

and then dragged in "reason as a *deus ex machina* for the making of the world."[22] So Albion's sons, having assigned the cause of generation to matter, introduce abstract reasoning to justify their principles, then declare it the right way to knowledge and eventually to perfect forms in art, making abstraction into moral law. The predicates *good* and *evil* belong to men's treatment of each other, not to art. A work may be banal, ineffectual, inconsequential, and so on; its forms may be well or poorly done. These are aesthetic, not moral judgments, a distinction Blake keeps making. Progressively—yes, even aggressively—Albion's sons negate spiritual perception and denominate its forms *evil*.

Employing battle imagery, Blake dramatizes the effects of Reynolds' "great ideal" of "perfection and beauty"[23]—a phrase Blake reorders and uses repeatedly; at the same time he indirectly confirms his own views enunciated earlier concerning the necessity of unfettered arts for a nation's vitality. In the war against imagination, Albion has been wounded:

> Outstretch'd his Giant beauty on the ground in pain & tears:
> His Children exil'd from his breast pass to and fro before him,
> His birds are silent on his hills, flocks die beneath his branches,
> His tents are fall'n; his trumpets and the sweet sound of his harp
> Are silent on his clouded hills that belch forth storms & fire.
> . . .
> Where once he sat, he weary walks in misery and pain,
> His Giant beauty and perfection fallen into dust. [18:46-19:1-8]

One hears strains of David's harp in these lines and other passages of the poem.[24] Blake selects images from the Psalms connected to Israel's history in time of trouble to depict Albion's affliction. Because tents were used by Israelites for holy worship, they here symbolize spiritual inspiration. Denying it and binding musicians, artists, and poets to iron rules is ruinous to the arts and pernicious to the nation.

---

[22] Aristotle, *Metaphysics* 1.4 (985ª): this is his criticism of pre-Socratics, to which Berkeley alludes in *Siris*.286.

[23] Reynolds, Disc. Three, p.45.

[24] *Jerusalem* is rich not only in psalmody but also in echoes of Jeremiah's lamentations for captive Israel. However, this study limits itself to those images bearing directly on Blake's aesthetics.

Controlled by the Spectre, subjected to external forces, and deprived of his own power to act, Albion in vain tries to recover life: "In the dark world, a narrow house! he wanders up and down/Seeking for rest and finding none! and hidden far within,/His Eon weeping in the cold and desolated Earth."[25] Restless he searches for the source of existence; he finds no comfort because abstract philosophy has entombed him in matter, burying his soul within earth. [19:14-16]

In his metaphysical reflections Berkeley lamented the tenacious grip matter had taken upon men's minds. On analysis, he finds this doctrine is a combination of prejudice and error. "From the outward form of gross masses," natural philosophers examine minute parts and apply spurious reasonings to form hypotheses of corporeal substances.[26] These "veils of prejudice and error" interpose a screen between men's minds, the real agent of their acts and ideas.

This is the philosophic fabric of Vala's artful veil. The Spectre, Vala, and her veil are inextricably connected in the opposition to spiritual perception. As Jerusalem represents energy of spirit, so Vala personifies powers in nature, and her veil symbolizes abstract ideas of nature's forms placed between the artist's inspiration and his creations. Like Jerusalem, therefore, Vala is a key character in the development of the dramatic action. The image of the veil along with the related motifs of hiding, concealing, covering, separating, dividing, and burying perceived particulars recur throughout the poem. Blake expresses this thematic element through numerous fictional projections: Jerusalem is "hidden" by Albion; she is "shut within" him; she is "Embalm'd in Vala's bosom"; Albion is dying because "his Emanation is divided from him"; and so on. Jerusalem is causally related to Vala, but natural philosophy has placed energy within nature itself. Previous to Albion's repudiation of spirit, Jerusalem "soft repos'd/In the arms of Vala, assimilating in one."

---

[25] In this vignette of Albion, Blake wittily draws upon Bacon's description of men who do not put their "gift of reason" to practical use, do not dignify knowledge by conjoining "contemplation and action." Such men enter into learning "as if there were sought in knowledge a couch, whereupon to rest a searching and restless spirit; or a terrace, for a wandering and variable mind to walk up and down": *Philosophical Works of Francis Bacon,* trans. Robert Ellis and James Spedding, ed. John M. Robertson (London: Routledge, 1905), "The Advancement of Learning," p.60.

[26] Berkeley, *Siris.*295-296.

She reminds Vala that nature's forms issue from the "Lamb of God.../ ...he gave thee to Albion." [4:16, 19:29, 23:9, 12:6, 19:40-41, 20:39-40]

Since the veil on the most general level signifies all abstractions from perceived particulars, it is of immense proportions, extending from science into art. For Blake it is the veil of abstract generalizations that must be removed. For Reynolds, on the contrary, the "veil" is made up of errors in neglecting the general and of "prejudices" in favoring the "fashion of the times" that "cover" truth: an artist "is obliged to remove" this veil "before he can see the truth of things" and acquire "the unadulterated habits of nature, which give him simplicity;... he, like the philosopher, will consider nature in the abstract, and represent in every one of his figures the character of its species."[27]

Reynolds' approach to representing the human figure derives from Locke, whose concept of man was especially odious to Berkeley. He deplores the erroneous suppositions and reasonings to frame "the abstract idea of *man*, or if you please, humanity or human nature."[28] Locke says that only what is general is essential to man: "the abstract idea is the very essence" (Essay, III.vi.4). This generalized abstract idea, Berkeley observes, possesses only what man shares with all animals, primarily body since Locke regards man as a corporeal being and his acts as so many mechanical motions. But even this bodily quality has a most abstract meaning: a body without motion, without shape. According to Berkeley, the measure of man is man, not abstract science. Man is a complex being, whose identity resides in the "human mind, self, or person," indivisible. As the universal spirit cannot be separated from forms of existence in nature, so the individual spirit cannot be separated from human life and actions. Man in his essential nature is spirit; as such, his unique property is spontaneous creativity. With typical irony Berkeley points out that naturalists reject spiritual substance because we have no direct experience of it; yet without any hesitation they accept an unperceived material substance.

By virtue of his unity with the universal spirit, man communicates with God and with other men. Spirit for Berkeley is not

---

[27] Reynolds, Disc. Three, pp.49-50.
[28] Berkeley, *Principles*.Introd.9; *Siris*.358.

merely an aspect of man's nature in Plato's sense; rather, it is man's essence according to Christian doctrine: spirit is identical to love—the "force that unites" and causes all things to "move in harmony."[29] Berkeley was troubled by the inhumanity inherent in a materialist metaphysics and sought to reestablish man as a moral being responsible for his own acts, a created and creative spirit motivated by love, not merely a generated body of nature impelled by material forces.[30]

The separation of spirit from the human form, and hence from human perceptions and acts, is a central issue in *Jerusalem*. Blake's moral as well as his aesthetic position is intricately connected to his concept of man as spirit. Not that morality and art are identical, as Blake repeatedly points out; rather, humanity and divine inspiration emanate from the same source. Because he experienced gross inhumanity in attacks upon his art and person—also vindictiveness in political accusations brought against him[31]—humanity, which at first seems tangential to his theme is in fact intrinsic to it and becomes a constant in his epic. In the defense of imagination against abstraction, individual genius against rules of reason, particular ideas against abstract ideas, the contrasts between spiritual power and material causality, between body of life and body of death, perception and reasoning, love and hate, peace and war, humanity and inhumanity make up the poem's counterpoint rhythm and embody much of its dramatic quality.

As the First Gospel, symbolized by a creature-form bearing the face of man stresses the discordance between legalistic morality and compassionate spirit, so *Jerusalem's* Chapter 1, taking its impress from the same creatural symbol, focuses on the difference between the inhumanity of naturalists and the humanity of spiritual beings. In a dialogue, which is part of the epic action, Jerusalem and Vala, representing opposite causal principles and opposite concepts of man, are pitted against each other. Jerusalem "in pleadings of Love" asks why Albion has shut her "into the winter of human life," closing up the world's perceivable beauty and man's "love and sweet affection." Appropriately, Vala's answer reflects naturalists' views: nature is not

---

[29] Berkeley, *Siris*.259.

[30] It is interesting to compare Berkeley's and Blake's concept of man, of existence, and of outward objects with Heidegger's views.

[31] Blake was indicted for sedition but found not guilty.

the creation of a providential being; it is the effect of material powers, cruel, not merely indifferent to man. She describes this self-subsistent world in terms of winter's heavy snows and natural man as a lost soul, a "wanderer" mourning for his former happy life. Metaphorically, Albion's land now lies covered over with cold matter; it is without guidance, hiding the paths of man and beast, burying the fields of food and ending in bitterness, hunger, and death.[32] [20:4-14]

The composite form of man, body held together by an indivisible essence from which emanate love and creativity, Blake correlates with the creatural animals of the fourfold Gospel held together by one spirit and connects it directly to God's providence or humanity: "the Four Points are thus beheld in Great Eternity" and are "the four Faces towards the Four Worlds of Humanity."[33] But this is not what the poet beholds in Albion's land; there, he sees "Humanity in deadly sleep" because of its "fallen Emanation"; Albion's "rocky form" militates "against the Divine Humanity." In defining the imagination as spirit, Blake not only bestows universality on the artist and his works; he also posits a universal audience, which he calls the divine humanity, the universal family, the universal humanity, and so on. The essential relationship between spirit, imagination, art, love, and humanity is explicit in the second part of the conversation between Jerusalem and Vala. Jerusalem speaks: she was once loved by Vala; now, because naturalists consider spirit to be an abstract idea and belief in spiritual power to be an intellectual fault, Vala looks upon her as a "Sin," implying that such belief is a crime against mother nature. Jerusalem enumerates the precepts of the New Testament, which propounds the 'law' of spirit, while she pleads with Vala: "O, unfold thy Veil in mercy & love!" Pity, kindness and mercy are not sins; they are spiritual forms of love without the naturalists' veils. As spirit, Jerusalem "cannot put off the human form"; whichever way she looks, she sees humanity. [12:54-57, 15:6-7, 19:35, 20:22-29]

In the same scene and in obvious opposition to Reynolds' maxim that artists should imitate their predecessors, otherwise "art would... remain always in its infant state,"[34] Blake incorporates the restraints put upon his original creations, alluding to them metaphorically as

---

[32] Blake's description of winter is much like James Thomson's in *The Seasons*.
[33] For a historical background of the gospel tradition, see the essay cited at n.4.
[34] Reynolds, Disc. Six, p.87.

infant loves. Jerusalem begs Vala, "Slay not my little ones"; and again, "Slay not my infant loves & graces." She recalls the past when she was caught in a "beautiful net" of gold and silken twist Vala had woven "with art" according to the Divine Vision rather than to rules of imitation and abstraction; when in brightness the beauty of perceived particulars showed through the veil; and when Albion beheld his "beauty & perfection" in these works. "Then was a time of love"; it has passed away and with it great art; therefore Albion lies in shadows of oblivion. [20:27-40]

Contrasts between Albion's glorious past and dreary present reappear at periodic intervals against the background of the irrepressible conflict. With a design to secure sympathy for Jerusalem and emphasize the dangers attending Albion, at plate 21 Blake draws together life, art and morality. Freely intermixing the current situation with the story of Job and of Eden, he dialates on the consequences of denying spiritual perception as he expands the action. Responding to laments of Jerusalem and Vala, Albion recognizes they have prepared his "death-cup" because they are separated. He recounts the events leading to his downfall. First (like Job, who doubted divine providence), he was assailed by doubt concerning spiritual power; then denying divine inspiration, he was (like Adam and Eve, who transgressed the divine law) overwhelmed by "Shame," shame for one so wise and great to fall into error and ruin the nation.[35] He has committed an offense against the eternal spirit, thus bringing desolation to his land, division among his people, misery to everyone, and threat of extinction to himself: "All is Eternal Death." He thought that all things are effects of natural powers; that truth in art as in science resides in abstract ideas of nature's forms; so "with costly Robes/ Of Natural Virtue" he covered "Spiritual forms," which are "without a Veil." Blake is here alluding to his representations of the human form that censorious critics judged "indecent," especially his depiction of a family meeting in heaven.[36] Critics had made Reynolds' doctrine of abstract ideas a moral virtue

---

[35] In this section Blake exploits Bk.IX.1120-1125 of *Paradise Lost*.

[36] Bentley quotes from Robert Hunt's review of Blake's designs for Blair's *Grave* (*The Examiner,* 7 August 1808): "At the awful day of Judgment, before the throne of God himself, a male and female figure are described in most indecent attitudes. It is the same with the salutation of a man and his wife meeting in the pure mansions of Heaven," pp.196-197.

ATTACKS UPON JERUSALEM

1. *The Meeting of a Family in Heaven*

and judged all arts accordingly. But like Berkeley, who always sought "to deliver the naked and precise truth" of things without the abstractionists' obscuration,[37] Blake presented the naked truth of his ideas without arraying them in dress woven by abstract reasoning.

In the events befalling Albion, Blake carries out the New Testament theological identity between human spirit and love, personified by Luvah. As the eternal spirit is the source of all art, so love is the eternal motive force of a compassionate public. Because he has "thrust Luvah" from his presence, Albion bears all the diseases of the soul—intolerance, cruelty, abhorrence, suspicion, revenge, hate, war. With Jerusalem exiled and Luvah driven "into the Deep" beyond the limits of human experience, Albion hears his "Children's voices" and sees "their piteous faces gleam upon the cruel winds" sweeping his land; he sees them "scourg'd along the roads" of natural philosophy; finally, he sees "them die beneath the whips of the Captains." And we see the flogging with tripartite philosophical lashes at the bottom of the plate. [21:2-41]

Conquering naturalist heroes make Albion's children their prisoners:

> Six months they lie embalm'd in silent death, worshipped,
> Carried in Arks of Oak before the armies in the spring.

The above problematic passage on the philosophical level refers to worship of nature and treatment of humans as its creatures, who are sacrificed in druidic (oaken) fashion. Allegorically, it alludes to the disrespect for Blake's individual creations. Like vegetation these captives lie dormant in winter and come to life in spring, when the captains who build their criticism on Reynolds' principles rise and in pride parade their conquests as they lead their armies against the imagination. The torment of a living-death Albion's children and concomitantly Albion himself suffer is never ending: in desperation he cries out, "O that Death & Annihilation were the same!"[38] [21:44-49]

Spreading her blood-stained veil over Albion, Vala informs him she has been deified: "Thy Sons have nail'd me on the Gates, piercing my hands & feet." Like a Christ figure on a cross, Vala's image is

---

[37] Berkeley, *A New Theory of Vision*, vol.1 (1948), §120.
[38] Cf. Eve's proposed self-destruction to evade the curse upon her offspring (*Paradise Lost*, Bk.X.999-1006).

borne by Albion's militantly crusading sons before their conquering armies. They track their enemy with the savagery of hounds in pursuit of wild boar: "Great is the cry of the Hounds of Nimrod along the Valley/ Of Vision..../ All Love is lost! terror succeeds, & Hatred instead of Love."[39] The allusions to Blake's experiences at the hands of hostile critics (exaggerated for purposes of the epic) need hardly be mentioned. [22:2-10]

Albion denies wrong-doing; his attitude is thoroughly scientific and his heart oaken hard. Why should he be blamed for bringing knowledge into a world of ignorance and beauty "into light of day"? He sent Jerusalem wandering because "Innocence is no more," no divinely inspired infant loves. This is an indirect criticism of Reynolds' remark that students who have ignored rules and depended on individual genius have "wandered... from the right way;[40] Blake alludes to this several times through various characters. In gentlest manner Jerusalem, for sake of humanity, begs Albion to readmit her: "Why should Punishment Weave the Veil with Iron Wheels of War/ When Forgiveness might it Weave with Wings of Cherubim?" At the bottom of plate 22 Blake illustrates this contrast: pairs of delicate angelic figures joined harmoniously, symbolizing divine love, float above wheels rimmed with sharp teeth, symbolizing Albion's notion of justice, rectitude in art and mechanical philosophy perfectly synchronized.[41] Driven by its wheels, Albion consigns Jerusalem to "impalpable voidness, not to be/ Touch'd by the hand nor seen with the eye," to the voids created by abstract philosophy: to Newton's absolute space, time and motion; to Locke's unknowable material substance; to Reynolds' "general" beauty, which "the sight never beheld,... nor has the hand expressed it."[42] Jerusalem in Albion's view is a "deluding shadow." Falsely he accuses her of reknitting Vala's veil, which he in druidic times of nature-worship rent, but which natural philosophers have made "more/ Perfect and shining with beauty!" Therefore he embraces Vala and prepares to sacrifice

---

[39] Blake here effectively combines biblical and Homeric imagery (cf.Gen.10:8-9 and Bk.17.281-283 of *The Iliad*). References to the Bible are from the King James version, and to *The Iliad* from Richard Lattimore's translation (University of Chicago, 1966).
[40] Reynolds, Disc. One, p.21.
[41] This illustration reflects also the description in 15:17-20 quoted earlier.
[42] Reynolds, Disc. Nine. p.151.

himself at her altar, expiating for his sin of ever having admitted Jerusalem and by the same act establishing the new religion and new art: "come, O Vala, with knife & cup, drain my blood/ To the last drop, then hide me in thy Scarlet Tabernacle." The cult of science had become a religion. [22:17-35, 23:1-7]

Although Albion has hidden Jerusalem, he has not disposed of her. From within the dark recesses of nature, as "from a sepulcher," her voice still is heard: spirit is ever-living and unconquerable. Whichever way Albion turns he beholds "Humanity and Pity." Momentarily, he has a glimpse of truth: "I have erred! I am ashamed!.../ I have taught my children sacrifices of cruelty:.../ I will hide it from Eternals!" He wildly fancies he can save his children by an extraordinary act manifesting miraculous powers. On analogy with Peter's spiritual net of the New Testament,[43] Albion casts Vala's veil into the "Atlantic Deep to catch the Souls of the Dead," but woven in errors it returns "in Errors." Why are the souls at the bottom of the sea? Blake here adds profundity to his theme by incorporating into his mythical scheme imagery deriving from Proclus to which Berkeley alludes in *Siris*.313-314: a human soul through false tenets and prejudices falls into "generation." This fall is like a man "diving to the bottom of the sea, and there contracting divers coats of seaweed... which stick close to him, and conceal his true shape." Nevertheless the soul inherently attempts to "emancipate herself from those prejudices and false opinions that so straitly beset and cling to her, to rub off those covers that disguise her original form." This is how Blake sees the followers of Reynolds' system, which conceals the true nature and shape of the human form. Albion tries to retrieve his errors, lift himself from his lapsed state, and save his children from eternal death; but he fails because only a spiritual act can bring back life to dead souls. [23:8-23]

Symbolically, Albion "stood between the Palm tree & the Oak," between Christianity and Druidism, between humanity and cruelty, between pity and enmity: "there Albion sunk," borne down by the weight of the new system. His state has some likeness to that of a soul Berkeley describes with respect to knowledge: a human soul finds herself "weighed down by sensuality"; if she lacks "some tradition"

---

[43] For a scholarly discussion of Peter's metaphorical net, see Wilhelm H. Wuellner, *The Meaning of Fisher of Men* (Philadelphia: Westminster Press, 1967).

to "sow the seeds of knowledge," she looks "through the dusk of a gross atmosphere." Clouded by false opinions, she "cannot see clearly. And if by some extraordinary effort the mind should surmount this dusky region and snatch a glimpse of pure light, she is soon drawn backward and depressed by the heaviness of the animal nature to which she is chained."[44] Albion, standing between two traditions, relapses: he affirms his naturalist convictions, drawing him *backward* into Druidism. "God in the dreary Void/ Dwells from Eternity, wide separated from the Human Soul"; Jerusalem is a "deluding Image." He rationalizes: God is punishing him because for her he rent "the Veil." Within Vala's veil, he enfolds his limbs, signifying all parts of the nation and all its arts, whose truth he believes only a high priest and his captains see.[45] Then, keeping to his code of natural morality, Albion utters a dying curse upon the "Blasphemous Sons" of Jerusalem as he sinks into the darkness prepared, in fact, by Vala's sons: "May God, who dwells in this dark Ulro & voidness, vengeance take,/ And draw thee down into this Abyss of sorrow and torture,/ Like me thy Victim." [23:24-40]

Albion suffers the supreme outrage: he is crucified by his own sons. They have taken vengeance, which belongs to God alone. Near death, Albion has second thoughts about the doctrines he has accepted and asks profound philosophical questions. Is life really only a certain combination of atoms, only certain motions of matter? Is man merely a passive object of external material forces? Are they the source of art and morality? Is death eternal? Is man "born to feed the hungry ravenings of Destruction?" The implied answer is no:

O Jerusalem, Jerusalem, I have forsaken thy Courts,
. . .
O Human Imagination, O Divine Body I have Crucified,
I have turned my back upon thee in the Wastes of Moral Law.

The rejection of spiritual power in *Jerusalem,* as in the Gospel's stories, is symbolized by crucifixion. Albion has repudiated art of the imagination as immoral. [24:14-24]

Distress and guilt lie heavily upon him. Following his impassioned confession and repentance, he agonizingly details in a long

---

[44] Berkeley, *Siris*.339-340.
[45] In Hebrew temples the veil hid from the eyes of all but the high priest the inner sanctuary of God (Heb.9:2-7).

monologue the idyllic state of earlier times, when "once happy Families" lived "in love & harmony," contrasting it with the present state of hate and discord. Yearning for the past and bewailing the present sounded by Albion here and earlier, by Vala, by Jerusalem, and by the poet will be echoed again and again by them and others until Albion restores Jerusalem. He recognizes the cause of his grievous state; he goes to destruction because naturalist "Builders" have taken over art; "they have forsaken Jerusalem." But despite this recognition, again like Job, Albion still doubts: "If God was Merciful, this could not be. O Lamb of God,/ Thou art a delusion and Jerusalem in my Sin!" Albion again struggles to uplift himself, but amidst confusions and strong affects he suffers a second relapse. As he falls back into the clouded and dark region of Ulro, he gives up: "Hope is banish'd from me." He despairs of salvation because, in accord with natural religion, he believes that punishment, cruelty, and eternal death await him. But Blake brings out in a touching scene the forgiving nature of spirit: Albion dies in the arms of the god he has slain. What Albion intends to extirpate, he confirms. [24:29-60]

At plate 25 Blake takes us inside Vala's temple to witness Albion's sacrifices.[46] The connections Blake has made between natural morality, art, and Druidism afford him opportunities to depict inhumanity at its zenith, sharply contrasting it to the compassionate character of spirit and intensifying our revulsion against the inhumanity of naturalist critics. In sensuous form he gives a vivid anatomical picture of unspeakable druidic rites offering human sacrifice to nature. Over Albion's body impressed with stars, sun, and moon presides Vala in the attitude of Michelangelo's creating God while her attendants Rahab and Tirzah draw out Albion's umbilical cord, symbolizing creativity, thereby giving birth to natural religion and art.[47] Albion's conversion is complete. "Thund'ring the Veil rushes from his hand, Vegetating Knot by/ Knot," entangling men's minds, decrying the imagination, and escalating the dismal war. Sorrow of death compasses Albion's people; lamentations abound; weeping and wailing are in season. [24:61-62]

---

[46] *The Illuminated Blake,* annotated by David Erdman (New York, 1974) is primarily descriptive rather than analytic; it does not discuss *Jerusalem's* illustrations contextually.

[47] M. Jackson interprets this scene as a mithraic ritual: "Blake and Zoroastrianism," *Blake Newsletter* (Fall 1977), pp.72-84.

Attacks Upon Jerusalem

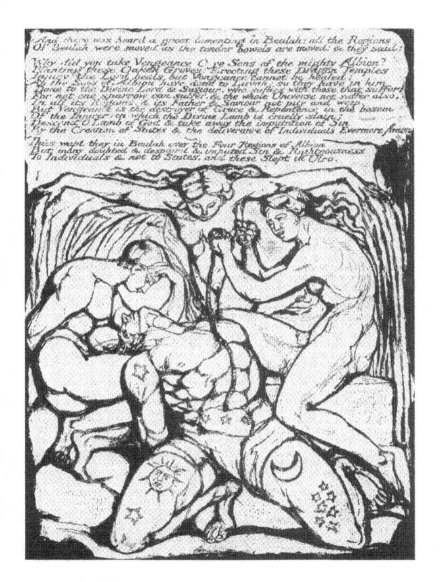

2. *Jerusalem* 25

PART FOUR

THE SATANIC TRIUMVIRATE

The leaders of Albion's war are Coban, Hand and Hyle: his giant sons of natural and rational philosophy. Blake fits these into his scheme of analogues by associating them with the Trinity. What is the connection? Berkeley, for whom the Trinity is the foundation of religion, claims that natural philosophy subverts this ancient doctrine. Countering "modern atheism" he asserts that no philosophers have ever "by the light of nature attained an adequate notion of the Holy Trinity"; nor were "those sublime hints, which dart forth like flashes of light in the midst of profound darkness... originally struck from the hard rock of human reason but rather derived... by a divine tradition, from the author of all things.... We are sprung from the Father, irradiated or enlightened by the Son, and moved by the Spirit."[1] Natural philosophers take this doctrine lightly and replace it with abstract reasoning and material substance.

In *Jerusalem* the hard rock is a persistent element associated with these two principles upholding Reynolds' system, which Blake epically treats. He selects cardinal features from the works of England's three most famous natural philosophers and ingeniously shapes these into characters parodying the Holy Trinity.[2] He slants his representations

---

[1] Berkeley, *Siris*. 354, 360-362. In his criticism of natural philosophy, generally he does not name the philosophers, except Newton on occasion; instead, he refers to them indirectly through their doctrines, sometimes quoting at length from their works. He respects the genius of Bacon, Newton and Locke; he criticizes them to the extent they erred in making reason the ultimate judge of truth.

[2] The discussion that follows presents the philosophical conditions and explains the doctrines surrounding Blake's art and bearing directly on the interpretation of his epic; it is not a complete comparison of the four complex philosophies involved—that in itself would require a huge volume.

towards a disagreeable connotation for purposes of the epic conflict, emphasizing the harmful consequences of misapplying scientific method to art. He is not hostile to science; like Berkeley, he is interested in advancing science but opposed to imposing its principles on all forms of human activity.

Bacon is the first of the philosophers, whose "terrors" the poet sees "hang" over the nation. Indeed an ardent interest in natural philosophy and its methods had been growing in England since the time of Lord Bacon. His fame as "the glory of his age and nation" remained relatively undiminished in Blake's day.[3] Reynolds esteems Bacon as a profound thinker and beautifier of all knowledge, bestowing on him the epithet "great."[4] Blake disagrees with this acclamation: "The Great Bacon—he is Call'd: I call him the Little Bacon—says that Every thing must be done by Experiment."[5] It can easily be seen why Blake, who held that forms are perfect in the artist's or poet's mind and that rules hamper individual genius, disparaged Bacon. [15.11]

In his seminal work, *Advancement of Learning,* Bacon charges that men have disgraced learning because they have tumbled up and down in their own conceits instead of contemplating nature. In addition to a consideration of nature, knowledge involves a rational function of the mind. Many men find the subject of methodology extraordinarily dry, yet "to speak truly of things as they are in worth, Rational Knowledges are the keys to all other arts."[6] Natural philosophy, upon which Bacon affirms all knowledge must be built, is badly in need of tools for penetrating the recesses of nature to discover causes. It is not strange, therefore, he concludes, that all branches of learning are now so barren.

Fifteen years later Bacon published his *Novum Organum,* supplying men with nature's own sapling along with "instruments and machinery" to impregnate and cultivate the tree, thereby reconstructing the sciences and providing fruit to all branches of knowledge.[7] In contrast to old (Aristotelian) induction, which

---

[3] *Philosophical Works of Francis Bacon,* "Dr. Rawley's Life of Bacon." p.1.
[4] Reynolds, Disc. Three, p.47.
[5] Blake, "Annotations to Reynolds," p.459.
[6] Bacon, p.111.
[7] Bacon, p.257;267 (Aphorism L)—he is alluding to Aristotle's analysis of forms; 297.

proceeds by simple enumeration of instances, the new method calls for gathering widely dispersed facts of nature, abstracting from them the phenomena in question, and arranging these qualities in conformity with tables of presence, absence, or degree. Only after the collected material has been thus prepared, digested, and confirmed by experiments can the cause of anything be inferred: "Matter rather than forms should be the object of our attention." Bacon refers to his method as "a rule or a pair of compasses" to aid men in the interpretation of nature and points to its objectivity: "my way of discovering sciences goes far to level men's wits, and leaves but little to individual excellence; because it performs everything by the surest rules and demonstrations."

He was convinced this mode of operation would lead men to knowledge of nature's secrets and therewith to mastery of her powers. By "arts and sciences" men can recover their "dominion over creation" and make possible new inventions to alleviate the miseries of mankind.[8] In this belief, at Aphorism I he issues two directives, one practical, the other theoretical, but mutually dependent:

> On a given body to generate and superinduce a new nature or new natures, is the work and aim of Human Power. Of a given nature to discover the form, or true specific difference, or nature-engendering nature[9] or source of emanation ... is the work and aim of Human Knowledge.

This peculiar covenant to human power in Bacon's philosophy, embodying a new physics as well as a new method and promising power to control nature for humanistic ends, inspired men to take up the new way of truth. Thus motivated, men engaged in various labors, isolating parts of nature, analyzing these by proper inclusions, exclusions, or degrees of a particular substance, and therefrom making Baconian inferences.

Although Blake's contemporaries looked upon Bacon as a prophet and his philosophy the means to useful knowledge, and hence to salvation, Blake regards Bacon a false prophet and himself,

---

[8] Bacon, p.387; by *arts* he means methods of inquiry and argumentation, not the fine arts: "logic and rhetoric being the arts of arts," p.77.

[9] Bacon, p.302: his phrase is *natura naturans,* by which he means nature is its own cause.

because divine inspiration is the source of his vision, a true prophet, a stance he regularly assumes in his poems: "I see the Past, Present & Future existing all at once." Bacon's philosophy, which sets down techniques for discovering nature without reference to spiritual causes, has contributed to the present dislocations in knowledge, religion, morality and art, and hence to Albion's ruin; it will in time lead to the "Abomination of Desolation," the total destruction of men and nations alike. Applying Bacon's anagrammatic method to his name, Blake calls Bacon also *Coban*. [15:8, 7:70]

Conjoining the present to the past through biblical analogues, Blake equates Coban with Cush; but he also makes him the father of Cush: "Coban's son is Nimrod: his son Cush is adjoin'd to Aram." Is this an error of fact? No. Blake is carrying out his mock Holy Trinity, a doctrine which holds that the Father, Son and Holy Spirit are united in one God.[10] Accordingly, he attributes this coinherence to Coban. The idea of a triune personality is continued by Blake in his characterization also of Hand and Hyle; like Coban, they possess three aspects of one demonic god in parody of one Lord, the person and work of Christ, and the person and work of the Holy Spirit. This accounts for the fluid identity and intrinsic unity of these characters within themselves and with each other. [7:15]

As Nimrod (according to one legend, which Blake evidently adopts) rejected worship of Elohim and established a new kingdom based on worship of nature's life-giving powers, so Coban rebels against spirit and founds Ulro, whose inhabitants regard nature to be the self-generating source of existence. Again, as the "mighty hunter" of mankind by conquest and loss of human lives extended his kingdom of Babylonia,[11] so Coban in depreciating individual inventiveness forcibly advances the dominion of Ulro. Finally, as Cush was joined to Aram, whose invasion, barbarities and near annihilation of Jerusalem are famous in the history of Israel's disasters,[12] so Coban is joined to the cruel attacks upon Jerusalem,

---

[10] To say more about this mysterious and complex theological doctrine would be out of place here; but it is hoped enough has been said to clarify the seeming confusion on Blake's part: for instance, see S. Foster Damon's *Blake Dictionary* (New York, 1971), p.300: "Blake... refers oddly to Nimrod's 'son Cush'."

[11] Cf. Gen.10:9.

[12] For details of this history see esp. Judges v.6 and 2 Samuel x.1-6.

threatening Albion's life. Here are the roots of Albion's "fatal Tree," which penetrates his art and eventually leads to his fall. Blake connects the biblical tree of knowledge to natural philosophy, conveying at once Coban's satanic character and the dire consequences for mankind.[13] [12:26]

Bacon's tree remained attached to nature's womb and received new nourishment from Newton. He added quantitative and generalizing tools far more comprehensive than the Baconian tables of qualities and thus opened a new road to human power and concomitantly a new form of knowledge. On the basis of four "Rules of Reasoning" in conjunction with abstractions from the senses, accurate experiments and mathematical computations, utilizing the laws of mechanics Newton characterized the forces with which bodies move toward each other.[14] These forces, which he calls *gravitation* or *attraction,* result from the "vis insita, or *innate force of matter.*" The power of all bodies whatsoever is proportionate to their mass. The motions of celestial bodies have exactly the same physical cause as terrestrial ones and are explicable by the same law: gravitation is the universal law of motion.

The precision instrument added to abstracting machinery for guiding men's understanding is mathematics. By deduction from the general theory he developed from axioms in Books I and II of the *Principia,* Newton mathematically demonstrates in Book III "the frame of the System of the World."[15] He explains the fluxes and refluxes of the sea; he derives the precise mathematical values of properties belonging to planets—their orbits, axes, planes, distances, weights, and so on; he accounts even for the phenomenon of fixed stars.

Suddenly, as if by miracle, Bacon's sapling became a huge tree, conspicuously increasing its mass; it spread and deepened its roots into earth; enlarged and elevated its trunk into the starry heavens; and multiplied its branches, filling them with green fruit, not one here and

---

[13] Though Bacon is certainly important in the development of natural philosophy, and though he is mentioned by Reynolds, Coban plays a comparatively small part in the epic conflict; his role is primarily formal: we rarely see him in action. Like Berkeley, Blake concentrates on the philosophies of Newton and Locke.

[14] Newton, p.398,2.

[15] *Ibid.*, p.397.

there but in clusters.[16] Bacon had prophesied that right method would result in a new philosophy of nature; he exhorted men not to rest content with a deficient science but to proceed determinedly to the discovery of nature's great form. He had declared that axioms rightly formulated would carry with them whole troops of inventions useful to men; he had not, however, foreseen that axioms could also lead to laws containing fecund bodies of new facts. Newton not only unearthed nature's form; through abstract reasoning, generalization of axioms, and mathematical ingenuity he revealed the structure of the universe as well. Bacon's figurative *rule* and *compasses* become literal: the world seemed truly the work of a geometer, who framed the universe according to mechanical principles expressible in simple mathematical form. *"Nearer the gods no mortal may approach."* This line from Edmund Halley's "Ode to Newton," prefixed to *Principia's* first edition, reflects the awe with which most contemporaries of Newton regarded his scientific insights. To them, his general law clearly manifested unlimited powers of human reason.

But Berkeley was immediately critical. Although he admired Newton's profound knowledge in geometry and mechanics, his exactness in experiments, and his original discovery of uniform motions, he rejected his explanation of them. Motions and various phenomena we perceive cannot be imputed to nature; rather, they are effects of "the immediate hand of God."[17] This "hand which actuates the whole is itself unperceivable to men of flesh and blood;... yet to an unbiased and attentive mind, nothing can be more plainly legible, than the intimate presence of an *all-wise Spirit,* who fashions, regulates, and sustains the whole system of being."

Because of the metaphysics implied in Newton's general law, Berkeley contests it at great length in *Siris*. He accepts the laws of attraction and repulsion but denies they have a natural cause, insisting and reiterating: "the principle of attraction itself is not to be explained by physical or corporeal causes."[18] Newton supposed the world goes like a "machine by itself, according to laws of nature, without the immediate hand of the artist." Berkeley criticizes the

---

[16] Bacon compares the partitions of knowledge to "branches of a tree that meet in a stem," *Advancement of Learning,* p.89.

[17] Berkeley, *Principles.* 150-151.

[18] Berkeley, *Siris.* 245,233,228,235.

deductive method by which Newton demonstrated the system of the world. "It is one thing to arrive at general laws of nature from a contemplation of the phenomena and another to frame an hypothesis, and from thence deduce the phenomena." Though there appears a uniform working of things, the particular laws are "diverse. And it is not known what other different rules or laws of motion might be established by the Author of nature." It seemed that Newton had presumed in making his observations of particular motions into a general law controlling the world as if it were actuated by his law.

The potential of representing Newton as a god is fully perceived and epically actualized by Blake, for indeed Newton's law had become a metaphysical principle widely accepted. Utilizing the ellipsis for 'hand of God,' Blake's alternate name for the second of England's natural philosophers is *Hand*.[19] Attributing gravitational forces to matter, Newton denies the power of spirit; imposing his law upon the world, he usurps the divine prerogative. Thus *Hand* is the demonic counterpart of the Divine Hand, the Godhead and Father almighty, creator of the universe, in the Holy Trinity. Blake projects the presumptuousness of generalizing abstractions from observed particulars into a universal law by picturing Hand as a satanic figure, arrogant and haughty, situating him in a hell-like mechanistic universe of hard matter: "Hand sits before his furnace; scorn of others & furious pride/ Freeze round him to bars of steel & to iron rocks beneath/ His feet." [7:71-73]

---

[19] This interpretation of the term *Hand* gives the symbol a significant meaning in the context of *Jerusalem's* main theme. Blake critics generally associate Hand with the editorial pointing finger used by Leigh Hunt of *The Examiner*. The identification of Hand as Hunt, which has become a convention in Blake criticism, is based upon speculations that have no factual support in Blake's works themselves. The biographer Alexander Gilchrist (1828-61) writes:

> It is true that the *Examiner* persecuted him [Blake], his publications and exhibition, and that Leigh Hunt was prone to tell 'good stories' of him;... and in some manuscript doggerel of Blake's we meet with the line: The Examiner, whose very name is Hunt.... But what form can the irate allegory be supposed to take in *Jerusalem*. Is it conceivable that that mysterious entity or non-entity, 'Hand' whose name occurs sometimes in the poem, and of whom an inscribed spectrum is there given at full length, can be a hieroglyph for Leigh Hunt? Alas, what is possible or impossible in such a collection?" (p.203)

In construing this symbol, we should not overlook Blake's own use of the pointing finger in his commentaries: see, for example, his annotation to §410 of Swedenborg's *Divine Love and Wisdom*.

Because Newton explains the system of the world by natural causes alone, "Hand has peopled Babel & Nineveh," the great cities in Coban's land: Babel signifies confusion with respect to natural causes; Nineveh symbolically and incisively conveys the status of England as a world power, the rapidity with which natural philosophy spread, and the resultant idolatry of nature, for Nineveh was not only an idolatrous city-state but also a powerful ancient empire exerting its authority upon successive generations of mankind. The great influence of Newton's philosophy Blake indicates in many other ways and places. For example, lines 8:43-44 through 9:1-2 comment on the overwhelming force of Newton's material causality upon the nation's religion and subsequently upon its art: "Hand has absorb'd all his Brethren in his might;/ All the infant Loves & Graces were lost, for the mighty Hand/ Condens'd his Emanations into hard opake substances,/ And his infant thoughts & desires into cold dark cliffs of death." Emanations, including those of the scientist, are inspirations and insights activated by spirit, the prime mover of every idea. *Infant,* like the word *children,* has an ontological meaning denoting spiritually related phenomena: thoughts and desires of the artist are conscious impulses originating from within him, from his imagination, and shaped by his genius, not by powers from without, nor by fixed rules of science. In an invocation, Blake makes a rare explicit reference to his art:

... O Divine Spirit, sustain me on thy wings,
That I may awake Albion from his long & cold repose;
For Bacon & Newton, sheath'd in dismal steel, their terrors hang
Like iron scourges over Albion: Reasonings like vast Serpents
Infold around my limbs, bruising my minute articulations.

Reasonings, abstractions and generalizations, the techniques of science that Reynolds made essential to art, are like steel swords plunging into the flesh; his laws constrict the artist pain by pain, damaging the particularizations of his spiritual perceptions. In the above passage Blake obliquely carries through the image of the fatal tree not only to suggest, among other things, the seductive quality of these reasonings and their evil effect on visionary art but also to reinforce the satanic nature of Hand, uniting him to Coban. [7:18, 15:9-12]

Hand is hailed as the divinely appointed saviour. Line 18:39 states this directly: "Hand mightily devour'd & absorb'd Albion's Twelve Sons." The allusion to Christ and his apostles is unmistakable; a parody of the historical Christ is made visible at plate 26. The complexity of metaphysical ideas Blake unites in this picture may be illuminated by turning again to Berkeley, who in his critique of natural philosophy had a lot to say about fire as God's instrument for energizing the universe. In *Siris* he undertakes an extended discussion (§130-202), which begins with an analysis of Newton's theory of attraction, passes to a consideration of air, then to fire, and ends with the doctrine of mind as the true and necessary cause of all existence. Newton attributes attraction "to all acids," which are diffused throughout the air; but air is never found pure; it "contains a mixture of all the active volatile parts" of everything, "that is, of all vegetables, minerals, and animals."[20] Air, from which all bodies "derive their forms," receives its power from a "pure invisible fire.... This mighty agent is everywhere at hand, ready to break forth into action, if not restrained and governed with the greatest wisdom."

Berkeley seems to be saying it is more plausible to explain motion in terms of immaterial "native spirit" than by movement of hard particles in space, in terms of processes of change rather than mechanics. Hence he interprets the natural cause to be secondary and delineates it as a pure invisible power symbolized by fire. Characteristically, he enlists the chief philosophers and wise men of antiquity; they reckoned fire to be the element of change, "yet they supposed a Mind or Intellect always resident therein"; they regarded the cause of "life and death, good and evil" as an "inward invisible force" or invisible fire, which they distinguished from culinary fire.[21] Finally, for added support he cites Holy Scripture. It contains many passages metaphorically representing the supreme Being "present and manifest in the element of fire" to convey His power in the operations of nature and affairs of mankind. Numerous places in "the inspired writings" describe God "as descending in fire, as attended by fire, or

---

[20] Quotations are from *Siris*.133,137,142,152. In passing, it is interesting to note Blake expresses ideas similar to these also in his *Milton:* "All the Wisdom which was hidden in caves & dens from ancient/ Time is now sought out from Animal & Vegetable & Mineral./ The Awakener is come outstretch'd over Europe: the Vision of God is fulfilled."[25:20-22]

[21] Berkeley, *Siris*.137,173,175,186.

with fire going before Him." Like some of the other prophets, "Ezekiel in his visions beheld fire."

Blake also beheld fire in his prophetic vision comprehending biblical, philosophical and aesthetic events. He depicts Newton as Hand with fiery flames issuing from his body in cruciform pose, demonically signifying God and Son. Since Newton explains forces operating in the mundane system by natural causes alone, Hand's fire is not restrained by the provident hand of a wise spirit; instead, it is a fierce and destructive fire.[22] This demonic deity aims to destroy the real agent, which to him is superfluous for explaining observed phenomena.[23] Therefore Blake pictures [plate 26] Hand invested with fire in the region of darkness and with a black scowl defying a terrified Jerusalem, "named Liberty" because freedom of thought and action emanate from spirit.

In relation to art the meaning is clear: divine inspiration denied; genius depreciated; Hand's law cruelly enforced. Such is Blake's vision of Reynolds' system and its consequences. Here illustration and text meet. Blake's riposte inscribed at the left edge echoes Malone's words in his "Introduction" to Reynolds' *Discourses*. Writing after the latter's death, Malone states he found among Reynolds' papers some notes for a new composition Reynolds "intended as a history of his mind, so far as concerned his art," along with "the advantages which he enjoyed, and the disadvantages he had laboured under, in the course that he had run."[24] Opposing Reynolds' system, Blake depicts the difficult *race* he has *run* so far as concerns his art. Like the other full-page illustrations punctuating *Jerusalem's* four parts, plate 26 brings out a crucial point in the narrative. From Newton's rules and law descend the doctrines that eventually lead to the conflict in art: "He [Hand] seiz'd the bars of condens'd thoughts to forge them/ Into the sword of war."[9:4-5]

The impact of Newton's law upon men's mind can scarcely be over-estimated. Both by attraction and repulsion it set off reverberations in all directions, ultimately touching everyone, and each

---

[22] Blake expresses a similar notion in his Epitome of Hervey's Meditations among the Tombs: "God out of Christ is a consuming fire."

[23] Rule 1 of Newton's *Principia* states: "We are to admit no more causes of natural things than such as are both true and sufficient to explain their appearances," p.398.

[24] Reynolds, *Discourses* (London, 1905), p.xiii.

THE SATANIC TRIUMVIRATE

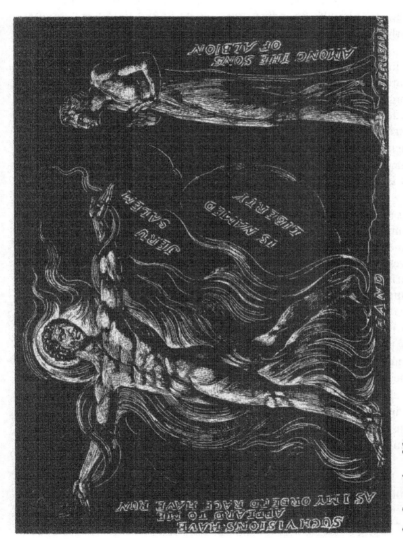

3. *Jerusalem 26*

naturally enough reacted according to his temper and inclination. The metaphysical implications of Newton's theory were so strong that one had either to combat or absorb its forces. His friend Locke was favorably impressed: here was a harmony of new truth, one law explaining by natural causes the operations of the whole world. Newton himself, sounding very much like Bacon forty-six years earlier, in his "Preface" to *Principia* expresses remarkable confidence in the method by which he discovered gravitation: "These forces being unknown, philosophers have hereto attempted the search of Nature in vain; but I hope the principles here laid down will afford some light either to this or some truer method of philosophy." Locke believed the "incomparable Mr. Newton" certainly had found the perfect procedure for inquiring into all things.[25] It seemed to Locke therefore he could hardly perform a more fruitful task for mankind than emulate Newton by extending his principles into a general theory of knowledge.

Locke's impetus for carrying out this work, however, came not from theoretical considerations; rather, it sprang from practical circumstances that were troublesomely urgent. Incompatible theologies among sects had flung the nation into civil wars for two centuries; even now after the Restoration fevered clamors and disputes of sectarian biases continued; each sect made fervid claims to privileged inner truths. In the dedicatory "Epistle" of his *Essay* Locke relates that under these turbulent conditions he became daily more absorbed in methodological debates about theology. Impelled by the certitude of Newton's law, Locke thought that a philosophy founded upon this demonstrated theory along with requisite rules of reason would stay the fury of religious quarrels among sects by exposing their intellectual deceits. Moreover, would not a system erected on Newton's principles advance all knowledge? Yes. Had not Newton's forerunner the great Bacon declared that all knowledge must be based on natural philosophy? Yes.

After clearing the ground of all that "rubbish that lies in the way to knowledge," and refurbishing it scientifically, Locke brings into full view a thickly branched tree deeply rooted in nature along with Newtonian machinery extensively applied.[26] Physical objects transmit

---

[25] Locke, "Epistle," p.14.
[26] Quotations in this paragraph and the two following paragraphs are from Locke, vol.1, "Epistle," p.14, bk.II.xxiii: §1-3;§5,11,6;§12,29,32.

into the mind simple ideas of sensation or reflection; but because we cannot conceive "how these simple ideas *can* subsist by themselves, we ... suppose some *substratum* wherein they do subsist, and from which they do result, which therefore we call substance." Of this general substance, however, we have no other idea than the sense impressions of "solid extended parts" that adhere in it. The same thing applies to any particular sort of corporeal substance, that which makes a thing what it is, let it be "man, horse, gold, water &c." Like general substance, particular substances or essences are ordinary observable qualities *abstracted* and put together *by reason* into a complex idea which includes a supporting substance, "though we know not what it is."

What about spiritual substance? This is pivotal in the religious disputes, Locke's primary worry. Immaterial substance is, Locke asserts, another complex idea and has exactly the same genesis as corporeal substance. Not apprehending how operations of the mind "can belong to body... we are apt to think these the actions of some other *substance,* which we call *spirit."* Of this substance, however, we have no more idea than we have of *"corporeal substance* in matter." In other words, "without knowing what it is," we suppose a *"substratum* to those simple ideas we have from without"; in like manner and with "like ignorance" we assume a substratum to those operations we experience within ourselves. Substances and their powers upon us we cannot doubt; but we can never know the proper attributes of substances because our senses are not "acute enough to discern the minute particles" upon which powers depend. Distinct sorts of substances are nothing but several combinations of simple ideas, the "cause of their union" is "unknown."

In constructing his system upon natural science, Locke solidly joins his labors to those of his countrymen. The objective of his work differs, however, from his two precursors. Bacon and Newton wished to extend the boundaries of knowledge, whereas Locke seeks to limit them. Bacon urged men to apply themselves unceasingly to analyzing matter until they discover all of nature's causes, a task to which Newton encouraged men by providing powerful machinery; but Locke counsels men to rest in ignorance concerning the real composition of things. Newton agreed with Bacon that by right method and human industry a science of nature is within men's reach; Locke disagrees, not because men lack adequate method or sufficient sedulity but because their faculties are "dull and weak." Though Locke realizes the Baconian ideal of superinducing upon nature a corporeal substance as the source of nature engendering nature, he warns that we can never know the true nature of things. Knowledge is power, as Bacon proclaimed in his famous apothegm, but, adds Locke, we are not capable of knowing much at all: "the simple ideas we receive from sensation and reflection are the boundaries of our thoughts." Our complex idea of corporeal substance is made up of these simple ideas; "and so it is of all our other ideas of substances, even of God himself."

By limiting knowledge, Locke aimed to resolve theological questions and thereby restore order to the nation. In Berkeley's opinion, however, Locke had not only failed in this endeavor, but through publicizing false principles had plunged mankind into far worse evils. He had undertaken his inquiry to establish the "certainty and extent of *human knowledge,* together with the grounds and degrees of *belief.*"[27] But in setting stringent measures to knowledge of our world, of ourselves, and of God, Locke had in fact, so it seemed to Berkeley, not only made knowledge of reality impossible and multiplied disputes in religion; he had also removed the foundations of religion altogether. His examination of the human understanding ends in a tragical irony: at one stroke he thrust man into error, atheism, and darkness.

Berkeley's severest criticism of natural philosophy is directed against Locke. He has led us into dangerous paths by supposing a two-fold existence of sense—the one *intelligible* or in the mind, the other *real* and without the mind, giving to unthinking things a natural subsistence of their own. All this Berkeley challenges: "We have no proof, either from experiment or reason, of any other agent or efficient cause than mind or spirit.... There is not any proof that an extended corporeal or mechanical cause doth really and properly act."[28] Added to this, "I know or am conscious of my own being; and that I my self am not my ideas, but somewhat else, a thinking active principle that perceives, knows, wills, and operates about ideas....

---

[27] Locke, Introd.2.
[28] Berkeley, *Siris.*154-155; *Third Dialogue,* vol.2, pp.233-234: he is not disproving the existence of matter; rather, he is offering a new analysis of what matter is, namely, that it consists entirely of sense-data; he denies it is the cause of ideas.

But I am not in like manner conscious either of the existence or essence of matter." Contrary to Locke, therefore, spirit is the only source of ideas, and we know more about this active agent than about any corporeal substance.

Everywhere it is Berkeley's purpose to remove this cornerstone of Locke's system. In the *Principles* he rebukes the enemies of spirit, "who lay so great a stress on *unthinking Matter,* and... use so much industry and artifice to reduce every thing to it."[29] In the *Dialogues* he projects himself as the immaterialist Philonous, who in continuous polemic opposes Hylas the Lockean materialist so that "atheism and scepticism *will be utterly destroyed*" and "the sublime notion of a God" made manifest. And most relentlessly in *Siris* he gathers support for the efficacy of spirit. Locke has unjustifiably extended Newtonian physical forces into a full-bodied metaphysics: "Sir Isaac himself insinuates" that even those ancients who took atoms for the principles of their philosophy attributed "gravity to some other cause distinct from matter." To Newton's testimony Berkeley adds the authority of ancients themselves: "Neither Plato nor Aristotle by matter, ὕλη, understood corporeal substance, whatever the moderns may understand by that word." To these celebrated thinkers, *hyle* "signified no positive actual being." To them and their followers, *hyle* is "made up of negatives, having neither quantity, nor quality, nor essence"; it is "known neither by sense, nor by any direct and just reasoning, but only by some spurious or adulterine method."

Appropriately, Blake styles the third of England's natural philosophers *Hyle*. As *Coban* represents Bacon's method, as *Hand* represents Newton's universal law, so *Hyle* represents Locke's concept of corporeal substance; each name catches the essential element of the three philosophies operative in Reynolds' system, which Blake sees as the apotheosis of errors. The satanic triumvirate heading this system is complete:[30] Hand is at the center, pictured as God, and "Hyle & Coban" are "his two chosen ones for Emissaries." [18:41]

The tree Bacon planted and Newton nourished, Locke indefatigably cultivated, producing a substance deadly to mankind.

---

[29] Berkeley, *Principles*.93; *Three Dialogues between Hylas and Philonous*, "Preface"; *Siris*.225,317.

[30] Cf. Crabb Robinson's record of Blake's remark: "*Bacon, Locke & Newton* are the three great teachers of Atheism or of Satan's doctrine," (Bentley p.313).

Hence, Blake singles out Locke for the harshest treatment, casting him in the most reprehensible role. Hyle is the evil one, the disseminator of falsehood because he has propagated matter as the sole power on earth.[31] Blake keeps intact the parallels with Judean history. Since Locke not only belongs to the same philosophical tree as Bacon and Newton but brings it to maturity as well, Hyle inhabits and extends Ulro, the kingdom of Coban and Hand: Hyle has peopled "Ashur" (another name for Nineveh) and "Aram," a land brought under Babylonian rule. Because Locke founded his system on Newtonian physics, and himself contemptuously disposed of spiritual causes, "Hand & Hyle rooted into Jerusalem by a fibre/ Of strong revenge." Then, to reinforce the parody between the Holy Trinity and Albion's sinister sons, Blake shows them "join'd in dark Assembly," laying out their strategy to bring the world under their rule, for "Ulro is the space of the terrible starry wheels of Albion's sons." Like "Three Immense Wheels," mechanically moved by abstract reasoning and "turning upon one-another," these sons, reminiscent of ancient gods in conclave, plot to destroy Jerusalem. [7:18, 15:1-2, 18:5, 12:51, 18:8]

Unwittingly, however, they plot to "murder their own Souls" and "build a Kingdom among the Dead" since spirit is the principle of existence. Confounded, Albion's sons dismiss it as a mere product of deluded minds; so they shout: "Cast, Cast ye Jerusalem forth! The Shadow of delusions!" Because they believe spiritual causes are false explanations of observed phenomena, these giant sons call Jerusalem Vala's "Harlot daughter." Determined to expunge this "sin and shame," they declare an all-out war against the universal family to suppress acts of spirit. Let there be "father now no more,/ Nor sons, nor hateful peace & love"; let there be only "War and deadly contention Between/ Father and Son, and light and love!" Let no one be spared; break all bonds of love: let there be hate and "deadly strife" between "age & youth,/ And boy & girl,.../ And city & village, and house & family." [18:10-26]

Piling up symbols and images that incorporate principles of natural philosophy, Blake elevates to epic proportions the attack upon spiritual perception and his 'sinful' forms depicting love, for Bacon's tree branched heavily over art. Cloaked in Babylonish garments

---

[31] From Blake's point of view, it is natural philosophers who are the rebels.

woven of corporeal substance, Coban, Hand and Hyle remorselessly pursue their goal to obliterate Jerusalem "To build/ Babylon the City of Vala, the Goddess Virgin-Mother./ She is our Mother! Nature!" Babylon belongs to the long line of metaphors, epithets and similes generated by the doctrine of corporeal substance and hence is a continuing image; it is Vala's city because Babylonians worshiped forces of nature personified in deities, such as Ishtar. Vala is a demonic counterpart of the Virgin Mary; as the self-sufficient cause of existence she is at once virgin, mother, goddess. So the founders of Ulro clamor for Jerusalem's death: "Cast, Cast her into the Potter's field!" becomes their war cry. She must be destroyed and her "little-ones," namely divinely inspired works, taken captive. As those enslaved by Babylon were compelled to build the city of Babel out of bricks and slime, so the captives of Ulro are forced to build Vala's city out of a substance "struck from the hard rock of human reason" (Berkeley's phrase, *Siris*.360). Through biblical parallels Blake indirectly transmits his criticisms of Reynolds' canon: material forces as the origin of ideas and the artist's bondage to these forces is conveyed by Babylon; confusion and presumption associated with abstract reasonings are represented by the jumbled language among the builders of Babel, by the tower's great height reaching to heaven, and by its subsequent destruction. [18:28-32]

Continuing his description of assaults upon spiritual power, Blake again conjoins these to his art: since his experiences as artist span several years, they are a constituent part of a long narrative. In pride of victory, Albion's formidable sons prosecute their hateful war "to destroy the Divine Saviour"; out of inanimate matter they build "Castles in desolated places" devoid of human perception and everywhere erect strong defenses, rapidly taking over Albion's land. Consequently, "his Affections now appear withoutside," determined by external objects. Equalizing themselves with gods, "Hand, Hyle & Coban" take possession of Albion's mountains, infusing a moral tone into their laws. From this commanding position they devour "Human majesty and beauty" of the Divine Vision, turning it "into solid rocks with cruelty and abhorrence,/ Suspition & revenge." They have relegated causes of ideas to corporeal forces, bound human thought to simple impressions of these, and shut out the light from which radiates existence. Hence "Albion's Circumference was clos'd; his Center began dark'ning." [18:37-38, 19:17-26,36]

Proud of their accomplishments and fearful lest they lose their authority, Coban, Hand and Hyle marshal their "warriors in the Vale of Entuthon-Benython." Here is another of Blake's portmanteau words, a play on the phrase *into-nothing-beyond-nothing,* significative of eternal death into which Albion is headed. Anxious for quick victory and absolute control, his dread sons expand their war, striking with fury everywhere. They "Reason in Cruelty" against spiritual power and "Demonstrate in Unbelief." In so doing they not only disavow certainty in knowledge but also deny the creative imagination and undermine humanity. Albion sees his people "in tortures of Doubt & Despair"; he sees Cordella, Sabrina, and Conwenna—personages of Albion's past imaginatively recreated by historians, poets, and artists—driven through the streets of Babylon into captivity. Everyone fears the attacks by the champions of Albion's satanic sons. Who will defend Jerusalem's children against the terrors of Entuthon-Benython and rescue Albion from the darkness into which he has fallen? [5:12,21:34-36.]

PART FIVE

DEFENDERS OF JERUSALEM

Albion's fall is not unique in the history of nations; others have fallen. We are told in *Siris*.302 that "λύσις," "φυγή," and "παλιγγενεσία," the ancient concepts of *setting free, escape,* and *regeneration* imply that in past human kind perhaps many times had fallen into error but had recovered. Thus encouraged, Berkeley directed his energies towards bringing men out of their "lapsed state" and "into a state of light." Probably drawing upon the term *Lüsis,* which suggests the English word *loose,* and on *lux* as well, Blake names his hero *Los.* As defender of spirit, he will loosen the fetters that chain the artist to Reynolds' rules.[1] Setting free the artist from them will assist him in his flight towards spiritual perception, a necessary condition for the perfection of both art and nation. To Los Blake assigns the epic task of awakening Albion, thereby restoring his emanation, regenerating him, and saving him from eternal death. Fittingly, Blake's engraved frontispiece shows Los embarking on this brave deed: like a sun bringing light to profound darkness, with his globe of fire Los enters the door of death to awaken Albion to eternal life.

Los has heard Jerusalem's lamentations. But in defending Jerusalem against the strong enemy, Los himself always is in danger of being taken captive: "His Spectre driv'n by the Starry Wheels of Albion's sons, black and/ Opake divided from his back." Blake supplements these words with an illustration: the bat-winged Spectre and darkness of night indicating Albion's blindness to the truth of spiritual power and his sleep of death are recurrent images. In the ensuing confrontation between Los and his Spectre, Blake dramatizes the struggles

---

[1] See Pt. Three.

4. *Jerusalem* 1

Defenders of Jerusalem

5. *Jerusalem* 6

to keep his commitment to divine inspiration in face of Reynolds' influential aesthetics. The Spectre tries to "devour Los's Human Perfection," the human essence actualized in his art, but finds Los is one of the "living," one animated by spirit: the constant participle *living* keeps alive this notion in the poem. By "arguments of science," an obvious allusion to Reynolds' *Discourses,* the Spectre attempts to lure Los into the enemy's camp. Failing to persuade by argument, the vaunting Spectre employs more drastic tactics: he reminds Los how he is mocked and how his "once admired palaces," his artistic creations, are now scorned by Albion's people. Why then should Los forgive and rescue Albion, who having cast out Jerusalem, denies friendship and love? Los's Spectre goes further: know that Vala "in cruel delight" now feeds Luvah, who is preparing "the Spectre of Albion to reign over thee." [6:1-2,14; 7:1,6,16,31,40]

The situation is critical. Los acknowledges that Albion has divided him from his Emanation and thus repudiated divine inspiration; nonetheless, he regards Albion a victim of his sons, not an enemy. Albion has been betrayed by them; he is therefore worthy of compassion: "the time will arrive/ When all Albion's injuries shall cease, and when we shall/ Embrace him, tenfold bright, rising from his tomb in immortality." Here is a reflection of Blake's apocalyptic view of history: time will tell that his view of art is right and Reynolds' is wrong. Here also is another reminder of immortality embodied in spiritual art and another instance of the frequent contrast between humanity and inhumanity: Los's attitude differs from the cruelty of Coban, Hand and Hyle, who punish Albion for what they interpret as a crime.[2] Expressing his humanity in a speech that matches his heroic stature, Los solemnly affirms his sublime task: "In anguish of regeneration, in terrors of self annihilation!/ Pity must join together those whom wrath has torn in sunder,/ And the Religion of Generation, which was meant for the destruction/ Of Jerusalem, become her covering till the time of the End." Like Berkeley, Blake uses the

---

[2] One is reminded especially of Aeschylus's *Prometheus Bound:* there, Zeus punishes Prometheus for his man-loving disposition; however, the moral situation in the two works is fundamentally reversed: Zeus inflicts eternal torment upon Prometheus, whereas in *Jerusalem* a compassionate God frees Albion from the suffering imposed by men.

natural philosophers' own weapons against them. Working within their systems, Los will join together what has been separated, namely cause and effect, spirit and nation, Jerusalem and Albion. Empowered by the eternal spirit, Los's "Mace/ Whirl'd round from heaven to earth;" he commands his Spectre to assist in crushing the enemy "on the Anvils of bitter Death," for the sake of art, and hence "for Albion's sake," whose life and perfection depend on the spiritual perceptions of his creative sons and daughters. In this belief Blake was convinced he stood upon firm ground, unshaken by mockery to accept naturalist aesthetics. So we hear Los's repeated phrase, "I am one of the Living," and his warning to the Spectre, "dare not to mock my inspired fury." This fury is not the unbridled fierceness motivated by the personal pride of an Achilles or by the narrow-mindedness of a naturalist critic; rather, it is enlivened by the divine wrath of one in the service of the eternal spirit. [7:54-64;8:16-17,35]

The Spectre is well-known to Los: "Thou art my Pride & Self-righteousness." Whenever reason separates from spirit, it becomes rebellious self-idolatry, assuming to itself all "magnitude & power." He denounces the Spectre: "Thy Uncircumcized pretences to Chastity must be cut in sunder." Blake is extending the biblical analogy between uncircumcision and the heathen into naturalist art,[3] and alluding to "the quietness and chastity of the Bolognese pencil," which Reynolds contrasts with the ineffectual "bustle and tumult" of Venetian painters to illustrate the superiority of generalized forms over minutely discriminated figures.[4] Blake's seemingly absurd metaphors therefore refer to corporeal substance and abstract ideas. These two doctrines—generating bodies and purity of conception—account for the remarkable persistence of sexual imagery in *Jerusalem. Uncircumcision* and *chastity* here apply to Reynolds' ideal of "unadulterated" and simple forms, which he consolidates in the phrase "simple chaste nature."[5] Since these metaphors derive from

---

[3] In "Propagation of the Gospel," Berkeley makes an analogy between "fleshy circumcision and the spiritual" (p.125). He thought that abstract ideas should be "pared off" because they conceal the true form of things: *Principles*.131.

[4] Reynolds, Disc. Four, p.61. Bacon describes his method as "the legitimate, chaste, and severe course of inquiry," *The Great Instauration*, p.253.

[5] Reynolds, Disc. Three, p.50,48.

doctrines of natural philosophy, they include natural religion and morality as well as natural art. [8:30-32]

Los vows his Spectre shall never control him; nor his spirit "ever assume the triple-form of Albion's Spectre" embodied in Coban, Hand and Hyle. Los's Spectre, any spectre, is clearly satanic as evidenced by his sentiments reflecting those of Satan in *Paradise Lost*. However, Blake artfully adapts satanism to his own purposes: the Spectre has not only asserted his own rational power; in his utmost abstraction he has replaced the eternal spirit with material substance, threatening both the divine inspirations in art and the future of mankind. Commensurate with this supposed substance, which in truth is inanimate matter, the Spectre is "a black Horror"; denying spirit as the true cause of existence, he is "all evil, all reversed & for ever dead: knowing/ And seeing life, yet living not." As such, he necessarily despairs of enjoying life and realizing human desires—an allusion to Reynolds, who warns that a student shunning imitation and depending on "native power" will "let fall his pencil in mere despair."[6] Even more than *doubt, despair* is used repeatedly to describe the state of intellect in Albion's land. [8:34;5:68;10:57-58]

Los must restrain the envious Spectre at every turn "lest he should devour Enitharmon," the source not only of Los's creativity but of his very life, for spiritual perception is not simply a mode of being; it is existence itself: "What shall I do, or how exist, divided from Enitharmon?" This name is most probably Blake's collocation of *En* and *harmony*. Berkeley appeals to these concepts in support of his metaphysical theory: as "the world is held together by harmony, the cause whereof is God," likewise "we are one... by our τὸ ἕν or unit," by virtue of our indivisible essence or spiritual substance.[7] Blake apparently conceived of personal identity in similar terms. In separating the artist from his spiritual perceptions and positing natural causality, the Spectre has divided Los from himself. Thus the poet tells us "Enitharmon is a vegetated mortal Wife of Los,/ His Emanation, yet his Wife till the sleep of Death is past." Like all vegetated mortals, she will in this state cease to exist when Los has successfully completed his mission, when he has joined men to their essence, and artists to their imagination, bringing the world under the

---

[6] Reynolds, Disc. Six, p.86.
[7] Berkeley, *Siris*.279,345.

harmonious direction and unity of the eternal spirit. [17:18; 12:9; 14:13-14]

As bearer of the globe of fire, Los is also "Demon of the Furnaces," in the sense of genius or daemon, for genius is the child of imagination, not "the child of imitation."[8] Like the artificer Hephaistos, who fashioned armor for sons of divinities, Los will forge the weapon of defense for Jerusalem's sons. With his "hammer of gold" and "anvil of adamant," imperishable metal and stone, this divinely inspired smith of words takes "the sighs & tears & bitter groans,/ ... to form the spiritual sword," against "the thundering cannon" and "the murdering gun" of mighty Hand.[9] Preparatory to this stupendous undertaking, Los works a mass of sorrow on his anvil and heats "it in the flames of Hand & Hyle & Coban/ Nine times" since each of these three dread sons in himself represents the Trinity. In this scene Blake plainly alludes to his sufferings and fully exposes the prevailing system of art strictly enforced by Reynolds' disciples against particularizations of the human form and against the Divine Vision. The natural philosophers' tree of knowledge has become an all encompassing tree of good and evil, a tree of moral virtue cultivated by critics: abstractions from study of nature are good; particularizations of inventive genius are evil. Albion's sons have assumed the prerogative of God by passing *moral* judgment upon the artist and punishing him. Looking into the furnaces, Los sees "the limbs form'd for exercise contemn'd & the beauty of/ Eternity look'd upon as deformity, & loveliness as a dry tree./... Inspiration deny'd, Genius forbidden by laws of punishment." Los has suffered and knows death's ambience. He is terrified, yet furious and indignant. So that "Enthusiasm[10] and Life may not cease," he orders his Spectre not to tempt his "own Children" (inspirations), to eat the fruit of Albion's tree; "Reason not against their dear approach/ Nor them obstruct with thy temptations of doubt & despair"; he commands him to labor at the great furnaces, for the work of redemption

---

[8] Reynolds, Disc. Six, p.87.

[9] Here is another interesting reversal of *Prometheus Bound* that reinforces Blake's contrast between pagan-like Hand and Los's merciful God: in Aeschylus's play the smith is commanded by Zeus to throw chains around Prometheus, fettering him to a rock; in *Jerusalem* the smith is inspired by the Almighty to loosen Albion's fetters that enchain men to the hard rock of reason and to matter.

[10] For the meaning of this term in relation to Reynolds, see p.20.

involves "the Spectre of the Living pursuing the Emanations of the Dead." Upon realizing that Los is "the sole, uncontroll'd Lord of the Furnaces," the averse Spectre obeys, kneeling "before Los's iron-shod feet," which enable Los to 'walk' on the hard rocks of Ulro among Albion's rebellious sons.[11] [32:6; 9:3-31; 10:31-33, 17:13; 8:26-27]

To protect Jerusalem's sons and daughters and save Albion from eternal death, Los must do more than repel the advances of Albion's Spectres; he must conquer the forces of Coban, Hand and Hyle, destroy the oppressive system of art, and construct a new one that does not constrict individual creativity. This is why Los boldly exclaims,

> I must Create a System or be enslav'd by another Man's.
> I will not Reason & Compare: my business is to Create.

Patently, the allusion is to Reynolds' system. In combating it, Blake aims to demolish the Lockean principles upon which this system rests and at the same time promulgate aesthetics based on immediate perceptions of the imagination, the divine principle of creativity, free from rules and doctrines of science. [10:20-21]

Using battle imagery Berkeley opposed abstracting, reasoning and comparing and replaced them with spiritual perception, the new machinery of knowledge. By light of examination he not only exposed the false principles of natural philosophy; he also erected a "firm system" based upon true principles, which would be proof against the "assaults" of abstractionists into religion and morality.[12] By this means he strove to deprive materialists of their "grand support," drive them from their "fortress," and then build a structure philosophically impregnable to material substance, the most pernicious enemy of all knowledge because it gives existence to objects independent of mind or spirit. Berkeley hoped his philosophy would bring peace to the Commonwealth torn by fierce disputes resulting from naturalist doctrines.[13] It is not surprising therefore that Blake

---

[11] By implication Blake invites comparison of Los's work to Jesus's walking among the Philistines.

[12] Berkeley, *Principles.* 89;93.

[13] In "Bishop Berkeley on Existence in the Mind" of the publication cited in Pt. Two, n.27, Karl Aschenbrenner suggests that Berkeley's philosophy developed out of

implements this philosophy in *Jerusalem*. As Coban, Hand and Hyle represent the philosophy of Bacon, Newton and Locke, giant sons of Albion and resolute sons of nature, Erin represents the philosophy of Berkeley, native son of Ireland and faithful son of spirit.[14]

Accordingly, when Los prepares for his labors at the forge, "Erin came forth from the Furnaces." While it is the goal of Coban, Hand and Hyle to remove spirit and propagate matter as a substance, it is the goal of Los and Erin to overturn this doctrine and restore spirit, the cause of all ideas. As Albion's spectrous sons obtain their authority from Coban, Hand and Hyle, bringing contention and hateful war among Albion's people, so Los elicits Erin's assistance to effect harmony and peace. To Los's wonder and amazement, along with Erin came "all the Daughters of/ Beulah." Etymologically, *Beulah* means "marriage" (Isa.62:4); philosophically, it imaginatively signifies the unity of soul and body; aesthetically, it refers to the intimate connection between spirit and inspiration; societally, it connotes an earthly paradise where artist and the public live in consort with each other.[15] These harmonious unions are manifested in the "Spaces of Erin." As Coban, Hand and Hyle are connected to Ulro, so Erin is joined to Beulah. By remote analogy Erin is associated with Dinah, Jacob's daughter, whom a Shechemite took by force in Canaan (Gen.34);[16] also by remote analogy, Albion's land is compared to the Promised Land of Canaan (now Israel), around which his sons set druidic rocks and force their principles to the

---

his ardent concern to settle some of the intellectual disputes arising out of Newtonian science: "He thought he had the key to peace with common sense without violating his learned convictions."

[14] The philosophical significance of this symbol has not heretofore been noted. Erdman gives it a political interpretation: "The prominence of Ireland in Blake's symbolism can be explained by the renewal of the struggle for Ireland's independence," (*Blake, Prophet against Empire* [Princeton, 1969], p.445). Yet, Erin has an added meaning on the philosophical level: the fact that Berkeley was an Irishman is an obvious clue to Erin's identity. Berkeley was born, bred and educated in Ireland, where he served "at the altar of Truth" (last words in *Siris*), opposing materialist doctrines of the English philosophers with his own metaphysical principle.

[15] Feminist critics include this image from Blake's allegorical poem to draw out implications of "anti-feminism": see *Blake Newsletter* (Winter 1982-83), Anne K. Mellor, "Blake's Portrayal of Women," pp.148-155; and Alicia Ostriker, "Desire Gratified and Ungratified: William Blake and Sexuality," pp.156-165.

[16] Blake alludes to this incident in biblical history also at other places in *Jerusalem:* e.g., 55:65:66.

utmost extremity upon Beulah's daughters, muses of divine inspiration. In their "perfection," their completeness, these daughters walk among Erin's spaces of particularized objects created by the eternal spirit, which reaches "from the starry heighth to the starry depth," contraposed to Newton's system of the world, which explains motions from the deepest sea to the highest heaven by material forces operating mechanically in an absolute space. [11:8-12]

Absolute space was contended at length by Berkeley because of its religious implications. He argues "that the philosophic consideration of motion doth not imply the being of an *absolute space,* distinct from that which is perceived by sense, and related to bodies." As there is no absolute time, so there is no absolute space: space and time are coordinates of visible or tangible objects.[17] He again brings up the subject in *Siris.* 270: "The doctrine of real, absolute, external space induced some modern philosophers to conclude it was a part or attribute of God, or that God himself was space." But the negative predicates that describe pure space belong to nothing.

Blake agrees with Berkeley that pure space has no meaning in terms of experience; and to correlate it with God is another enormity growing out of natural philosophy. The chief advantage of putting an end to absolutes is that it frees the artist from Reynolds' imperative of abstract forms. The "abstract Voids between the Stars are the Satanic Wheels," which turn the iron wheels of war in art. But the inspiring daughters of Beulah are everywhere, ready to restore spirit to its rightful place; they appear "within & without" the furnaces, inside and outside Erin's spaces, "incircling on both sides/ The Starry Wheels of Albion's Sons," prepared to make "Spaces for Jerusalem/ And for Vala the shadow of Jerusalem." Los stands in awe of this sublime wonder; he recognizes the immensity of his venture, feels anxiety lest he fail, and looks for divine encouragement to proceed with the redemptive task. [13:37, 12:17-19]

Faced with the challenge of restoring spirit to philosophy, Berkeley, who was well-versed in scriptural texts, at times gave more than a biblical air to his criticism of natural causality. He lamented that, notwithstanding what Holy Scripture itself relates, some philosophers continue to deny the world is actuated by an eternal

---

[17] Berkeley, *Principles.* 116.

spirit. To combat these obdurate naturalists, who twitted him about his causal principle, Berkeley retorts that "the immediate hand of an *almighty Agent*" is not apparent to them.[18] Although God is concealed from corporeal men, his "intimate presence" is "plainly legible" to those who possess "comprehensiveness of mind." In a solemn and prophetic tone he warns that *"the finger of God is not so conspicuous to the resolved and careless sinner"* and reminds materialists *"that the eyes of the Lord are in every place beholding the evil and the good."*

To Blake's hero the divine sign is plainly visible. Though the strong forces of Albion's sons terrify Los, they do not deter him because he perceives the time for judgment has come:

...I saw the finger of God go forth
Upon my Furnaces from within the Wheels of Albion's Sons,
Fixing their Systems permanent, by mathematic power
Giving a body to Falsehood that it may be cast off for ever,
With Demonstrative Science piercing Apollyon with his own bow.
God is within & without; he is even in the depths of Hell!

Again Blake welds together philosophical and biblical materials. However, in creating poetic lines for his epic, he does not merely repeat the same notion; he continually compounds the chief events with more instances. Here, adopting a moral tone, he charges naturalists with impiety and on their own principles destroys their system to make way for a new system. It is not difficult to see that in the above passage Apollyon alludes to Locke, who built his philosophy on Newtonian science. Though Newton was concerned with the efficient cause of nature, not with its ultimate cause, Locke made these equivalent. Moreover, in furthering his own project, he interpreted not only the scientific knowledge but also the principles of science prevailing at that time as limitations to any future knowledge.[19] Hyle therefore is natural philosophy's "angel of the bottomless pit,"[20] trapping individuals who must be delivered from

---

[18] Berkeley, *Principles,* 151,155.

[19] Newton himself was optimistic about making further discoveries concerning particles; what he plainly said was that he did not know the ultimate cause of gravitation, though he hoped the principles he "laid down will afford some light" to this: "Preface" to the *Principia,* p.xviii.

[20] Rev.9:11.

oppressive systems. So in the very presence of the enemy, Los prepares with art the ground for building Golgonooza in Erin's spaces. [12:10-15]

Golgonooza, another instance of Blake's penchant for word-blending to create names, is apparently a conflation of *Golgotha* and *ooze* to signify the place from which will flow the beneficial fruits of the eternal spirit. As such, it is the poem's geographic and imaginative center. Unlike the city of Vala, built out of matter according to mathematical proportions and embodying natural virtues, the city of Golgonooza is built according to spiritual perception and incorporates New Testament ethical ideals. The palace of Golgonooza exemplifies these ideals and at the same time Blake's concept of great art, founded on divine inspiration and minute discriminations: a synthesis of religion, morality and art. In the long passage [12:25-13:29] picturing the great work, Blake luxuriates in particulars. With an overwhelming precision of detail, he describes every feature of the palace, from its exterior to its inner chambers: its materials, structure, and ornamentation.

> The stones are pity, and the bricks, well wrought affections
> Enamel'd with love & kindness, & the tiles engraven gold,
> Labour of merciful hands: the beams & rafters are forgiveness:
> . . .
> The curtains, woven tears & sighs wrought into lovely forms
> For comfort; there the secret furniture of Jerusalem's chamber
> Is wrought.

These humane values are held together by visual and verbal art, by illustrations and lines: "the nails/ And the screws & iron braces are well wrought blandishments/ And well contrived words." The immortal beauty and perfection of the human imagination is objectified in Golgonooza, bringing aesthetic pleasure to men and conveying eternal human values. [12:30-41]

Building this permanent fortress is part of the action within the poem and at the same time an analogue to the poem itself. The construction of Golgonooza, which lodges the spiritual army's camp, and the composition of *Jerusalem,* which synoptically presents the whole story, are coterminous and intrinsically related to the creation of a

DEFENDERS OF JERUSALEM

system, allowing us to share in the adventure of a creative act.[21] Los's fourfold sons who help build Golgonooza spiritually evoke the four evangelists; in turn, *Jerusalem's* four chapters architecturally correspond to the four-part structure of the Gospel. This parallelism is meticulously carried out in Golgonooza's design. Its four points "beheld in Great Eternity" are "the Four Worlds of Humanity," symbolized by the four apocalyptic animals. "Ezekiel saw them by Chebar's flood"; the poet sees their images formed by Los as they appear on the frieze above Golgonooza's four gates facing four directions. In accord with his philosophical principles which connect the imagination to sensory particulars, Blake correlates the four geographical points to four human senses, relating them in bold relief to the eternal spirit and contrasting Golgonooza to the world of mechanical philosophy. The "North Gate," the ear or divine voice representing inspiration, has "four sculptur'd Bulls"; and the "South Gate," the eyes of Divine Vision representing the organs of spiritual perception, has "four Lions" wondrously carved. From these gates, looking towards Generation one sees the mystical symbols are cast in iron (mechanical philosophy); towards Ulro, they are baked of clay and continuously turning "upon the Wheels of Albion's sons with enormous power" (earth turning upon abstractions); but towards Beulah and Eden, the four bulls and lions are moulded from four diverse metals (symbolizing four aspects of spiritual man). The "Western Gate," the merciful tongue or word, "has four Cherubim" like men. But this gate is "clos'd up" because Albion has ruled out humanity. Looking from this gate towards Generation and Ulro, one sees the living creatures again of iron and of clay; towards Beulah, they are of stone (signifying man as a passive object of material forces); and Eden is closed to mortal man until Jerusalem is recalled. The "Eastern Gate," the nostrils or breath of life representing the eternal spirit symbolized by the eagle, now takes its form sevenfold from the "Wheels of Albion's Sons." Towards Eden, therefore, this gate fronts seven "forms of death" frozen in eternal ice; towards Beulah, "seven diseases of the earth" carved in stone; towards Ulro,

---

[21] Frye, *Fearful Symmetry,* calls Golgonooza a "watchtower of art," p.357. Paley, *The Continuing City,* characterizes it as "the central embodiment of Blake's millenarian theme" and compares its architectural features to "the Temple of Solomon," p.136,141.

"forms of war, seven enormities"; and towards Generation, "seven generative forms" all rooted in pride: selfishness, jealousy, hypocrisy, hate, cruelty, revenge and murder, all practiced by critics to advance Reynolds' system. The essential task for Los and Erin is to restore spiritual power to the Eastern gate and open the Western gate now "clos'd as with a threefold curtain," woven by natural philosophy threefold.[22] [12:54-13:23]

The source of life, humanity, creativity, and eternity—typified in the architecture and ornamentation of Golgonooza—is concomitantly the source of nature, of all existence, inner and outer. Blake transmits this cardinal principle through an ornament of nature:

The Vegetative Universe opens like a flower from the Earth's center
In which is Eternity. It expands in Stars to the Mundane Shell
And there it meets Eternity again, both within and without.

In this cosmographical simile he employs an image from Proclus used by Berkeley (*Siris*.345) to express the individual's participation in divine unity. This spiritual center in Blake's system is the originating and controlling imagination in contrast to Reynolds' fixed rules based on nature's powers and on abstraction. The floral form suggests how inspiration arises, develops and blooms into a work of art: the perceptions of the imagination coincide with the beauty of the universe, which is like the beauty that lies inside every flower. From the imagination issues Golgonooza; from it, like a flower blossoming into lines of minute details and delicate colors, radiates the exuberance within and without to combat the forces of Coban, Hand and Hyle; from it will come Albion's salvation. [13.34-36]

Around Golgonooza and in contrast to its beauty and convexity arching up towards heaven "lies the land of death eternal, a Land/ Of pain and misery and despair and ever brooding melancholy" because Albion's sons make it a crime for an artist to express his own ideas and impossible for anyone to attain salvation. In the detailed description of this land, Blake helps himself to Milton's hell in *Paradise Lost* but adds imagery specifically associated with Reynolds' system animated by zeal of naturalist critics. "The Rocks of solid fire, the Ice

---

[22] Probably a reference to Bacon's threefold aspects of nature: nature generating, nature varying, and nature mechanical; these three divisions recur repeatedly in his writings: e.g., p. 80, p.427, and pp.678-679.

valleys, the Plains/ Of burning sand, the rivers, cataract & Lakes of Fire,/... The trees of Malice, Revenge/ And black Anxiety," are features that have evolved in Ulro; the "woven labyrinths" and "snares" are products of specious reasonings.[23] "The Voids" no less than "the Solids" derive from a mathematical treatment of mechanics; and the "clouds" are formed by unknown corporeal substances. All in all, it is an inhospitable world fashioned by abstract reasoners. Their "Concave Earth wondrous, Chasmal, Abyssal, Incoherent" has characteristics of the modern physicists' *black hole*: trapped in Ulro, there is no escape from extinction. The conglomerate of material forces and abstract reasonings militate "against the Divine Vision." In self-righteousness of their theories, "Hand & Hyle & Coban" along with their armies gather "before the eastern gate bending their fury/... to desolate Golgonooza,/ And to devour the Sleeping Humanity of Albion." Therefore "Los walks round the walls, night and day"; he will neither slumber nor sleep until Albion awakens. [13:30-31, 40-55; 5:28-30]

From his vantage point on the mount of Golgonooza, Los beholds "all that has existed in the space of six thousand years"; all those prodigious events of future days Adam saw in the panoramic view from a hill of Paradise have occurred.[24] Los sees past and present contrivances of those who turned away from spirit to enslave mankind: he sees the "Looms & Mills & Prisons & Work-houses of Og & Anak," potent rulers of Bashan and Hebron; and in Ulro he sees the inventions built by the spectrous sons of Albion, imprisoning Jerusalem's sons. Just as the topography of the Miltonic hell is adapted to the current situation in art, so is the catalog of underworld gods. Los scrutinizes the three demons guarding the dark world of Coban, Hand and Hyle: "the Cherub at the Tree of Life, also the Serpent/ Orc," and "the Dragon Urizen." The Cherub (which in gospel tradition symbolizes the four faces of man) here is Satan in disguise; through this image Blake implies that abstract reasoners conquer by guile. Orc, an abbreviated form of Orcus (the name

---

[23] In Berkeley's *First Dialogue*, vol.2, p.207, Hylas, admitting he is "ensnared and as it were imprisoned in the labyrinths" of his own making, is challenged by Philonous to "invent any new means to extricate" himself.

[24] For details of Adam's vision see *Paradise Lost*, XI.357-867.

Roman poets used for Pluto) is a devourer of emanations.[25] Urizen, the dragon of flaming fire, is another example of Blake's adeptness at inventing descriptive names; it is probably a confluence of two concepts: of the Hebrew *UR* (fire), by which Berkeley tells us that "in the Chaldaic oracles all things are supposed to be governed,"[26] and of human *reason*, which natural philosophers have made all-powerful. Bacon declared it the key of knowledge; Newton made it the main tool of modern science; Locke enthroned it as the ultimate judge of everything, even of divine revelation; and Reynolds made it the criterion of form and judgment in art. All now accords with the movement of abstract reasoning; no other way is lawful. Albion's champion is Urizen, like fire, "ever consuming" all things while the Spectres build new inventions of destruction to extend the frontiers of Ulro. Urizen strives to usurp universal power; hence at 16:31 Blake refers to "the Conflict of Luvah & Urizen," of eternal spirit and overblown human reason. The three demons comprise "the Vegetated Tongue, even the Devouring Tongue," propagating falsehoods about the "brain," the "heart" and "bowels"—about intellect, love, and compassion—intent on bringing every human activity into the system of natural philosophy, engulfing mankind in "seas of sorrow" and leading it to eternal death. [13:57-62; 14:2-9]

"Such are the Buildings of Los and such are the Woofs of Enitharmon" because the true principles in art cannot prevail unless its false principles are seen, acknowledged, and rejected. This brief interruption in the narrative reminds us that visionary art is important. It tells us about the latest revolt against the eternal spirit. Albion and his sons have entered upon an evil path because they have rejected the Divine Vision. [14:15]

Besides Albion's demoniacal sons and their dark, deadly world, "Los beheld his Sons and he beheld his Daughters." As creations of spirit, they are free of disguise and falsehood: "Every one a translucent Wonder, a Universe within,/ Increasing inwards into length and

---

[25] Blake's Orc is very likely an imitation of Lodovico Ariosto's Orc (Italian *Orca*), the ravening monster that feeds on woman's flesh: *Orlando Furioso*, tr. William Stewart Rose, ed. Baker and Giamatti (New York, 1968), VIII.li,liv.

[26] Berkeley, *Siris*.179. *Urizen* is usually written off simply as *your reason*. But this overlooks the connotation of destructiveness Blake attaches to abstract reasoning. Swedenborg makes *Ur* a symbol of "external worship in which are falses," *Correspondences, Representatives, and Significatives,* 6th ed. (Boston, 1872), p.406.

breadth and heighth,/ Starry & glorious." Spiritual perceptions have length, breadth and height because they are existent objects;[27] they are translucent because they are immediately perceived and known by the mind: existence and perception are one and the same phenomenon. These sons and daughters look towards the East, "inwards" towards the eternal spirit; hence, "in their bright loins" each has "a beautiful golden gate, which opens into the vegetative world" of life. Through allegory and anatomic metaphor Blake conveys the stellar power of imagination to perceive realities of the physical world and to create beautiful things. Perceived particulars and works of art are effects of the same cause. [14:16-20]

Blake then [14:25] relates this principle specifically to his practices in art. Every one of Los's children "has the three regions, Childhood, Manhood & Age":[28] another allusion to Reynolds. Following Locke, for whom man is an aggregate of qualities abstracted from animals, Reynolds advises students of art to abstract certain qualities from the human figure to arrive at a general form representative of a class:

> as there is one general form, which... belongs to the human kind at large, so in each of these classes there is one common idea and central form, which is the abstract of the various individual forms belonging to that class. Thus, though the forms of childhood and age differ exceedingly, there is a common form in childhood and a common form in age, which is the most perfect, as it is more remote from all peculiarities.[29]

Blake rejects this approach to human forms. For him, as for Berkeley, every man is a particularized spiritual being in space-time. Childhood, manhood and old age therefore are three definite and visible

---

[27] Cf. Gorgias' statement: if a thing exists, "at least it is threefold, having length, breadth and depth," 'On Nature,' *Ancilla to The Pre-Socratic Philosophers,* tr. Kathleen Freeman (Oxford, 1956) p.128.

[28] Karl Kiralis, "The Theme and Structure of William Blake's *Jerusalem,*" ELH (June 1956) pp.127-143, takes this phrase as a hint of the poem's form, correlating Ch. II, III and IV resp. with the three ages—Jews with a state of mental childhood, Deists with maturity, and Christians with senility. Though the poem does not bear out these correlations, there is a thematic connection between Blake's concept of childhood, maturity, and old age and of creation, redemption, and judgment.

[29] Reynolds, Disc. Three, pp.47-48. His concept of classes is based on Locke's *a posteriori* philosophy and hence is not as Platonic as it seems.

manifestations of human life; these cannot be abstracted and reduced to one generalized form. Particulars are not merely details of stylistic discernment of character; they define realities.

Because Albion's sons do not acknowledge the reality of spiritually perceived particulars, "Los beheld the mild Emanation, Jerusalem" like a "pale cloud" bending eastward in Albion's tomb (visible at plate 14), for its arches, Erin tells us [49:52], are built by the Lord. Los recruits an army to labor at the divine furnaces to restore Jerusalem. Those who proffer themselves for Albion's sake are long to tell; therefore the willing participants are given in terms of counties from England, Wales, Scotland, and Ireland, each divided into twelve gates named for the twelve tribes of Israel. These, however, are not presented as a mere list; even in this catalog Blake keeps alive the action in the poem: "Los fix'd down" the counties on his anvil. [14:31-35;16:28]

Following the long section of some two hundred lines [12:25-16:60] describing Los's building of Golgonooza, his perception of the current situation on all sides, and his enlistment of troops, the poet temporarily suspends his narrative to comment on the expansive power of the imagination particularized and to assert that great works of art are spiritual acts comparable to the divinely inspired and inspiring verses in the Old and New Testament.

> All things acted on Earth are seen in the bright Sculptures of
> Los's Halls, & every Age renews its powers from these Works
> With every pathetic story possible to happen from Hate or
> Wayward Love; & every sorrow & distress is carved here,
> Every Affinity of Parents, Marriages & Friendships are here
> In all their various combinations wrought with wondrous Art,
> All that can happen to Man in his pilgrimage of seventy years.
> Such is the Divine Written Law of Horeb & Sinai,
> And such the Holy Gospel of Mount Olivet & Calvary.[30]
> [16:61-69]

---

[30] It is interesting to compare this passage to Canto XVI.2 of Torquato Tasso's *Jerusalem Delivered,* tr. Joseph Tusiana (Fairleigh Dickinson, 1970), describing the doors of a fair garden, where two warriors are sent to rescue the great knight Rinaldo, whom Armida through guile imprisons as her lover: "Through the main portal (for the ample home/ has full a hundred of them) pass the two./ The doors of storied silver on their hinges of lucent gold give out a strident sound./ The warriors watch those figures

DEFENDERS OF JERUSALEM

Again we meet Blake in person of the artist. The above lines state his fundamental principle in response to painters and critics who denigrated his works. Art is more than a scientific rendering of nature and more than technique fixed by rules. Great art is a treasure of insights and information about the human condition; it records significant events in the history of man as a spiritual being. By implication *Jerusalem* is such a work; it speaks to universal humanity.

At plate 17 the narrative is resumed, heavily embedded with more allusions to Reynolds' theory and its bearing upon Blake. Having secured the supporting counties, Los directs his Spectre to search out "the Daughters of Albion" and drive them away from "the Children of Los," literally constrain the attacks by adherents of naturalist generalizers and make way for art based on spirit and particulars. "Los himself against Albion's sons his fury bends, for he/ Dare not approach the Daughters openly, lest he be consumed/ In the fires of their beauty & perfection & be Vegetated beneath/ Their Looms in a Generation of death & resurrection to forgetfulness."[31] As artist, Los is susceptible to the beauties of nature and thus sensitive to the seductions of Albion's naturalist daughters; but he recognizes the false love of those who also destroy. The charming daughters are part of the naturalists' ambuscade to waylay Los and destroy his emanation in the same way that Vala seeks to destroy Albion's emanation. "Such is that false/ And Generating Love, a pretence of love to destroy love." In this scene one cannot fail to perceive the indirect references to attacks by contemporary artists and critics upon Blake's art, the attempts by people, Hayley and others, to persuade Blake to take up the popular form of art, his recognition of the undeniable practical advantages in becoming a naturalist artist, his resistance to these inducements, and, finally, his epic attack of Reynolds' principles. [17:3-9,25-26]

---

eagerly,/ for matter has been vanquished here by art;/ only the speech is missing; but, if you believe your eyes, the lively scenes speak too." Art instructs: the warriors see depicted the story of Alcides, who once ruled the stars and now twirls a spindle; and of Anthony, who aspired to an empire but forsook his armies to follow a wanton queen and invite death. "Such are the stories sculpted one by one/ on the bright silver of those regal doors." Such is the sad fate awaiting false and heedless lovers. It should not be surprising that Blake puts to his own use other images that also occur in Tasso's poem. Perhaps from this work Blake received a hint for the title of his epic; however, the former has a strictly religious theme, whereas Blake's main subject is art.

[31] Blake seems here to be applying to naturalists the Platonic doctrine mentioned

95

Los's soliloquy [17:29-47] reviews these principles and contains important philosophical points and attitudes Blake shares with Berkeley. In his criticism of material substance, the latter refers to Lockeans as those who hold to an "unknown support of unknown qualities," an unknown something, "we know not *what*, and we know not *why*";[32] strangely, their instrument of knowledge leads to ignorance. Having nullified spiritual powers and reduced the whole series of events in the universe to impulses of one body on another and all action to unknown forces in "minute particles on bodies" acting on one another, they fit man into this same system and regard him a body composed of these forces. Through his hero, Blake expresses similar thoughts with respect to art. Communing with himself, Los observes that Albion's sons "know not why they love nor wherefore they sicken & die."[33] First, they separated spirit from nature, making it the effect of an unknown substance; then, they separated it from man, leaving him "a little grovelling Root outside of Himself," controlled by external forces. [17:29-32]

Blake does not deny the existence of bodies. He denies matter is the source of power in bodies: this is the metaphysical issue. Not to recognize this fact along with the fundamental distinction between bodies and matter, or between things and matter, or between nature and matter leads to a misunderstanding of his position, and consequently to inconsistencies in interpreting his works.[35] The metaphysical conflict in *Jerusalem* is not between nature and spirit, nor between body and spirit; rather, it concerns corporeal and spiritual *substance:* opposed principles of causality. For Blake, as for Berkeley, bodies really exist, but the cause of their existence is spirit or mind.

---

by Berkeley in *Siris*.313: "sowed in generation" and immersed "into animal nature," a human soul in this "slumber forgets her original notions."

[32] Berkeley, *Principles*.77; *Siris*.250. For an analysis of Locke's substances, refer to Pt. Four.

[33] It should be clear by now that Blake's quarrel with Reynolds involves the source of nature's forms and manner of depiction, not nature as a subject of art.

[34] In terms of its Gospel analogue, this passage echoes Luke 23:24 referring to unbelievers in spirit, who know not what they do.

[35] For instance, Barbara Lefcowitz's "Blake and the Natural World," PMLA, vol.89, Nr.1 (Jan. 1974); or Jackson's essay cited in Pt. Three, n.40; or Ostriker's essay, *supra* n.15; or Eaves' *William Blake's Theory of Art:* "Blake's argument is a strong opposition between nature and imagination," p.32.

Berkeley gives us a clear philosophic statement of this distinction: "Ideas imprinted on the senses are real things, or do really exist; this we do not deny, but we deny they can subsist without the minds which perceive them."[36] Spirit or mind is temporally prior to ideas; it stands in irreversible causal relation. Claiming existence for both body and spirit does not imply they are in any way alike: they are at once different and complementary. Locke considered body and spirit mutually exclusive. Berkeley and Blake regard them as *contraries* which cannot exist independent of each other. Referring specifically to bodies, Berkeley states: "Body is opposite to spirit"; both are necessary to human life. Body itself possesses no power: "So far forth as there is real power, there is spirit. So far forth as there is ... want of power ... there is a negation of spirit." Locke maintained that spirit does not denote anything subsisting in itself; rather, spirit and related concepts, such as morality and virtue, are but verbal constructs for mixed modes of affections and unobservable qualities: nothing more than "abstract complex ideas, made arbitrarily by the mind"; hence, all that "pudder" about "*essences*" is only about the meaning of "sounds."[37] In reply Berkeley applies Locke's nominalism to his own idea of corporeal substance, words signifying no existent thing: a perfect description of a *"non-entity."*[38]

The above distinctions implied in Blake's metaphysics are made explicit in Los's philosophical reflections. "Negations are not Contraries." The difference between negation and contrary is the difference between corporeal substance and body: body and spirit are *contraries*; corporeal substances are *negations* of spirit. Therefore, "Contraries mutually Exist;/ But Negations Exist Not." If Los be separated from spirit, he becomes a corporeal body composed wholly of matter, "a Negation, a meer/ Reasoning" and a "Derogation" from spirit. Heroically, he pledges that corporeal substance, a distortion and inversion of the true cause of existence, shall remain a non-entity forever:

---

[36] Berkeley, *Principles*.90; *Siris*.290.
[37] Locke, III.5.xv-xvi.
[38] Berkeley, *Principles*.68.

> ...O thou Negation, I will continually compell
> Thee to be invisible to any but whom I please, & when
> And where & how I please, and never! never! shalt thou be
>   Organized
> But as a distorted & reversed Reflexion in the Darkness
> And in the Non Entity.

Indignant, he sends his Spectre to challenge the enemies of spirit and agents of evil motivated by hate: "Go thou to Skofield: ask him if he is Bath or if he is Canterbury./ Tell him to be no more dubious: demand explicit words./ Tell him I will dash him into shivers where & at what time/ I please; tell Hand & Skofield they are my ministers of evil/ To those I hate, for I can hate also as well as they!"[39] [17:33-43,59-63]

Meantime Albion lies in death-like sleep. Vegetative fibers of Coban, Hand and Hyle spread, enrooting into every part of the world. The cries of war, howlings in pain, and lamentations of sorrow one hears along with the sufferings, incessant tears and death one sees will continue until Albion awakens to the truth that spirit is the power actuating all bodies, all ideas. To end this hateful war Los and his strong guard unresting walk in the spaces of Erin beneath the moon of Beulah. Its inspiring daughters plead with the vengeful sons of mighty Albion and send up a devout prayer for delivery from oppression, not for vengeance, but a prayer to the Lamb of God for "the deliverance of Individuals." [25:13]

Thus ends Chapter 1, with which Parts Three through Five of the present study deal, explaining the situation together with its causes and identifying the main characters. Repetition is an essential element in the structure of this fourfold poem presenting a broad view of the prolonged war on several fronts conveyed through interchange of verbal and visual forms. The main ideas introduced in *Jerusalem's* first chapter recur in subsequent chapters, where through affiliated meanings and increments of action Blake develops these ideas, describing the varied strategies employed in repeated attacks by enemies of divine inspiration and individual genius; the calamitous consequences for a nation and for humankind; and the spiritual artist's responses.

---

[39] According to S. Foster Damon, *A Blake Dictionary* (E.P. Dutton, 1971), Skofield is a fictive projection of John Scholfield, a vengeful sergeant who accused Blake of treasonable utterances; as such, he is one of Albion's vengeful sons.

PART SIX[1]

ENCOUNTERS WITH THE ENEMY

Having revealed to the public at large the intrinsic philosophical unity between Jerusalem and Albion—between spirit and a nation's humanity, its art, and its survival—and keeping to his literary form (cf. Mark's gospel to the Jews), Blake addresses Chapter 2 to the Jews, making explicit the religious basis of their unity with Christians. Besides the assumed general historical parallel between Israel's and England's circumstances (Jerusalem's capture by heathens in ancient times and her exile by naturalists in the present age), Blake now points to the continuity of faith—faith in a new and living way promised in the Old and revealed in the New Testament, an item upon which the Evangelists laid great stress: "the Lamb of God, the Saviour became apparent on Earth as the Prophets had foretold." Jews and Christians are united by a belief in the immutable counsel and promises of a spiritual god, signified by "Elohim" as the creator of the whole world and by *Jehovah* as the father of all spiritual beings and source of everlasting strength.[2] On these doctrinal grounds, Blake makes a practical appeal importuning Jews to join the struggle against Albion's invading sons: "Ye are united, O ye Inhabitants of Earth, in One Religion, the Religion of Jesus, the most Ancient, the Eternal & the Everlasting Gospel." The poet's entreaty includes a series of ballad stanzas, which take their general impress from the Psalms praising

---

[1] From now on the explication will proceed consecutively by plate, obviating the necessity of references to *Jerusalem* at the end of a paragraph.

[2] For passages referring to Israel's god see Gen.33:20, Num.16:22, Isa.26:4, and Paul's letter to the Hebrews, which calls attention to their faith in spirit and gives many examples (11:1-39).

Israel's god, exulting over its past grandeur, deploring its distresses under heathen oppressors, and giving thanks for its subsequent deliverance. Correspondingly, Blake's lyrics recount the joyous and peaceful past when Jerusalem dwelt in Albion's land and walked its "meadows green"; they bemoan the "War & howling, death & woe" since her expulsion occasioned by Albion's Spectre; and, fittingly, terminate in her prospective reunion with Albion.

Following these recollections of Albion's past and intimations of his future, Blake visually conceives the causal connection between spiritual perception and nature, and concomitantly between imagination and art, again representing creativity by a flower. At plate 28 we see Jerusalem and Vala embracing within the whorling petals of an elaborately structured lily of Havilah, a peculiarly edenic symbol. This "ornament of perfection" and "labour of love," in fine a work of minute discriminations inspired by the imagination, is become "a Crime, and Albion the punisher & judge." He enforces a new rule dictated by Reynolds for expressing sublime ideas: "care must be taken not to run into particularities" lest they "degrade the sublime."[3] He devotes the greater part of Discourse Four to this subject; he demeans "minute particularities," associating them with the "merely ornamental" or "sensual style." Its "seducing qualities... debauch the young"; unfortunately, now this style "has been disseminated throughout all Europe." By contrast to the ornamental, he exalts the grand style, juxtaposing it to *general form, sublimity,* and *nobleness.* The ornamental, though of lower rank than the grand style, has merit if "the general and particular ideas of nature be not mixed." In line with Newton's statement that "Nature is pleased with simplicity, and affects not the pomp of superfluous causes,"[4] and with Locke's leading principle that nature furnishes the mind with ideas "simple and unmixed."[5] Reynolds' presiding principle is "simplicity." And consonant with demonstrative truth in science, Reynolds compares taste in art to "demonstration in geometry." Iron-minded Albion declaims these criteria of art, denying the efficacy of spiritual perceptions and sublimity of particular ideas: "I therefore condense them into solid rocks,

---

[3] Reynolds, Disc. Four, pp.58-67; Disc. Seven, p.109.
[4] Newton, p.398 in support of Rule 1.
[5] Locke, II.ii.1.

6. *Jerusalem* 28

stedfast,/ A foundation and certainty and demonstrative truth,/ That Man be separate from Man, & here I plant my seat." Demonstrable forms containing one uniform conception, like the simple impressions of nature on which these forms are founded, represent sublimity; affinities between man and spirit are unnatural consanguinities. Works of those who do not acknowledge demonstrated natural causes will be censured.

Then in a few lines [28:14-19] we have a superb verbal picture of natural philosophy as it thrives under Albion's tyrannical reign: the naturalists' tree springs up from "underneath his heel." It is a "deadly Tree"; but unlike the causative tree of Eden created by the universal spirit, Albion's tree created by his mighty sons yields neither knowledge nor salvation. Because natural philosophers attribute universal power to impenetrable particles, Albion worships a "God who dwells in Chaos hidden from the human sight." Albion's sons promised a foundation for certainty in knowledge and religion; instead, they have grown a fruitless and sinister tree in the midst of Albion's fair country, clouded his heavens, desolated his land, ruined his cathedrals, taken control of his universities and academies, bringing scepticism into all parts of knowledge, doubt into revealed religion, and suspicion into spiritual art. Alas, Albion finds himself miserably rooted in an unknown matter of indefinite qualities and hopelessly lost in speculative difficulties of intricate reasonings:

> The Tree spread over him its cold shadows, (Albion groan'd)
> They bent down, they felt the earth, and again enrooting
> Shot into many a Tree, an endless labyrinth of woe.

Bacon's tree had, primarily through Locke's work, grown into a bewildering labyrinth operating on many levels. Berkeley used this image to describe the nation's doubtfulness and uncertainty resulting from natural philosophy's abstract ideas, which purportedly remove "prejudices and errors of sense."[6] But do they? With great irony Berkeley points out:

> "endeavouring to correct these by reason we are insensibly drawn into uncouth paradoxes, difficulties, and inconsistencies, which

---

[6] Berkeley, *Principles*, Introd.1: an allusion to Newton's *Definitions* and "Scholium" (*Principia*, pp.2-6).

multiply and grow upon us as we advance in speculation; till at length, having wander'd through many intricate mazes, we find ourselves just where we were, or, which is worse, sit down in a forlorn scepticism.

Applying Newtonian rules, Locke aimed to lead us to clear and definite truths in knowledge and religion; instead, he eliminated whatever we had of both, leaving us with nothing. With spiritual substances removed, causes concealed, senses diminished but reason extolled, all is fruitless speculation and controversy. "Abstraction" has always led to "manifold inextricable labyrinths of error and dispute."[7]

Blake conveys this situation in art by joining Albion's philosophic tree to the Daedelian image. Labyrinths wind their way through the whole of *Jerusalem:* the melancholy words *doubt, despair* and *suspicion* resound throughout the poem. Controlled by his Spectre, Albion erects altars to powers in nature while his sons build fortifications against humanity and art. "In Shame & Jealousy"—two more motifs in the poem, two more evils, the disposition to pass moral judgment on works of art and to jealousy exploding into hate because men do not respect individual talents—Albion's sons strive "to annihilate Jerusalem," inexorably leading Albion to eternal death. Reynolds' machinery enthralls, entangles, and eventually destroys. But divine mercy intervenes [plate 29]:[8] like a sun in human

---

[7] Berkeley, *Principles,* Introd.17. He uses this image also in other places, e.g., *Alciphron,* Dialogue VII.20 (Euphanor, who represents Berkeley's view, is speaking): "if we begin with generalities, and lay our foundation in abstract ideas, we shall find ourselves entangled and lost in a labyrinth of our own making," vol.3, p.316. See also the reference at n.23, Pt. Five.

[8] V.A. DeLuca, "The Changing Order of Plates in *Jerusalem,* Chapter II," *Blake, An Illustrated Quarterly* (Spring 1983) pp.192-205, speculates that Blake rearranged the order of plates in Copy D to correct the imbalances of printed text and illumination in copies A-C and believes the change weakens narrative continuity. In my study of the two arrangements, I find the order of D, here observed, results in a more logical narrative connection than the arrangement in A-C. In D, Albion is hopelessly entangled in natural philosophers' metaphysical tree and entrapped in their epistemological labyrinth (28); divine power intervenes, and forthwith come two immortal forms (29); they are Enitharmon and Urthona, who report to Los on Albion's critical state (30); Los goes in search of the enemy (31); he sees Albion on the brink of Non-Entity; Albion's sons bear him from the bloody field and place him on a couch (32); near death, he experiences an apparition (33). The twenty-eight kneel around

form the eternal spirit appears over Albion's dark rocks; the divine voice goes forth assuring the "Human Family" that Jerusalem shall be restored; hence Albion shall be saved and his fame perpetuated. The way to Albion's salvation, however, is tortuous because the "Reactor hath hid himself thro' envy"[9] and cannot be apprehended "till he be reveal'd in his System." Presumably, the Reactor refers to Reynolds and the chain reaction initiated by his system and maintained by nameless critics. The full discovery of this system and its perpetrators constitutes Los's heroic action and consequent fall of Ulro at a set time. Meanwhile Albion must sleep; all is confusion; all is tumult.

Simulating conditions of war, Blake presents the details as a report from two fugitives, who are none other than Enitharmon and Urthona, Los's emanation and his Spectre, pictured at the top of plate 30 as two flying human figures, spirit equipped with wings of a butterfly and reason with those of a bat. These "Immortal forms" who have escaped from the turbulence give an account of what they have witnessed. Lordly conquerors have taken Jerusalem; Ireland alone remains her holy place. They saw Albion walk arm in arm with Vala; they saw him "prostrate before" his "wat'ry vision." Albion is like Narcissus, who took his reflection for an actual being; his vision of natural powers is but a "wat'ry Shadow" of "his wearied intellect," a mere reflection of his interminable abstractions. To this "sweet entrancing self-delusion," which he has endowed with divinity, Albion humbles himself in an act of complete submission:

Albion's couch of death, and the four zoa combust in rage (41); they see Albion in his pale disease brooding on evil (42); they see their wheels rising up poisonous against him (43). Pl.47 tells us "the Furnaces of Los/Began to rage," and takes us to the site of the furnaces. The four plates following 28 in A-C are placed after 42 and thus numbered 43-46; though I find this arrangement presents a less direct narrative connection between 28-9, 41-2-3, and 46-7, it does not negate the progression of Los's incessant labors directed towards rescuing Albion. The hypothesis of visual design as Blake's governing principle cannot be consistently applied in view of the fact that pl.29 in both orders consists primarily of text; that in D, pl.42 predominantly text is followed by a textual plate; and that in both copies, 46 and 47 are largely textual. A pattern of alternating text and designs does not seem to hold for the whole of *Jerusalem* either.

[9] Envy is one of the motivating characteristics of the Pharisees in opposing Jesus: see Mk.15:10.

> O I am nothing when I enter into judgment with thee!
> If thou withdraw thy breath, I die & vanish into Hades;
> . . .
> O I am nothing, and to nothing must return again!
> If thou withdraw thy breath, Behold, I am oblivion.

They saw Albion struggle with Luvah over Vala's body; they saw Luvah strike Albion; and they heard "the fallen Man" threaten Luvah:

> ...Go and Die the Death of Man for Vala the sweet wanderer.
> I will turn the volutions of your ears outward and bend your nostrils
> Downward, and your fluxile eyes englob'd roll round in fear;
> Your with'ring lips and tongue shrink up into a narrow circle,
> Till into narrow forms you creep.

Albion's pathetic confession of his utter insignificance and his zealous acceptance of natural powers at once criticize corporeal man and strike subtlely at Reynolds, who like Locke condemns enthusiasm of divine inspiration and dismisses man's inner powers to perceive realities. Albion exaltingly affirms Lockean man, a passive body played on by external objects. In *Siris.295* Berkeley tells us why this concept of man is false: naturalists suppose a material substance, they are deluded to think bodies exist independent of mind upon which material forces impress ideas; what they take for "substances and causes are but fleeting shadows."

In the lively report by Los's messengers, Blake continues the satanic connotations and biblical parallels introduced earlier. The doctrine of material substances, represented by Coban-Hand-Hyle's deification of Vala, is likened to the serpent's fallacious argument that beguiled Eve. Albion's surrender to Vala is likened to Adam's capitulation to Eve. As the two informants fled from Albion, they saw "the vast form of Nature like a serpent" roll between Jerusalem and Vala: they saw the separation of spiritual power from nature. The "jealous fears & fury & rage & flames" they saw roll round the feet of Luvah and Vala suggest the disturbing passions that subsequently arose between Adam and Eve (*Paradise Lost*). In the expulsion of Luvah or "Pity & Love" and in Albion's reverence for natural philosophy, Enitharmon and Urthona saw "Sexual Religion in its embryon Uncircumcision"; they saw the inception of natural and abstract religion.

The epithet *sexual* is rich in meanings. Generically it is related to Newton's general abstract law, which organizes the structure of the universe in terms of attraction and repulsion: in Blake's language *sexual organization*. By this ingenious combination of metaphor and literalness Blake conveys not only naturalists' worship of powers in physical bodies but also their devotion to abstract general ideas. *Sexual* therefore covers the total set of relations linked to the law of gravitation and by extension encompasses the philosophical principles associated with it. He applies the multivalent term to a wide range of concepts and acts as they relate to Reynolds' system, particularly to critics who regarded the bare and naked spiritual forms of human love in his art sexually and thus morally offensive (for example, see Part Three, n.36 and Plate I, which critics saw as a sexual embrace).

Coincident with the Second Gospel, Blake activates the powers symbolized by the lion, persistently showing Los as a divinely inspired artist progressively demolishing the oppressive system and accomplishing Albion's delivery [Plate 30]. Upon hearing the messenger's dire report, Los prays to the Savior for aid and laments Albion's depressed state because of his "Opressors." Lightly masking the attacks upon his art, Blake again comments upon the nation's apparent inhumanity towards spiritual perception. Abrogating spirit in the world and treating men and their acts as merely motions of corporeal bodies destroys men's creative powers, nullifies humanity, and degrades art. "Humanity knows not of sex"; its essence is love. As man is spirit so his art and morality are expressions of it. But Albion has made the divine body of imagination into a "Rocky Law of condemnation & double Generation & Death./ Albion hath enter'd the Loins, the place of the Last Judgment"; he has entered the place of human creativity and infringed the prerogative of God.

With his globe of fire, Los goes in search of "the tempters" to generation [plate 31]; walking among Albion's hard rocks and in his caves, he

> ...saw every Minute Particular of Albion degraded & murder'd,
> But saw not by whom; they were hidden within in the minute particulars

Of which they had possess'd themselves, and there they take up
The articulations of a man's soul and laughing throw it down.

The above quotation contains conspicuous allusions to Reynolds' ideal of abstract general figures and autobiographical references to anonymous critics' ridicule of particularized art, infusing this section with an intensity of personal feeling. Since reality consists of perceived particulars, to interdict them is to deny their existence, murder them. Closed from the minutiae of actual objects, which abstractioners have, along with themselves, hidden, Los had no sure footing; "he walk'd difficult." Nonetheless, he continues his explorations and views with alarm how completely reasoners have appropriated the world and transformed it into a network of abstractions based on a generalized material substance underlying all phenomena, hence connoting divine power: "Every Universal Form was become barren mountains of Moral/ Virtue, and every Minute Particular harden'd into grains of sand, /And all the tendernesses of the soul cast forth as filth & mire." Reynolds lies also behind these lines; his metaphysical principle and notion of the mind as "a barren soil" (see page 20) have brought the wasteland into art.

Blake's concept of universal forms follows from his metaphysics. For a clarifying perspective we may cite Berkeley: universality consists "in the relation it bears to the particulars signified or represented by it; by virtue whereof it is that things, names, or notions, being in their own nature *particular,* are rendered *universal.*"[10] Whereas Locke held that universals are select qualities formed into abstract ideas according to a man's peculiar interest and rationally demonstrable, Berkeley contends they signify actual things, which are creations of God. He thus reinstates what Locke cast out of human experience: the immediate presence of a spiritual agent and perceivable universal forms.

But natural philosophy prevails. Coban, Hand and Hyle wield their power; their principles dominate art. So Los sees "the house of bread," the spiritual food that nourishes creativity, reduced to "Dens of despair" and humanity abolished: all is turned into "stones and rocks." He cannot find the enemy because there is no "human form," no living being of whom he can inquire about "these

---

[10] Berkeley, *Principles,* Introd.15.

Criminals" who slay those who believe in spiritual power. Yet, were he successful in finding them, his ethics forbid him to take vengeance, indeed impel him to show pity and compassion; he will not stoop to their tactics. So once again Blake, as he keeps doing, reverses Reynolds, attributing to his rules the cause of despair; once again he interjects the spiritual code of conduct, contrasting it with the moral law exercised by murderous anonymous critics; and once again he points to the distinction between art and morality, which, however, nowise excludes it as a subject of art.

Continuing his search, Los overhears Jerusalem affectionately remind Albion: "I cannot be thy Wife; thine own Minute Particulars/ Belong to God alone."[11] She makes explicit what has already been implied: as visible objects in the world are creations of God, so particularized visions in art are the creations of the eternal spirit. As such, their reality is a question "of Faith & not of Demonstration," Ulro's test of true forms.[12] She tries to make Vala realize this fact. But Vala claims Albion as her own; she has been given to him by Urizen, the father of demonstration; hence the "House of Albion" wages war to keep her as his wife, the fertile mother of all one sees in his land. Vala calls Jerusalem a harlot, literally a false principle, and holds her responsible for the raging war. By these allusions to Helen as the cause of the Trojan war initiated by the House of Atreus, Blake underlines Albion's tragic fate. Because, according to Vala, Jerusalem is a troublemaker in the House of Albion, she and her children must "sustain the glorious combat & the battle & war" to purify man by blotting out his "delusions" of spirit. The scene at plate 32 opens out the incident visually showing Vala shrouded, indicative both of hidden powers and of death, angrily condemning Jerusalem and her children. After pronouncing their doom, Vala, like another Clotho, casts her inflexible "dark threads" over Albion, subjecting his sons and daughters to inescapable material forces (using Berkeley's words, *Siris.* 271), to "necessity" and "fate, the idol of many moderns."

Despite his diligence, Los cannot locate the well-concealed enemy. But during his reconnaissance of its territory, he sees Albion on the brink of falling into "Non-Entity" for "his disease rose from

---

[11] Cf. Berkeley's Homeric allusion to "earth as the wife of heaven," *Siris.* 43.
[12] Locke, it will be recalled, maintains we perceive only secondary qualities, whereas demonstrable abstract ideas refer to hidden real qualities.

7. *Jerusalem* 32

his skirts" or outward garments: from the erroneous supposition that things are, in Berkeley's phrase, "clothed with sensible qualities" by a material substance and exist independent of the mind.[13] Seeing Albion on the verge of extinction though not past rescue, Los "siez'd his Hammer & Tongs, his iron Poker & his Bellows," striving to save him but met with "stern defiance" from his sons. Blake again renders in terms of combat the nation's precarious state; he creates another image of the conflict in art, recapitulates its cause, and carries further the imagery present in the rock. In this fierce war Albion is gravely wounded; his sons, headed by Coban, Hand and Hyle, bear him "from the bloody field" to the porch and on "the Couch" of contemplation[14] repose his trembling limbs, around which they rear "their Druid Patriarchal rocky Temples." While Albion lies dying, "his Spectrous Chaos" appears before him, "an Unformed Memory," an epitome of Reynolds' Lockean assumptions, with which the apparition identifies itself: with reason as an authoritative principle; with the concept of man as a quantitative object and lowly creature in the universe;[15] with the notion of the human mind as a blank tablet upon which nature writes simple ideas and the memory stores; and with the doctrine of abstract reasoning [plate 33].

> I am your Rational Power, O Albion, & that Human Form
> You call Divine is but a Worm seventy inches long
> That creeps forth in a night & is dried in the morning sun,
> In fortuitous concourse of memorys accumulated & lost.
> It plows the Earth in its own conceit, it overwhelms the Hills
> Beneath its winding labyrinths.

The Spectre creates chaos because he assumes that external objects impress disparate qualities upon a passive mind and because abstract ideas formed from these simple ideas have no actual referents; he builds labyrinths because he makes knowledge of forms circuitous and baffles by concealing particulars from sight; and, not least, he is "the Great Selfhood/ Satan, Worship'd as God" because in excessive pride

---

[13] Berkeley, *Siris*.316. Blake also expresses this idea in 10:9-10.
[14] For this allusion see Pt. Three, n.25.
[15] Locke theorized that the several species in the corporeal world are linked together closely, but that we are "more remote from the infinite being of GOD than we are from the lowest state of being, and that which approaches nearest to nothing," Bk.III.vi.12.

of reasonings he conspires to control mankind by subjecting it to material forces.

These forces were Berkeley's primary concern in his philosophical reflections. *Siris*.249 contains one of many statements about the problem accompanying Newtonian forces:

> And although a mechanical or mathematical philosopher may speak of absolute space, absolute motion, and of force as existing in bodies, causing such motion and proportional thereto; yet what these forces are which are supposed to be lodged in bodies, to be impressed on bodies, to be multiplied, divided, and communicated from one body to another, and which seem to animate bodies like abstract spirits or souls, hath been found very difficult, not to say impossible, for thinking men to conceive and explain.[16]

Blake considers these forces in relation to art and renders his criticism in a surrealistic parody of abstraction based on Newton's system of the world:

> ...a white Dot call'd a Center, from which branches out
> A Circle in continual gyrations: this became a Heart
> From which sprang numerous branches varying their motions,
> Producing many heads, three or seven or ten, & hand & feet
> Innumerable at will of the unfortunate contemplator
> Who becomes his food.

Such is the way of abstraction; such is the state of Albion because his rational power in overbearing pride has eclipsed the Divine Visions and narcissistically created a concave world of hypostasized abstractions which reflects back to him in "Sexual Reasoning Hermaphroditic." Here is an addition to the complex of sexual images triggered by abstract philosophy, which embeds power in corporeal bodies. Blake has created a perfect metaphor of the theoretic and actual situation: like the ambiguity of the term *sexual*, *hermaphroditic* encapsulates many nuances of meaning related to

---

[16] Berkeley, himself a keen mathematician, acknowledges mathematics is an important mode of knowledge. He and Blake object to turning abstractions into unknowable entities: such reifications do not help at all to explain how bodies act upon each other or on the mind; they feign an explanation.

blending the cause of motion and its spatial-temporal effects (natural phenomena) along with the indefiniteness of material substance and reduction of man to a vegetative and lowly state, for hermaphroditism occurs in many species of plants and invertebrate animals.

Albion's second apparition confirms this philosophical hermaphrodism; it appears "in gloomy pomp/ Involving the Divine Vision in colours of autumn ripeness." To Albion this phantom seems more lovely than anything he has ever seen; its attractive yet strange character perplexes him:

> I never saw thee till this time, nor beheld life abstracted,
> Nor darkness immingled with light on my furrow'd field.
> Whence camest thou? who art thou, O loveliest?

He does not recognize Vala in her sexual colours, death disguising life. Appareled thus, she intends to deceive, employing an artifice used by satanic figures, those angels of darkness who simulate an aura of light to beguile their victims.[17] Vala separated from Jerusalem is nature abstracted from life and from the particulars of "the Divine Vision," which she and Albion have "hid." Embracing the garment with which reasoners have clothed Albion, Vala informs him she has been raised to divinity, made the mighty goddess of life and creativity:

> Know me now Albion: look upon me. I alone am Beauty.
> The Imaginative Human Form is but a breathing of Vala.

Resurrected by naturalists, she has become the prime deity of the world: the most powerful, beautiful, perfect and holy thing men can behold. How can Albion possibly resist falling in worship at her feet? A series of rhetorical questions by him identifies her more precisely, bringing together the current philosophical situation, biblical parallel, religion and art [plate 34]. She is "Nature, Mother of All," another sobriquet for natural causality. She is "Babylon," built by worshipers of objects in nature. As natural phenomena, Vala is the "dweller of outward chambers," but abstracted she has ascended "inward," posing as a divine Being. She contains within herself an abstract unknowable material substance, which accounts for her illusive, enigmatic, and hermaphroditic nature as well as her autumnal col-

---

[17] A device used in *Paradise Lost, Orlando Furioso, Jerusalem Delivered, Don Quixote,* and other literary works.

ours, for matter is "a garment of death." Albion is baffled by her incongruous relationships: how can she in resurrection be wife of the son and mother of all? In eternity they do not marry.[18] Blake continues the sexual imagery in this dramatic episode he has created around Reynolds' notion of the divine principle as a phantom, nothing more than an "ungrounded conceit" of untaught minds, and his elevation of nature as the fountain of inspiration.[19]

Vala's pretentions to divinity, her peremptory claim to ideal beauty, and Albion's imminent death elicit a vehement aesthetic protest by Los to "the Sons of Albion & to Hand the eldest Son of Albion":

There is a Throne in every Man, it is the Throne of God;
This Woman has claim'd as her own, & Man is no more!
. . .
Hand! art thou not Reuben enrooting thyself into Bashan
. . .
Is this the Female Will, O ye lovely Daughters of Albion, To
Converse concerning Weight & Distance in the Wilds of Newton
    & Locke?

Los questions the application of scientific doctrines to art because they deny man's sovereignty, his innate powers of perception and creativity. Like Berkeley, who, objecting to Locke's correlation of mental and physical phenomena, argues "it is evident to every thinking man that human minds are not bandied about by corporeal objects without any inward principle of action,"[20] Blake maintains that man's ruling power is plainly evident from everyone's experience. But devotees of natural philosophy have hidden this "most evident God" and fashioned nature a controlling deity: they, notably Reynolds and his ilk, have immersed man in matter and relegated the artist to the mechanical and dehumanized world of Newton and Locke.

The action now centers on Reuben, a figure containing multiple meanings. Through it Blake not only conveys theories of natural

---

[18] An allusion to critics' moralizing joined to the Sadduccees' question and Jesus' answer in the Gospel, see Mk.12:25.

[19] Reynolds, Disc. Six, p.86.

[20] Berkeley, *Alciphron*, Dialogue VII.20.

philosophy but also imparts feelings of revulsion by anthropomorphizing nature and relating man intimately to the vegetable kingdom. Because Newton imbued matter with powers of motion, Hand is charged with infusing life into the womb of mother nature. He is likened to Reuben, Jacob's eldest son, who impregnated his mother, was sent wandering, settled in Bashan, relinquished the faith of Jehovah, and turned to idolatry. Tacitly, the superstition about mandrakes possessing potency to effect life is compared to belief in natural powers. Moreover, the poisonous properties of mandrakes suggest deadly consequences of material substances. All these associations implied in Los's accusations are exhibited in Los's acts described in the next seventy lines [34:43-55 and 36:1-54; plate 35 comments on these divinely justified acts involving Reuben and will therefore be discussed after plate 36].

Cut off from the eternal spirit, whose power has been transfused "into three Bodies" of a natural godhead, modern vegetative man is like Reuben, who slept "beside the Stone of Bohan," the block Reubenites set up as a rival altar to the sacred tent of Jehovah. Hence Reuben becomes an instrument in combating the enemy that must be revealed in its own system. Resolutely, Los heaves his thundering bellows and swings his mighty hammer into full action. He bent Reuben's "Nostrils down to the Earth... rolled his Eyes into two narrow circles... folded his Tongue/ Between Lips of mire & clay... bended/ His Ear in a spiral circle outward, then sent him over Jordan" into the enemy's ranks.[21] Blake employs the naturalists' own weapons against them; it is part of the complicated stratagem for quashing the enemy, who by the interposition of a thoughtless substance separates the human mind from its sovereign power. Through successive distortions of the human form Los demonstrates concretely natural philosophers' erroneous assumption that the mind considers a single sensory quality separate from others with which it is blended in objects and frames to itself an abstract idea of it. This is how material powers took control of the world: how nature was separated from "Divine Power," man from spirit, and the artist from his inspirations. This is why "Hand stood between Reuben & Merlin,

---

[21] Spirals appear in Swedenborg's system of rational knowledge; Blake adapts these along with other Swedenborgian concepts to natural philosophers' abstract reasonings about external phenomena.

as the Reasoning Spectre/ Stands between the Vegetative Man & his Immortal Imagination."[22] One after another Los warps Reuben's senses and in a series of forays sends this Lockean aberrant form into Ulro in search of realities. However, without belief in spiritual efficacy, without the initiating act of the mind and perceptive power of the imagination, but with senses separated and constricted, directed outward and downward, Reuben perceives neither unified real qualities comprising objects, nor their beauty and perfection, nor their true cause of existence; he experiences only disparate secondary qualities and dark impenetrable surfaces of some unknowable abstract substance called *matter*. Therefore, "in reasonings Reuben returned" and announced, "Doubt is my food day & night." Each time Los sent the misshapen man into Ulro "every-one that saw him/ Fled!" They fled in terror of what they saw: the "horrible Form" and evidence of Los's power. So "they hid in caves/ And dens; they looked at one-another & became what they beheld," encouraging one another in their evil venture against spiritual power, unmindfully hastening their own defeat.[23] "Hand, Hyle & Coban fled"; all who saw the hideous form "became what they beheld, fleeing over the Earth," spreading their theories.

While bending Reuben's senses, Los sees "the Four Zoas,[24] who are the Four Eternal Senses in Man," separate "from the Limbs of Albion" and his land divide "into Jerusalem & Vala"; he finds "Accident & Chance" hidden in objects "Fixed by the Divine Power." He thus advances the divine plan, for "Reuben is Merlin/ Exploring the Three States of Ulro: Creation, Redemption & Judgment," analogous to the poet explaining the three phases of natural philosophy in relation to Albion [36:31-42].

Blake supplements Los's deformations of the human senses with an interpretive statement: "If Perceptive Organs vary/ Objects of Perception seem to vary:/ If the Perceptive Organs close, their Objects seem to close also" [34:55-56]. This fact was demonstrated by Berkeley to "root out" the preconception that external objects have an independent existence and to support his own theory that "visible

---

[22] According to one tradition, Merlin possessed powers of insight and prophecy.

[23] This interpretation takes advantage of the situation described in Psalm 64 and gives to Blake's lines a meaning consistent with *Jerusalem's* theme.

[24] Blake uses the Greek plural (zoa) as an English singular.

objects are only in the mind."[25] To this end, he argues the nonexistence of absolute qualities, which figure in the abstract idea of matter, and fully illustrates that "variation" in the position of our visive or other perceiving faculty "may vary the judgment" we make about objects. In his continuing efforts to discredit abstract reasoning as a determinant of reality and extirpate belief in material substance, Berkeley astutely notes that as "life from different principles takes a different issue," so it is "in regard to our faculties." Naturalists assume "sensible appearances are all in all"; they employ their reasonings about them; their "desires terminate in them"; they "look no further for realities or causes."

Blake draws out the implications of such a philosophy in art. Reynolds and his followers take nature as their principle and from it seek to abstract the hidden essence of objects. But theories about the world affect not only its objects but also its perceivers: "Consider this, O mortal Man, O worm of sixty winters, said Los,/ Consider Sexual Organization & hide thee in the dust" [34:57-58]. If men believe everything depends on matter, they themselves must be composed of it; they become what they behold, both what they perceive and what they revere. So the Eternals looking down comment upon the doleful scene: because Albion's sons and daughters believe nature is the principle of life, they "are vegetable only fit for burning"; because they conceal minute particularities in abstract ideas, they despair of knowledge and depress sublime art, for "Art & Science cannot exist but by Naked Beauty display'd." Here is another allusion not only to natural philosophers' doctrine of abstraction but also to Reynolds' ruling that "particularities" be left out and "figures... be cloathed."[26] The observers "in Great Eternity"

---

[25] Berkeley, *Theory of Vision*.138.77,73; *Siris*.294: this is not a rejection of the senses; neither Berkeley nor Blake denies the normal mechanism of sensory perception—sensory data are real, but they cannot exist independent of mind.

[26] Reynolds, Disc. Four, p.55,57. Keeping to his criterion of reason, he attributes nakedness in ancient sculpture to "greater reasons" that preponderate over the rule of showing figures in native dress, adding that "Art is not yet in so high estimation with us as to obtain so great a sacrifice as the ancients made, especially the Grecians; who suffered themselves to be represented naked": Disc. Seven, p.114.

conclude that taking "What seems to Be" for a true principle "is productive of the most dreadful/ Consequences" [36:48-53].[27]

As in the first fall of man, so in Albion's fall the merciful Lord intervenes [plate 35]. Coordinate with Los's acts the Savior, who has power to preserve his creation, reaches beyond Hand's system. "Two Limits, Satan and Adam," death and life, set by the Divine hand, permanently stand in every human. "Albion hath enter'd the State Satan!" The notion of states derives from Swedenborg,[28] but Blake gives them an empirical content that fits Berkeley's theory of general

---

[27] Blake expresses this Berkeleian principle (*Siris*.278) more completely in *Milton* 26:44-45: "every Natural Effect has a Spiritual Cause, and Not/ A Natural; for a Natural Cause only seems."

[28] From the concept of states, Swedenborg constructs a complicated ontology, which like his science is deductive (see his *Principia*). Blake declares Swedenborg "did wrong in endeavouring to explain to the reason, what it could not comprehend" (Crabb Robinson's account of Blake: Bentley, *Blake Records*, p.540). This statement is supported by Blake's own notes to Swedenborg's works; especially pertinent are Blake's comments on §239, 241 and 257 of *Divine Love and Wisdom*. Swedenborg's system is Platonic to the extent that knowledge derives from abstract general forms, which man may come to know "by laying asleep the sensations" (§257). Blake rejects this principle and gives forms an empirical content, basing them on the principle of cause and effect, whereas Swedenborg's organizing principle is moral: "Evils and Falsities" in opposition to Goods and Truths" (§271).

In passing it may be useful to mention some other fundamental differences between their view of the world, of nature, and man. Swedenborg posits "two worlds, the spiritual and the natural.... The two are totally distinct"; he replaces Plato's theory of participation with a theory of "correspondences" (DL&W, §83); he speaks of nature as "clothed in matter" (§315), admitting it as a real entity; and, Blake notes at §181, "he speaks of Men as merely earthly Men" (Annotations to Swedenborg, p.92). In contrast Blake causally connects spirit to nature, does not posit intermediate realms of beings (as does Swedenborg), and rejects both material substance and earthly man. To show in detail what Blake accepts and what he rejects of Swedenborg's philosophy requires another study. Suffice it here to repeat Blake's statement concerning the ontological relations Swedenborg sets up: "This is certainly not to be understood according to the letter for it is false by experience." Blake may agree with Swedenborg on theological points, but on the principles of his philosophy he disagrees with him and agrees with Berkeley. Blake's most devastating criticism of Swedenborg's system occurs in *The Marriage of Heaven and Hell*, plates 21-22: it sprouts from "systematic reasoning. Swedenborg boasts that what he writes is new; tho' it is only the Contents or Index of already publish'd books.... Swedenborg has not written one new truth. Now hear another: he has written all the old falsehoods."

In "A New Heaven is Begun" (*Blake Newsletter* [Fall 1979] pp. 64-90) Morton Paley indicates that Blake "both appropriates and subverts" Swedenborg's ideas and after 1790 rejects his theological and ethical doctrines, p.80.

forms: they refer to particulars, not to abstract ideas (see page 127). *Satan* therefore is a form of evil, of selfhood or pride, a temporal event open to change, a state from which man may be delivered. Disavowals of spiritual power are errors of intellect created into permanent states occurring in space-time as visible particulars "to deliver Individuals evermore!" Through Reuben Los visibly displays the cause of the nation's fall: Albion's acceptance of a materialist metaphysics is satanic. Plate 35 with text superimposed shows God as crucified Christ in a Michelangelesque attitude setting limits to destruction and creating states, symbolized by the creation of Eve, from whose seed comes deliverance. The process by which individuals can be saved is carried out by God in human form. The design powerfully conveys God's humanity and reflects Blake's fundamental theological belief: we know God as man. Thus Los sees the "appearance of a Man" in his furnace and hears the voice of eternity promising that Albion will reenter the state of life and humanity; he will be saved from oblivion and his erring giant sons forgiven. But Albion must "pass thro' condemnation"; he must suffer his own deadly laws: "No individual can keep these Laws, for they are death/ To every energy of man and forbid the springs of life."

Blake uses the term *energy* in the same sense as Berkeley does, namely as a causal principle.[29] In *Siris*.250 he disputes Newton's hypothesis that there are "certain forces or powers" in "the minute particles of bodies"; he contends that "the force exists... not in them," not in the bodies moved, "but in the mover," which "the Peripatetics rightly judge... to be ἐνέργεια or act." And in *Siris*.261, opposing Locke's notion of man, he adds: this energy, from which "springs" the visible world and all its motions, is the same as the "spirit of man," the source of his existence, his creativity. For Blake this creativity is most evident in art: Los's exertions in the work of redemption epitomize this energy.

The divine voice provokes Los to fury. He calls upon Albion to rouse himself before it is too late: his reason is "most deform'd"; his

---

[29] In his book, *Energy and the Imagination* (Oxford, 1970), Morton Paley lists some typical antecedents as well as subsequent views of these two concepts, ranging from Plato's general view of imagination to Hazlitt's notion of the power of strong excitement. It should be kept in mind, however, that *energy* or *power* in the sense of cause is peculiarly modern and does not fully emerge as a causal principle until Newton's time.

"insane" Spectre has prepared out of hard matter a rocky sepulcher ready for Albion if he persists in forbidding men to exercise their springs of life and to express their perceptions in art, upon which Albion's own life depends. But despite "blue death"[30] hovering at his feet, Albion obdurately turns away from "Universal Love." Los, however, does not abandon him; in faithful service to the eternal spirit he protectively follows him. Albion has fallen, but Los prevents him from falling further. All this we see against a background of darkness at plate 37. Above the overlaid text is Los in "Divine Similitude" literally upholding Albion as he flees from the palm of love and peace towards the oak of hate and war; and below is the Spectre with outstretched bat-wings hovering over Albion's petrified body, his fate if he continues his present destructive course. Pleading with him, Los explains: the counter-attacks by himself and his sons are motivated by love, not hate, for sake of Albion's life, not his death; they do not strip with bronze the ears of the enemy, slash in two the tongue, or knock out the eyes with blows on the head; they fight with flaming words and visible particulars; they fight with powers of spirit: "Our wars are wars of life, & wounds of love/ With intellectual spears, & long winged arrows of thought./ ... We live as One Man; for contracting our infinite senses/ We behold multitude, or expanding, we behold as one,/ As One Man all the Universal Family, and that One Man/ We call Jesus the Christ; and he in us, and we in him/ ... he is all in all" [38:14-24].

Los's importunities restate Blake's basic tenet that the observed world is the effect of spirit, a substance we share with the Creator, making us one with Him (see page 82) and hence one with the spiritually inspired artist; they also counter Bacon's theory of natural phenomena as expansion and contraction caused by motion of particles,[31] against which Berkeley argued, maintaining that a vivifying spirit "contracting ... and expanding" produces multitude effects in the vegetable and animal system.[32] Granted, when someone investigates inward structures of objects or observes motions in

---

[30] This image occurs in *The Iliad;* exactly what Blake wishes to suggest by this allusion is ambiguous: perhaps several things—among them, elements of paganism in natural philosophy for which Albion fights his war.

[31] For details of Bacon's theory see *Novum Organum,* Bk.II.L-LII.

[32] Berkeley, *Siris.* 143, 295.

nature, he frames his hypotheses to suit natural science. These fit the occasion and answer the end of an experimenter or a mechanic. But if he "ascends from the sensible into the intellectual world, and beholds things in a new light... he will then change his system, and perceive that what he took for substances and causes are but fleeting shadows; that the mind contains all, and acts all, and is to all created beings the source of unity and identity."

Blake applies the concept of expansion and contraction to the human senses, which he has connected not only to the human mind but also to the eternal senses, the four zoa (cf. 36:31). He continues in plate 38 to develop these philosophical points contextually in aesthetic diction. London's appeal to Albion states explicitly that things have their existence in the imagination. It functions not merely to transform realities; it directly perceives realities: "My Streets are my ideas of Imagination" and "My Houses are Thoughts." Lest this seem like a fantastic allegory, the poet reassures readers he tells the truth; he knows it from experience: "I write in South Molton Street (a place associated with Blake) what I both see and hear." He confirms London's pronouncements: "Cities/ Are Men, fathers of multitudes, and Rivers & Mountains/ Are also Men; every thing is Human, mighty! sublime!/ In every bosom a Universe expands as wings,/ Let down at will around and call'd the Universal Tent," Blake's metaphor for spirit. These lines, therefore, are more than a restatement of London's utterances concerning acts of perception; they include essential metaphysical beliefs Blake shares with Berkeley, whom we may consult for a straightforward philosophical exposition.

Although Berkeley's doctrine of the mind equates reality with perception, it is not subjectivist in the sense that things are determined by individuals alone. Berkeley secures objectivity for his theory of ideas through the causal principle he enunciates in the *Principles* and reiterates in *Siris*. When things are not actually perceived by some "created spirit, they must either have no existence at all, or else subsist in the mind of some eternal spirit."[33] The continued existence of objects is divinely sustained; God is the universal perceiver or sublime cause of all things; created spirits or finite minds by their kinship to an eternal spirit or infinite mind are recipients of its effects perceived

---

[33] Berkeley, *Principles*.6,82,101-102; *Siris*.43,328.

as ideas. Berkeley informs us positively his doctrine in no way calls into question "the reality of timber, and stone, mountains, and rivers, and cities, and human bodies." All these exist. Further, our ideas of them are not copies of reality; rather, they are the real world because we perceive directly the creations of an eternal spirit. Natural philosophers belittle our faculties; they contend that the "real essence, the internal qualities, and constitution of even the meanest object is hid from our view; something there is in... every grain of sand, which is beyond" our comprehension. But this complaint is groundless; it is based on "mechanical causes" of bodies, "whereas in truth, there is no other agent or efficient cause than *spirit*." This "vehicle of power," of which nature is an articulate revelation, is so evanescent "as to escape" the "nicest search"; it is in fact an inward principle, not a quality such as figure or weight of bodies. The minutest particles as well as the greatest masses are governed in their natural motions by divine power: like "the driver in a chariot," God "comprehends and orders and sustains the whole mundane system."

Using imagery similar to the above, Blake existentially joins the active mind to sensory phenomena, the eternal spirit to created spirits, the sublime to the mundane. Things are men because objects literally consist of integrated sensible qualities having their existence in the perceptions of human imagination, not in an external world independent of mind, nor in a rationalized world of abstract ideas. These objects are also mighty and sublime since their form and continued existence depend on the eternal spirit. This translucent power "by vegetations viewless" is the cause of all existence and the gate to eternity. At plate 39 he communicates this causal principle through complexity of characters and intricacy of actions: "Satan's Watch-fiends, tho' they search numbering every grain/ Of sand... they never find this Gate./ It is the Gate of Los," the gate to great art and humane morality, to "Human beauty" and "Mercy." Albion has fled through this gate and "turn'd his back against the Divine Vision" because Coban, Hand and Hyle have seized the vehicle of power. Adapting the famous Platonic image to his own purposes, Blake pictures Urizen as the driver of a war-chariot, drawn by spectrous wild horses (human reason out of control) of the demonic trinity, a triple wave of ruin rising against Albion.[34] But Los, "not yet infected

---

[34] Unlike Plato's charioteer, Blake's driver is spirit: it, not reason, controls.

with the Error & Illusion" of zealous naturalists, does not forsake Albion.[35]

In the next plate [40], obviously alluding to tragic scenes in classical and biblical literature about revolts against heaven, Blake heightens the drama and expands the involvement in the conflict. The land itself cries out: "Albion is sick to death./ He hath leagued himself with robbers; he hath studied the arts/ Of unbelief." Coban, Hand and Hyle are thieves who have hidden spirit, stolen God's fire, depriving man of his essential treasure; they have persuaded Albion of falsehoods concerning causes of ideas and creativity; they have "sown errors over all his fruitful fields!" Upon hearing these wailings, "Twenty-four" agitated representatives of Albion's people come "trembling on wat'ry chariots," gather round his couch, shed tears, and shudder at the dreadful consequences that await mankind.[36] "For had the Body of Albion fall'n down" and let fly "the enormous Spectre," which satanically opposes with intent to devour "the Merciful," then "Man himself" must "become a Fiend," an unhuman form. He must needs suffer "the torments of Eternal Death," and Albion with "his mighty Sons chain'd down" to an eternity of fire were it not for "the Merciful One," for "the Divine Family," and for Los, who built "the stubborn structure of the Language."

This much quoted cryptic phrase relating to Blake's art has an affinity to a theory of vision Berkeley developed and justified in conjunction with his criticism of abstract matter. Natural philosophers, observing that certain qualities recur in nature, suppose these possess powers that determine existence. Further, assuming that every name must have only "one definite signification," they abstract the recurrent qualities and gather them under a general name, making its meaning consist in a determinate abstract idea.[37] This precision of

---

[35] In calling Los "the twenty-eighth" and "four-fold" [38:13], is Blake implying *Jerusalem* is the twenty-eighth book, fourfold, of the New Testament? Possibly so.

[36] The scene is reminiscent of Oceanus and his chorus of daughters, who, out of kindness visit the "malefactor" who stole the element that devises all, advise him to cease his obstinacy and acknowledge the sovereignty of the ruling god, *Greek Tragedies*, vol.1, ed. David Greene and Richard Lattimore (University of Chicago, 1967), "Prometheus Bound," 1.3-10.

[37] Berkeley, *Principles*, Introd.18: he is here pointing to the difference between (1) the visible object, e.g., a particular star, and (2) the meaning of the word *star*. We use this word according to a single definition without assuming a third thing, such as an

meaning is misleading because it suggests that an abstract idea stands for a particular thing; but it has no exact correspondence to anything in space-time; it is only a general name, a term for the sum of particular occurrences. There is no intermediate cause between perception and sensory particulars. To escape "that fine and subtle net of *abstract ideas,*" Berkeley promises he will make as little use as possible of general names in his own philosophizing.[38] Instead, he will depend on what he actually sees: "whatever ideas I consider, I shall endeavour to take them bare and naked into my view."[39] Communication based on perceived particulars with minimum abstraction, a language close to visible things, is an epistemological principle directly related to his theory of reality. Since words not only are signifiers both of existent and of non-existent things but also have variable meanings, the universal language is, according to him, not linguistic but visionary: "objects of Vision constitute the Universal Language of Nature."[40] Vision and reality are both at once. On this same principle he connects the spiritual and physical, the infinite and finite, God and man.

Berkeley elaborates upon his theory of language in *Siris*.252. He contends mechanical principles do not solve the real cause of phenomena; they only reduce appearances to rules fixed by the Author of nature.

> There is a certain analogy, constancy, and uniformity in the phenomena or appearances of nature, which are a foundation for general rules: and these are a grammar for the understanding of nature, or that series of effects in the visible world whereby we are enabled to foresee what will come to pass in the natural course of things.

---

underlying starness; in fact there are only individual stars. These distinctions are directed at the abstract general idea of an underlying matter: Berkeley does not allow this third independent entity.

[38] Berkeley, *Principles,* Introd.22.

[39] Berkeley, *Principles,* Introd.21; he makes a similar claim for his exposition in *Theory of Vision* (see Pt. Three, n.37). Bacon compares his plain and perspicuous presentation in *Novum Organum* to "nakedness of the mind," *The Great Instauration,* "The plan of the Work," p.248. Much of the imagery Bacon used against old induction Berkeley uses against abstract reasoning. It is not impossible that Blake also may have read *Novum Organum,* at least parts of it.

[40] Berkeley, *Theory of Vision*.147. Nature as the language of God perhaps derives from the Fourth Gospel, "the Word was God," 1:1.

The universe is like a book written by the finger of God: particulars are metaphysically tied to vision in Berkeley's system.

The world of particulars as a meaningful visual language of divine creation is inextricably bound to Blake's view of reality as vision and his notion of poet and artist as prophet: "Length, Bredth, Highth... Obey the Divine Vision" [36:56].[41] Because Blake equates imagination with spirit, he extends the universal language of vision to all objects and all people: the vital act in art as in science is vision, which the poet-artist makes eternal: vision, reality, and the divinely inspired poem are coextensive. Direct perception of visible objects unencumbered by the net of abstract reasoning is both the philosophical subject and method of Blake's epic. Hence the repeated use of *behold:* to apprehend through vision. The reader is asked to "behold the Vision of Albion" [1:7], the nation's events bare and naked, which the poet and Los clearly see. Neither Berkeley as philosopher nor Blake as poet denies the role of verbal language in communication; for both men visual forms are a metaphysical preference. Blake carries out the substantive nature of vision in the interaction between illustrations and verses, between images and words. The illustrations therefore are not gratuitous; they manifest an essential part of Blake's system. As art, visual forms are not of a higher metaphysical level than poetry. Both forms are effects of imagination: imagination is to vision as vision is to a work of art, whether formed by writing, drawing, engraving, painting, sculpting or by other media.[42] The illustrations supplement the variable meanings of words. Blake avoids indefiniteness, stays free of illusions, and aims to free others from the abstractioners' entangling net, which he engraves at several places, most prominently on plate 4, 31 and 45. His protreptic poem is built entirely on the concept of Divine Vision; both heaven and earth have set hand to his poem. Visions of the imagination are not outside the actual world: the poet sees the series of events involving Albion, sees the shuttles of reason weaving "black

---

[41] For Blake, as for Berkeley, communicaton with God is not through mystical experience; rather it is through perception of visible objects. In "A Descriptive Catalogue," he states: "A Spirit and a Vision are not, as the modern philosophy supposes, a cloudy vapour, or a nothing: they are organized and minutely articulated beyond all that the mortal and perishing nature can produce," p.576.

[42] This is a complex topic that needs detailed psychological and philosophical investigation.

melancholy as a net" over Albion to enmesh Jerusalem and ensnare her children. Therefore, "acting against/ Albion's melancholy, who must else have been a Dumb despair" because he has turned his back on the Divine Vision, Los builds the stubborn structure of the universal language.

At the bottom of plate 41 we see Albion completely in his Spectre's power. "Ulro" threateningly rolls "round his skirts from Dover to Cornwall," round his Southern borders, where Urizen has assumed control [plate 42]. Albion is at a low point in his melancholy and broods on evil. He accuses Los of hypocrisy: "O thou deceitful friend,/ Worshipping mercy & beholding thy friend in such affliction!" Whereupon Los shows him that the "accursed things" plaguing him result from false principles he so fondly perpetrates in art to his own detriment, indeed to his extinction. But Albion remains adamant; he angrily but mistakenly blames Los for the dying nation and commands him to return its emanations. Seeing himself as a providential father, Albion charges Los with ingratitude and demands justice. Los will not be intimidated; while retaining his compassion, he retaliates with harsh words in yet another attempt to awaken Albion: "Righteousness & justice I give thee in return/ For thy righteousness, but I add mercy." Again he reminds Albion he was "the Image of God surrounded by the Four Zoas," three of which he in his selfhood has slain—humanity, divine power, and forgiveness through self-sacrifice. Los is the fourth; he is the spirit of prophecy and cannot be put out of existence. Albion is "in Error," because he has banished Jerusalem; Los comes to rectify this error by defending imagination, the true source of creativity; he comes to instruct those who lack this knowledge.

Blake reintroduces and expatiates upon the concept of limits. The doctrine of matter represents "a limit of Opakeness" named *Satan* because its proponents engage in open war with intent to destroy the substance that joins men not only to God but to each other as well. Limiting perception to sensory appearances is "a limit of Contraction"; as a form of human error, it is named *Adam*. Both limits exist in every man and if exceeded lead to eternal death. But the Savior in his infinite power and mercy creates generation out of "Contraction's Limit" to save man by displaying to him the power of spirit, an inner power of unlimited range and luminosity. Because spirit begins and ends in eternity, "there is no Limit of Expansion;

there is no Limit of Translucence/ In the bosom of Man." But Albion has imposed limits by instituting laws based on physical science. Los will no longer endure these outrages, no longer tolerate the repressive laws in government any more than in art;[43] he outrightly challenges Albion: "I break thy bonds of righteousness. I crush thy messengers/ That they may not crush me and mine;.../ ...I defy thy worst revenge./ Consider me as thine enemy."

It is not an easy battle to combat Albion's powerful forces. Like a vengeful god, Albion in accord with his iron laws peremptorily orders his mighty sons to arrest Los: "Go Hand & Hyle! sieze the abhorred friend/ As you have siez'd the Twenty-four rebellious ingratitudes/... Man lives by deaths of Men." But Los, who wears the superior invisible armor of spirit, escapes the ferocity of Albion's sons. The "Divine hand was upon him"; he "drew his Seven Furnaces around Albion's Altars" to try the naturalists' forms seven times.[44] Against their raging war conceived in dreams of Ulro, he fearlessly continues to build "the Mundane Shell/ In the Four Regions of Humanity" to reveal in visible particulars the reactor in his own system, which places an outside covering over the artist's inspirations. Because the cover is composed of abstractions from nature, it is "the Net & Veil of Vala." So ends this long plate.

As the intensity of the war and danger to Albion's life mount, Los's fury and activity increase [plate 43]. While he desperately works to save Albion, the twenty-four in captivity, hearing Albion's sons shout in pomp of war and glory of victory, anxiously curb their Spectres (another implied comparison between uncontrolled reason and wild horses): they inquire after Jerusalem; they pray for salvation; they weep. But they act not, rationalizing that if they voice anger "Albion will destroy Jerusalem"; on the other hand, if they display mercy towards him, he will destroy them. Their dilemma sits on an unfounded fear because as spiritual beings they have power to repel the enemy. Therefore Los reproaches them for their timidity and lack of confidence: "Why stand we here trembling around/ Calling on God for help, and not ourselves, in whom God dwells," reach out "to

---

[43] See Pt. Three, n.31.
[44] An allusion to Ps.12:6: "The words of the Lord are pure words: as silver tried in a furnace of earth, purified seven times"—another reminder that Los's words are divinely inspired.

save the falling Man?" Los's long speech [43:12-80] is an impassioned criticism of abstract generalization and a fiery defense of minute particulars. Why do the sons of Jerusalem remain aloof while generalizing abstractionists build a world of "Swell'd & bloated General Forms repugnant to the Divine-/ Humanity who is the Only General and Universal Form."

This wrathful rebuke to Reynolds' forms has philosophic support in the general and universal forms Berkeley opposed to Locke's theory. According to Locke, "general and universal belong not to the real existence of things"; they are contrivances of the human understanding "and concern only signs."[45] Berkeley is of another opinion: "a word becomes general by being made the sign, not of an abstract general idea but, of several particular ideas."[46] Since general terms owe their justification to particulars and conform to all instances of the object represented, they have a direct connection to existent things. There is no dichotomy between the general and particular. The issue is crucial because it bears on Newton's general law of motion. Berkeley wishes to take forces out of material particles, and universals out of Newton's hand: force or energy of "this mundane system" has its source in spirit; and "laws of attraction and repulsion" are "general rules" established by a universal mind.[47] The "mutual relation, connexion, motion, and sympathy of the parts of this world" show it is "animated and held together by one Soul... and directed by a Mind." The notion of existence independent of mind not only retards knowledge by placing it in uncertainty but also subverts religion and morality by destroying "the αὐτεξούσιον [free power] of God or man."

Because general forms occupy a central place in Reynolds' system, Blake returns to them again and again, casting his criticisms into emotive and metaphorical language. Los berates the naturalists' forms; they are nothing but abstract ideas, all of them based on corporeal substances, itself an abstract idea contrived of such qualities as

---

[45] Locke, III.iii.
[46] Berkeley, *Principles*, Introd.11; cf. the quotation on p. 201. He does not reject general ideas; he disagrees with Locke's concept of them. This is also Blake's position. Hume refers to Berkeley's criticism of abstract ideas and his concept of general ideas as "the greatest and most valuable discoveries" made of late years in philosophy (*A Treatise of Human Nature*, 1.i.7).
[47] Berkeley, *Siris*.154,231,273,271.

hardness, extension and motility. Albion's sons have puffed up these abstractions into a really existent universal power, repellent to God, the prime mover. A divine energy moves the whole and all its parts, which "seek with love & sympathy" the general forms set by the benevolent Creator, "Who protects minute particulars every one in their own identity." Now this energy "is clos'd in by deadly teeth" of mechanical wheels that turn to destroy and replace it with a "net" of reasoning and a "trap" of hard matter, rendering friendship, love, and, not least, Divine Vision abhorrent. Blake regards Reynolds' method mechanical despite the latter's denial (see Part Two). In lines 43:28-29 he symbolically alludes to Reynolds' opinion (cited at page 20) regarding the intoxicating but dangerous effects of divine inspiration: love, the "wine of Spirit," has been turned into cruelty, and perceived particulars, the "vineyards" of God, into stupefying matter. Naturalists' generalized forms are "A pretence of Art to destroy Art; a pretence of Liberty/ To destroy Liberty; a pretence of Religion to destroy Religion" because these unique values flow from the human spirit, not from forces external to it, nor from rules. The beauty of form is particular; the glory of imagination is liberty; and the inspiration of religion, as of art, is love.

To inspire his cohorts, Los speaks with the conviction of a Christian soldier; they fight for truth because they fight with spiritual arrows of love and bow of life, literally with God's power and covenant, whereas Albion's armies contend for false doctrines leading to eternal death. Everywhere dead corpses lie before them because in a world determined by physical forces men are by nature enemies to each other. Albion's generalizing sons grind the living and the dead in their "rumbling Mills" much as they crush particulars until the "minutest powers" of perception in art and science are lost. Los adds persuasiveness to his argument by contrasting these consequences with those emanating from spiritual acts. Instead of "Mutual Forgiveness" he sees punishment; instead of "Minute Particulars" he sees barrenness; "instead of heavenly Chapels," he sees bodies of hard particles, which Albion's sons mathematically demonstrate. Their rational power has driven them into doubt of their own powers of creativity, into unknowable abstractions, and hence into "incoherent despair." Los concludes the fighting address to his men with the command and subtlety of an Odysseus: "why do you all stand silent? I alone/ Remain in permanent strength. Or is all this goodness & pity only/

That you may take the greater vengeance in your Sepulcher?"

Fourfold the twenty-four respond [plate 44]: "with kindest violence" they surround Albion and strive to bring him back to life and peace, symbolized by Noah's ark, which in contrast to the bat-winged Spectre, Blake illustrates as a dove-winged floating house threatened by a billowing dark sea. Still, Albion resists divine influence; he rolls "his Wheels backward," historically, back into spiritually unenlightened times. The divine family anxiously hovers around him; it delegates Los as watchman, naming him "The Spirit of Prophecy, calling him Elijah," who admonished his nation's king and predicted the latter's death if he did not mend his rank ways. Like this great prophet of Jehovah, Los watches over Albion, who is fast propelling himself into a world of eternal death with his sons "ascending & descending in the horrid Void."

For this vivid image of Albion's sons and their modus operandi, Blake joins Bacon's description of his method, a "road that ascends and descends,"[48] and Berkeley's explanation of plant life (page 119): abstraction and nature conjoined. On analogy with the "ascending and descending juices" of vegetable bodies, Blake pictures Albion's naturalist sons as a part of the world they investigate: "Such is the nature of Ulro, that whatever enters/ Becomes Sexual & is Created and Vegetated and Born." Like Baconians, who by the light of axioms educed from natural phenomena deduce many new things below and above the earth, these sons alternately ascend to immense spaces among the starry wheels of abstraction and descend from there to Ulro among its dark satanic wheels to invent more abstractions. Blake again presents the chief events but as always adds new imagery to characterize naturalists' methods and doctrines in the sphere of art, building up the narrative with each instance. In their "Spectrous Uncircumcized Vegetation," Albion's sons have formed "a Sexual Machine, an Aged Virgin Form." Through these hyperboles Blake both gives concrete expression to his criticism of Reynolds' system and emphasizes its preposterous rules. *Uncircumcision* is again semantically linked to materialism (cf. page 81); *sexual,* like Babylon, belongs to the imagery that clusters around Vala as a self-generating

---

[48] Bacon, *Novum Organum,* Bk.I.CIII: rules for this new logic were planned though never accomplished as part of this work. Newton carried to perfection the new way of inquiry; Berkeley questioned its validity (*Siris*.228).

body (cf. page 112); *machine* refers to the mechanical operations of copying other works in imitation and of gathering impressions from scientific observations; *virgin* is another allusion to chaste forms abstracted from nature.

Again Blake brings out the mingling of science with religion and art that turns Jerusalem's holy places in Erin's land into worship of natural powers; again he comments on the consanguinity of humanity, art and spirit; again he renders philosophical principles in psalmodic tones:

> Man is adjoin'd to Man by his Emanative portion
> Who is Jerusalem in every individual Man, and her
> Shadow is Vala, builded by the Reasoning power in Man.
> O search & see: turn your eyes inward: open, O thou World
> Of Love & Harmony in Man: expand thy ever lovely Gates![49]

The above conviction and appeal sounded by twenty-four spiritual sons, whom Blake calls by English place names representing cathedral cities, the protectors of spirit in Albion's kingdom—north, south, east and west—are developed in Bath's long speech [plate 45]. Because Bath is also a place of mineral springs, it is both "healing City" and "mild Physician of Eternity," healer of body and soul.[50] As spokesman for the divine family, Bath pleads with dying Albion, whose sons have closed his "Western Gate" of humanity. Albion was in the past a paragon of benevolence, trust and brotherhood; now he is a "piteous example" of suspicion and mistrust headed for oblivion because in giving free rein to his reasoning power he set in motion selfhood. This "dread disease" only spirit can heal. But Albion is deaf to Bath's solicitude. The illustration at the top of plate 45 shows Albion helplessly enrooted in a substance woven by abstract reasoning's ensnaring net drawn by Vala.

In a desperate move to save Albion, another member of the divine family approaches him [plate 46]. Oxford, associated with a long tradition of divinely inspired poets, implores Albion: "Thou art in Error." Ulro rises from fallacious principles; this one error destroys the human soul and debases spiritual art. Oxford begs Albion

---

[49] Cf. Ps.34:8.
[50] Bath is a peculiarly rich symbol, encompassing not only medical and church history but also biblical parables and Arthurian legend.

Both, mild Physician of Eternity, mysterious power
Whose springs are unsearchable & knowledg infinite.
Hereford, ancient Guardian of Wales, whose hands
Builded the mountain palaces of Eden, stupendous works!
Lincoln, Durham & Carlisle, Councellors of Los,
And Ely, Scribe of Los, whose pen no other hand
Dare touch: Oxford, immortal Bard! with eloquence
Divine, he wept over Albion; speaking the words of God
In mild perswasion: bringing leaves of the Tree of Life.

Thou art in Error Albion, the Land of Ulro:
One Error not removd, will destroy a human Soul,
Repose in Beulahs night, till the Error is removd
Reason not on both sides. Repose upon our bosoms
Till the Plow of Jehovah, and the Harrow of Shaddai
Have passed over the Dead, to awake the Dead to Judgment.
But Albion turnd away refusing comfort.

Oxford trembled while he spoke, then Fainted in the arms
Of Norwich, Peterboro, Rochester, Chester awful, Worcester,
Litchfield, Saint Davids, Landaff, Asaph, Bangor, Sodor,
Bowing their heads devoted: and the Furnaces of Los
Began to rage, thundering loud the storms began to roar
Upon the Furnaces, and loud the Furnaces rebellow beneath

And these the Four in whom the twenty-four appeard four-fold:
Verulam, London, York, Edinburgh, mourning one towards another
Alas!——The time will come, when a mans worst enemies
Shall be those of his own house and family: in a Religion
Of Generation, to destroy by Sin and Atonement, happy Jerusalem
The Bride and Wife of the Lamb. O God thou art Not an Avenger!

8. *Jerusalem* 46

not to reason on "both sides," not to make divine power into a material force, and vice-versa, thereby destroying the human spirit, whose immortal beauty great art objectifies. Have faith in spirit, for "the Plow of Jehovah and the Harrow of Shaddai" will pass "over the Dead," awakening them to divine judgment. At the bottom of the plate is Blake's vision of this event, revivifying the imagination and giving credence to Oxford's words: in a dark world passing over the dead are grieving Jehovah and mournful Jerusalem seated in a cart, its tongues formed of three serpents, representing the specious reasonings of the demonic trinity; the cart is drawn by creatural animals mounted by eagles, symbolizing spirit of prophecy; the reins are held by Jehovah, governing even the rage and folly of Albion's sons to the fulfillment of His wise aesthetic purposes.[51] Oxford's expostulation avails not. Implacable, Albion refuses counsel and comfort. Los steps up his work at the furnaces; Albion's warring sons bellow loudly; Los rebellows their thunder.

The war against spirit intensifies and spreads, spawning natural religion and vitiating divine inspiration [plate 47]. "Luvah tore forth from Albion's Loins in fibrous veins, in rivers/ Of blood over Europe:.../ Animating the Dragon Temples." Presumably, the illustration showing Albion in violent motion and Vala trampling on Jerusalem refers to this catastrophe. The contorted bodies attest the ferocity of the attacks. Loud the cries of war as the living contend with spectres of the dead. The poet hears the "mingling cries of Luvah with the Sons of Albion" and comments on the irony of this tragic war: Albion in vengeance fights victims whom he himself has already "murdered" by denying their springs of life and spiritual perceptions. These selfsame reasons explain why the more Albion triumphs in war the closer he moves to eternal death; they account also for his last words, "Hope is banish'd from me."

Albion has been crucified by his sons, but his death is "for a period" only even though he rejects spirit since it is indestructible [plate 48]. The merciful Saviour builds "a Couch of repose," which is none other than Blake's fourfold poem, "Spiritual Verse, order'd &

---

[51] Erdman believes that the driver is Albion and the design reflects the prophetic artist's desperation "to construct a vehicle of life," *Illuminated Blake,* p.320. Paley believes the passengers are Vala and Albion making "their way as Pluto and Persephone into the lower world," *The Continuing City,* p.110.

measur'd" and ornamented "with emblems" displaying momentous events prophesied in the Old and New Testament and manifested in Albion's history. As Albion expires, his spirit necessarily but temporarily separates from him. Blake describes the separation and subsequent reunion mythologically in terms of his world view: space and time are particularized creations of spirit. It is not the aged virgin form of mother earth, nor the force in particles that saves Albion. His salvation comes from the spiritual acts of his grievously stricken friends. Their "Emanations" concenter in "an Aged pensive Woman" of imagination to attend "the pale limbs of his Eternal Individuality." She takes a "Moment of Time," drawing it out to cover eight-thousand-five-hundred years filled with human history, from the Book of Genesis to *Jerusalem,* from Adam's to Albion's fall; she then takes an "Atom of Space," opening it into Beulah, signifying the union of art and imagination. Blake always refers to space and time in terms of events, never in the abstract. For him, as for Berkeley, time is a relation between particulars in space; absolute space and time are phantoms. The creative "labours/ Of sublime mercy in Rephaim's Vale,"[52] prepare for defeat of Albion's giant sons, his redemption, his reunion with Jerusalem, who is safely hidden "among the Spaces of Erin."

At this crucial moment Erin addresses the Daughters of Beulah. Concordant with Berkeley's causal principle stating that "the animal, vegetable, and mineral kingdoms" as well as all the assemblage in heaven are actuated and held together by spirit, not by "vortexes," Erin bewails the fatal consequences upon Albion resulting from his sons' materialist philosophy.[53] The speech of one-hundred-five lines [48:54-50:17], sustained by the informing aesthetic theme, begins with an allusion to the vortical theory. Because it has been extended to include existence of humans and their acts, Albion's land has become "the Vortex of the Dead," which interestingly behaves much as an *event horizon:* like particles in vortical motion, men are pulled by gravity, whirled around, swallowed up, and lost in the boundless extent of space. Hand's law of motion "freezes sore" upon Albion's sons and daughters, solidifying them into passive bodies. Those who

---

[52] The Valley of Giants, where David encountered and defeated the Philistines.

[53] Berkeley, *Siris.*162,260. For Newton's hypothesis on vortices, see *Principia,* p.389 ff.

dare exercise their creative energy are regarded unforgivable enemies and murdered. Erin bids the daughters mourn for their neighbor upon the lakes of Ireland, where contraries are equally true, where spirit and body, divine inspiration and art, exist in harmonious relation as cause and effect. Since Albion's sons have thrown out the source of creativity, his valleys, mountains, and "the Bodies in which all Animals & Vegetations, the Earth & Heaven/ Were contain'd in the All Glorious Imagination, are wither'd & darken'd."

Throughout, Erin supports the views and sentiments expressed by Los earlier. Because Albion's sons attribute existence to unperceivable material substances, they turn the earth into an "Opake Globe," reduce visible creations of an eternal spirit to abstract ideas and embroil continents in furious war. Referring to the doctrine of matter and abstract reasoning, Erin cries out: "O Polypus of Death! O Spectre over Europe and Asia,/ Withering the Human Form." In their extravagant conceit of rational powers, Albion's sons strive to drive out a substantial god, create a pure and chaste world of absolutes, and destroy the sensory particulars perceived by human spirits, figuratively "to murder the Divine Humanity." Lacking comprehensiveness of mind and restricting themselves to appearances, these sons shut out "True Harmonies" of spirit and bodies. Taking the senses one by one, Erin describes the Lockean limitations that Los concretely displayed by deforming Reuben's senses and directing them downward into earth's interior. The satanic doctrine of Coban, Hand and Hyle has rooted all existence in a self-sufficient nature and reduced man to a contemptible form that creeps "in reptile flesh upon the bosom of the ground!" Albion must be delivered from his deathly state and deadly war. With an abundance of biblical images and in language suited to deliverance, Erin sounds the call of redemption: "far remove these terrible surfaces" of abstractions and make room for Jerusalem that Albion may live in love and peace. Entangled in the inextricable nets of false reasonings and in great perplexity of mind, not knowing the true cause of existence, yet thinking they do good, abstract reasoners have captured the universe of the intellect and spin it in concentric circles. "They are beginning to form Heavens & Hells in immense/ Circles, the Hells for food to the Heavens, food of torment,/ Food of despair." Blake does not believe in a conventional heaven and hell separate from existence on earth; nor can he accept the linkage of godhead to punishment. Heaven, earth and hell are all together; freedom of spirit is heaven, is life; possession by corporeal forces is hell, is death.

"Iniquity must be imputed only" to states, not to individuals. The concept of states relating to the Christian doctrine of salvation uttered earlier by the Divine Voice [plate 35] is applied here to Albion's sons. Erin instructs the daughters "to distinguish the Eternal Human/ That walks about among the stones of fire in bliss & woe/ Alternate from those States or Worlds in which the Spirit travels"; distinguish between man as a spiritual being and the temporal states through which he passes in the world. Why? Because spirit is "the only means to Forgiveness of Enemies" and to eternity. Coban, Hand and Hyle do not distinguish between human forms and natural phenomena since they exclude spirit and regard man as a material body. In Albion's fallen state "Luvah is named Satan" because he has entered the world of Coban, Hand and Hyle, who oppose spirit with material powers. Albion has deified these, allegorized nature, and reverted to druidism, which thrives on death; he "is now possess'd by the War of Blood!" Had Albion not cast out Jerusalem, he would not have died. As this philosophic discourse comes to a close, "Erin's lovely Bow" promising life encloses the deadly "Wheels of Albion's Sons," who appear in the distance, issuing from the great body of their much perplexed triune God, ascending among the stars, then descending into Albion's sea of death. The entire process is graphically portrayed at plate 50.

The text of Chapter 2, as of Chapter 1, ends with a chorus of Beulah's daughters praying for quick delivery from the satanic world and its attendant evils. Plate 51 depicts that dark world: in the center of a subterranean pit sits its creator Hyle with his faculties directed downward; Vala is its ruling power; and man, who is chained to it, is its prisoner.

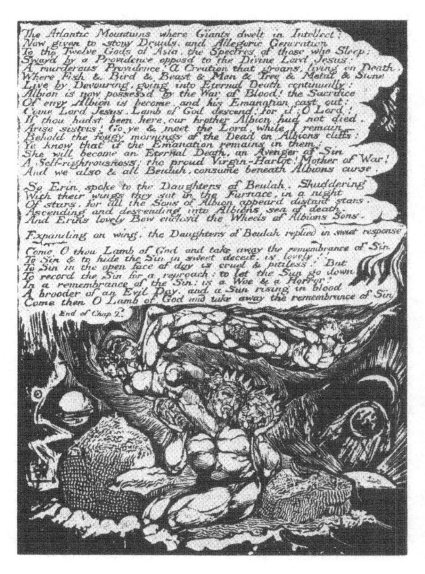

9. *Jerusalem* 50

Encounters With The Enemy

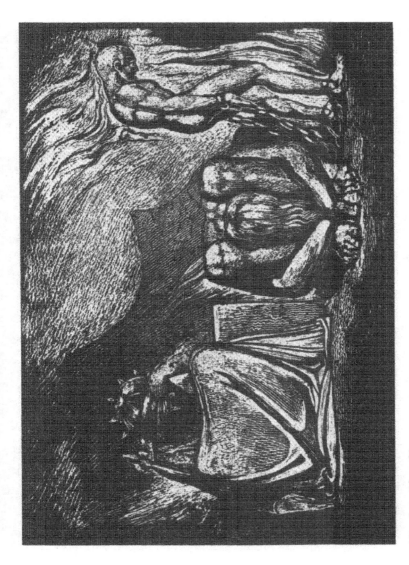

10. *Jerusalem* 51

PART SEVEN

GRIM WAR CONTINUES

Taking his cue from the Third Gospel addressed to the Greeks, who defined man as a rational animal, Blake directs Chapter 3 to the Deists, with a parenthetical reminder of the difference between man's essential property and his spatio-temporal states. The Deists' self-righteousness and vindictiveness are called *Rahab,* Egypt's poetical name signifying pride and insolence. This state Blake contrasts with self-sacrifice and forgiveness assiduously preached in Luke's gospel, from which this chapter takes its dominant tone.

Because Deists, following Locke, base their religion on material powers, which they call *God,* they are enemies of Christianity; and because they teach the Lockean doctrine of reason as man's natural faculty, they are enemies of the human race. Deism is begot on pride of physical science, which interprets the operations of the universe as just so many mechanical motions of bodies. Upon this supposition Deism grounds its morality. But Blake contends man is not naturally born forever faultless; virtue depends on continuous spiritual acts. Deists pretend to be virtuous by speaking about the human heart and feelings, but they idealize the corporeal man.

First on Blake's list of philosophic Deists is Voltaire, who gave literary shape to Locke's materialist doctrine. He regarded men as completely corporeal and spiritual religion as hypocrisy. For him, feelings and acts of men are only special cases of objects actuated by particles; therefore mechanism is the basis of both religious feelings and moral acts. Next in order of pretenders, according to Blake, is Rousseau, who constantly talked about virtues of the human heart, yet held that men come forth from nature good and pure, that the preponderant human passion is an innocent *amour de soi.* Gibbon is another enemy of spirit because he interpreted the Middle Ages as a retrogressive movement in human history and charged the monks with war. Though Hume criticized moral systems based on science, he argued that morality arises from artificial virtues which appeal to some abstract notion of sympathy. The ballad that follows Blake's reproof tells the sad story of revealed religion attacked by its enemies, from Titus to Rousseau, reverses Gibbon, and charges Deists with the present divisions and religious contentions carried into art.

Heading plate 53 is Blake's rendition of a deistic goddess, taking his point of departure from Berkeley's critique of naturalism: "The Egyptians, who impersonated nature, had made her a distinct principle and even deified her under the name of Isis"; they symbolically represented this "supreme Divinity sitting on a lotus," a gesture "to signify the most holy and venerable Being" (*Siris*.268-269). With minute fidelity to particulars, Blake artfully represents Vala as such a divinity, modifying the common iconographic formula to reflect specific doctrines of natural philosophy. In contrast to Jerusalem and Vala embracing in the lily of Havilah at the beginning of Chapter 2, here Vala lone reposes on a huge Egyptian water lily,[1] representing the vegetative universe. The equally huge shell within which she sits symbolizes her natural genesis together with her hard impenetrable surfaces. Her three-tiered crown of the demonic trinity with its incised sun, moon, and stars signifies commingling natural philosophy and religion. Thus regally sits the prime deity of the universe and tutelary goddess of art: nature is the totality.

Immediately below this illustration, after telling us Los is a vehicle, a spirit incarnate serving to combat the strong spectre, Blake returns us to the poet's narration of another episode in the grim war, for the war against spirit is not one simple battle. Naturalists' metaphysics infiltrated art to its core: "the roots of Albion's Tree enter'd the Soul of Los," painfully dividing him from his inspirations and attacking his creations "time after time." But unlike Albion's sons, Los does not take vengeance; instead, he weeps and mourns for Albion; clothed in sackcloth of hair he sits labouring at his seven furnaces, building Golgonooza "Spiritual Fourfold" to avert the disaster looming over the nation. His glowing furnaces are incomprehensible

---

[1] Erdman takes this to be a sunflower rising out of water.

11. *Jerusalem* 53

to the vegetated eyes of Albion's sons, who in their "perverted & single vision" do not look beyond physical objects to perceive the cause of creativity.[2] Depriving an artist of his creative powers is tantamount to consigning him to death. Blake conveys the vitality of imagination in art through visceral imagery: "The Bellows are the Animal Lungs, the Hammers the Animal Heart,/ The Furnaces the Stomach for Digestion." Works of art are products of inspiration, love, and process, all dependent on inner powers.

Once again Blake interrupts the action to restate allegorically, and categorically, his fundamental principle translated into art [plate 54]. "In Great Eternity every particular Form gives forth or Emanates/ Its own peculiar Light, & the Form is the Divine Vision." Art is by no means a mimetic reproduction of nature or of other works according to fixed rules. Every work is a unique expression of an artist's vision, an effect of spiritual perception. This source cut off by Albion's sons "is Jerusalem in every Man" and "is called Liberty among the Children of Albion" because spirit is free. Blake's concept of liberty, therefore, goes beyond practical freedom from bondage of thought and action; it has a metaphysical meaning in Berkeley's sense of a causal principle. Berkeley insisted upon innate human liberty because it concerns moral accountability: unless man be a free agent, he is not answerable for his acts. He thus reiterated and inculcated his tenet that man is a spiritual being possessing an inner power to determine his own conduct. As an empiricist, Berkeley is ever alert to confirm his theoretical statements by experience; the notion of liberty is no less philosophical than pious: "We are conscious that a spirit can begin, alter, or determine motion; but nothing of that appears in body" (*Siris*.291).

Nevertheless, the principles of corporeal philosophy endured in Reynolds' system, shackling the artist. From this circumstance Blake extracts another concrete example of sexual organization, creates another incident in the aesthetic conflict, and another subtlety of biblical association. Through inordinate pride, Albion has fallen from spirit into matter, hurled by "his own Spectre." Deep in a chaos midst three abstract philosophies, Albion "tosses like a cloud," under a mass of bat-winged Spectres—a situation Blake pictures at the bottom

---

[2] In a letter of 22 November 1802 to Butts, Blake refers to Newton's "Single vision," p.818.

of the plate. In a society ruled completely by laws abstracted from nature, men do not communicate with each other directly as spiritual and hence as humane beings; Locke has interposed "Memory between Man & Man." Seeing his people trapped in abstractions, "from which springs Sexual Love as iron chains" because abstract reasoning places the source of inspirations as well as emotions in physical forces, Albion attempts again to uplift himself. But the omnipotent and ubiquitous Spectre ever reminds him: "I am God, O Sons of Men! I am your Rational Power!/ Am I not Bacon & Newton & Locke," who teach reason is the key to all the arts, nature the root of all ideas, and abstraction the true method of all knowledge? Blake names the Spectre *Arthur,* a mighty monarch, a *dux bellorum.* Against this conquering power and compacted philosophical authority Albion tries to protect his land. He "drew England into his bosom," but controlled by his giant sons she stretched out like a "long Serpent in the Abyss of the Spectre," the infernal regions of Coban, Hand and Hyle. They continue to plow the earth in their conceits; they mock "an unknown Eternal Life" and accuse those who believe in spiritual powers of building a "World of Phantasy."

This accusation was brought against Berkeley's theory of ideas time and again. His adversaries charged him with sweeping away the physical world. In reply, Berkeley retorted that his world of sensory qualities actually perceived is far more real than their world of unperceived material substances. He pointed out that according to his theory evidence of the senses is as trusty as ever; in fact, belief in them is much stronger than is admitted by Lockeans, who hold ideas of sense to be mere images of objects. It is the materialists themselves, therefore, who fabricate a fanciful world; they have relinquished perceived particulars for the sake of dreams and vain fictions. Repeatedly, Berkeley had to clarify his position: objects perceived by the mind are real—real stones, and if kicked they occasion real pain, which not even Dr. Johnson will pretend can exist without a perceiving mind: "there are bodies"; but they are passive.[3] Materialists captivate followers by teaching that the cause of existence is a mysterious power in bodies.

---

[3] Berkeley, *Principles.* 82. Cf. Blake's statement, "I question not my Corporeal or Vegetative Eye any more than I would Question a Window concerning a Sight. I look thro' it & not with it": [A Vision of the Last Judgment], p.617.

Blake too had to contend with captious and unyielding critics; he too would not be slave to another's system. At plate 55 he is especially bold in his allegories and indulgent in his allusions to Reynolds, who dispelled the "phantom of inspiration" by instituting rules of procedure:

> ...that Veil which Satan puts between Eve & Adam,
> By which the Princes of the Dead enslave their Votaries
> Teaching them to form the Serpent of precious stones & gold
> To sieze the Sons of Jerusalem & plant them in One Man's Loins,
> To make One Family of Contraries, that Joseph may be sold
> Into Egypt for Negation, a Veil the Saviour born & dying rends.

Reynolds' rules negate spiritual perception, worship nature's powers, hide in abstraction the visible particulars of naked forms, cut off the artist from the Divine Vision, and force his creative powers into imitation of geometrical philosophers or master painters, thereby denying Albion access to eternity.

Alarmed at this progressively dismal end, the immortals meet in conclave and with one accord decide to enter the war on Albion's behalf.[4] Their thunderous voices are heard throughout the Newtonian universe; and every part of it, from the remotest star to the deepest sea, responds. This is a cosmic war. Confronting the warriors of Ulro, who restrain their horses (sources of power) with iron bits (rules of reason), in battle cars the soldiers of eternity, "Curbing their Tygers" (emblematic of superior strength) with "golden bits" (spiritual powers), speak, and "their Words stood" arrayed like men in chariots: "Let the Human Organs be kept in their perfect Integrity," complete. If men do not trust the sensory particulars perceived by the human mind, they can at will devise whatever reality they choose, either taking nature as the all in all and themselves "Contracting into Worms," or making human reason the standard of everything and "Expanding into Gods." Such ludicrous extremes result from "Ulro Visions of Chastity": oddly, chastity has its origin in natural science. Whether we contract space-time into natural phenomena or expand it into infinity, one unalterable fact remains: as humans we belong to "One Family" united by virtue of spirit.

---

[4] Unlike the Greek pagan gods in *The Iliad*, the immortals do not oppose one another; there is no conflict among them; the rebellion instigated by men is against god.

How prevent the errors and consequent judgment issuing from Ulro? "Labour well the Minute Particulars." Its laborers, presented allegorically as Christ's plowmen, are led by the Living Creatures, who defy "the Reasoner to Demonstrate with unhewn Demonstrations," that is, prove the existence of his general ideas without his cutting tools of abstractionism: "Let the Indefinite be explored, and let every Man be Judged/ By his own Works," not by those of others or by some general standard. Art no less than science can exist only "in minutely organized Particulars"; and judgments about art cannot be made without considering the specific circumstances and purpose of the artist. Blake subsumes evaluations of art under the doctrine of particulars to preserve the integrity of individual creations as Berkeley had done with moral acts.

Berkeley criticized Locke's proposal to "place *morality* amongst the *sciences capable of demonstration*" by "setting down" some qualities and defining what "every term shall stand for."[5] He saw that rules of reasoning are tautologous, and morality founded on arbitrary definitions and generalization is only a demonstrable science of words, not of particular actions. It is impossible, according to him, "to frame an abstract idea... of goodness" prescinded "from every thing that is good."[6] The opinion that moral terms "stand for general notions abstracted from all particular persons and actions" perverts morality. This Lockean approach applied to forms, in Blake's view, perverts also art. While sharing Berkeley's impatience with abstractions and generalities, here as elsewhere Blake exhibits his usual indignation against Reynolds' criterion of excellence, which rates art in proportion to its generality. "General good is the plea of the scoundrel, hypocrite & flatterer"; it does not take into account native talent; an artist can feign genius by appealing to a general rule even though his disposition of circumstantial particulars is faulty. *Good*, like the term *evil*, refers to particular works, not to art in general. Those at the plow, echoing Los's dictum sounded earlier, remind us truth in art depends on "Circumcision, not on Virginity," on trimming off excess surfaces that cover the determinate, not on the unknown. Blake's metaphoric expressions for truth value in art are part of the configuration of concrete sexual imagery linked to

---

[5] Locke, IV.iii.18,20.
[6] Berkeley, *Principles.* 100.

individual creativity and particularized forms against set rules and abstract ideas.

While those at the plow protect bare and naked forms of imagination and cry down abstract entities, Los labours at his furnaces and chants "his song." It poses fundamental questions about existence in its totality, which Blake raised earlier in another context [plate 34]; here [plate 56], in a complex play of ideas he poetically embellishes within Christian myth his metaphysical position concerning man, the world, and art. When Los rhetorically asks the daughters of Albion whether man is generated, cared for, nourished, and wholly governed by mother nature, the answer is *no*. Man is neither a product nor a captive of nature, personified as a "woman" such as the great goddess Isis or Ishtar. Nor is the world itself a product of random natural forces. Rather, this world is a providential creation of an eternally active spirit, "a Cradle for the erred wandering Phantom," who seeks to extract forms from nature. Lest the Divine Vision and Albion be lost irretrievably in "Non-Entity's dark wild" of abstraction, Los pleads with the daughters of Albion to turn their iron reels towards the "golden Loom of Love," joining the inspired artist and poet's muses in preparations for redemption, when the enslaving system shall be mowed down as grass. At that divinely appointed time the liberating system created by Los shall be revealed: in apocalyptic language, "The Sun shall be a Scythed Chariot of Britain: the Moon, a Ship/ In the British Ocean, Created by Los's Hammer, measured out/ Into Days & Nights & Years & Months." The daughters jeer at Los's prophecy and mockingly reply that spirit is lost forever: "it came/ And wept at our wintry Door." The daughters who turned away spirit, represented here by the infant Jesus, are the emanations of Coban, Hand and Hyle, namely Ignoge, Cambel and Gwendolen. Their taunting reply to Los's questions about the artist and his powers, therefore, conforms to Locke's natural man: "look! behold! Gwendolen/ Is become a Clod of Clay! Merlin is a Worm." Together the three daughters comprise the "Female Will," universally embodied in Vala; they hide the "Divine Vision with Curtain & Veil & fleshy Tabernacle": like *veil, curtain* or more precisely "curtain of words" is Berkeley's metaphor for abstract ideas, and *fleshy* his term for materialism;[7] Blake again engages these

---

[7] See Pt. Five: n.3, p.90, and n.22.

metaphors aesthetically, showing how natural philosophy has become a religion controlling art. In parody of events surrounding Christ's crucifixion, the emanations of the demonic trinity are the "Three Women" at the cross, the guardians of naturalism.

At the next plate [57] we see against the vault of heaven two of the women, presumably Cambel and at her right Ignoge, with vegetative fibers streaming from their fingers, positioned atop the revolving earth; they are in evident possession not only of science but also of religion and art, symbolized by the cathedral, as well as of man, represented below by Gwendolen's embedment in earth. Natural forces have taken over the world completely because spirit has been separated from the human body. Therefore one hears "Bath & Canterbury & York & Edinburgh" question this separation: "What is a Wife & what is a Harlot?" Are not both spiritual beings? And are not church, theater, religion and politics expressions of the imagination reflecting human existence itself? Despite these outcries resounding throughout the nation, Albion continues to flee from the Divine Vision. The illustration on plate 58 shows him "Plowed in among the Dead" while the three-headed Spectre of natural philosophy rises above,[8] dividing, abstracting, demonstrating and judging, thus prolonging Albion's war and its cruelties.

A vivid verbal description of these cruelties extends over several plates beginning with 58, an exceedingly complex plate that brings together the cutting away of spiritual perception in science, philosophy, religion and art cast into acts of war. While Albion's sons advance their divisions of "Rational Philosophy" supported by their artillery of "Mathematic Demonstration" on the battlefield, pushing their machinery into every domain, his daughters, dancing to the timbre of war, perform their duty at the altars. Natural philosophy had become a bizarre religion: "Naked & drunk with blood" as if at a vintage festival of a heathen cult, these daughters at will divide from Jerusalem's sons and in cruelty unite with Albion's sons, who regard mind as nothing more than particles subject to relentless bombardment by external forces. "The Inhabitants of Albion at the Harvest & the Vintage/ Feel their Brain cut round beneath the temples, shrieking,/ Bonifying into a Scull, the Marrow exuding in dismal pain."

---

[8] This interpretation correlated with the poem's stated theme differs from that suggested in Erdman's *Illuminated Blake*, p.337.

IMAGINATION UNBOUND

12. *Jerusalem* 57

Thus Albion's people are converted to the "Hermaphroditic Condensations" of his sons.

On the intricacies of this metaphorical characterization, a philosophic light is thrown by *Siris.* 299. There in reflective judgment of natural religion, Berkeley refers to certain pagan sects who mixed religion with superstition; they did not distinguish "the female from the male," the creating power from the created phenomena, "their Isis or τὸ πᾶν comprehending both Osiris the author of nature and his work." He sees a curious analogy between these unenlightened sects and Deism because it subscribes to a doctrine that makes nature its own cause, unwisely mixing science and religion, confounding both. In the *Principles.* 93-95 he is direct, severe, and explicit in his criticism of those "impious" persons, who have fallen in with a system that favours their inclinations. They deride "immaterial substance"; taking man to be an epiphenomenon of nature, they suppose "the soul to be divisible and subject to corruption as the body"; they "exclude all freedom, intelligence, and design from the formation of things, and instead thereof make a self-existent, stupid, unthinking substance" the cause of all beings. Their *"idolatry"* derives from the principle that bodies exist unperceived, upon which they construct a cosmology. The fantastic "mingling" of demonstrative science and articles of "faith" in Christianity, thereby impairing revelation, incensed Berkeley: "Did men but consider that the sun, moon, and stars ...are only so many sensations in their mind, ...they would never fall down, and worship their own *ideas.*"

Blake makes a like criticism of zealous naturalism in art, projecting yet another image of Reynolds' system dedicated to nature. Vala is the all inclusive Isis in modern garb. Out of a hermaphroditic substance, naturalists erect a mighty temple to Vala, combining in her the dual functions of conception and generation. The temple's architect is Urizen, who gives the substance an abstract form according to rules of reason; through its porticos pass the revolving sun and moon, shining forth nature's great powers. As with Golgonooza, Blake allegorically describes the building in detail. Its architectural parts are given names of ancient and modern countries whose culture exemplifies naturalists' values: for example, "Canaan" is Urizen's "portico," but it is not a pleasant ambulatory because "Rational Philosophy and Mathematic Demonstration" war even against each other. To bring down Urizen's grand edifice, Los, whose forge is "Britain," fixes on his anvil "stones & timbers" from the temple's entranceway and superstructure, striking these materials with strong blows "To Create a World of Generation from the World of Death,/ Dividing the Masculine & Feminine," the creations from the creative principle, "for the comingling/ Of Albion's & Luvah's Spectres was Hermaphroditic," leading to death: human generation is hermaphroditically impossible. Hence, underneath the temple springs the fountain of Jordan, symbolizing human creativity and prefiguring redemption. A fierce battle ensues: Los, as with a spear or an arrow, fixes "Hand & Koban" over the sun, then "Hyle & Skofield" over the moon; "terrified the Spectres rage & flee." But inflamed with their reasoning power, they return and defiantly rear "their dark Rocks among the Stars of God, stupendous/ Works! A World of Generation continually Creating out of/ The Hermaphroditic Satanic World," in their abstractions laying a whole nation in blood for their own glory.

In this unequal combat, Los undaunted fights valiantly to save Albion and his people [plate 59]. Unlike Peter, who cast the spiritual net to catch living souls, Albion had cast the "Veil of Vala" to snatch "Souls of the Dead." Out of the abstractionists' veil, which stretched from Albion's tree, vegetated, and petrified around the earth, Los forms "the Gates & mighty Wall" of imagination between "the Oak" and "the Palm," between the rocky destiny of naturalism and the eternal life of spirit, progressively creating "in process of time" the means to save Albion by liberating the artist from the "Mundane Egg," the hard-shelled universe of natural philosophy, and opening the gates to immortality. Meantime, Albion lies in his tomb; the four spheres of existence in his land remain chaotic, for when he "was slain upon his Mountains" and Jerusalem exiled, the distinct and orderly parts of the land, delineated by Generation (nature) in the north, Beulah (harmony of spirit and body) in the south, Eden (paradisic creations) in the east, and Humanity (man) in the west, all fell into ruin. Natural philosophy had relegated Urthona (man) to the north, installed Urizen (human reason) in the south, excluded Luvah (eternal spirit) altogether, and placed Tharmas (body) in the west. Consequently, north is a "solid Darkness" of impenetrable particles in an "unfathomable" space; south is "a burning Fire" of fierce war; east is "a Void" of abstract ideas because Urizen has displaced Luvah; and west is "a World of raging Waters," of torment and cruelty, for

Albion's sons have confounded religion with science and now confound art with both.

Midst this confusion is the "sublime Universe of Los & Enitharmon." Lines 59:21-55 clearly focus on art; again Blake ingeniously weaves into the main action attacks upon his art, his defense of it, and his resistance to Reynolds' theories. In the western part of the north, where the artist is enslaved to nature, Los forms a gate to Beulah, to inspiration; then he sets up "Cathedron's Looms" facing his furnaces in the south. Cathedron, a "wondrous golden Building immense with ornaments sublime" is another appelation for *Jerusalem:* in proportion and architectural features like a cathedral, a work of art divinely inspired. Concomitant with Los's furnaces creating visible forms are Enitharmon's looms weaving a beautiful panorama to reunite the artist and his imagination. Spinning and weaving dominate the action in the next several plates as Blake draws out the Temple's veil, which he has connected to Reynolds' system. Los's daughters assist in bringing life, peace, and immortality to Albion; hour upon hour, one daughter sits at the reel; another turns the wheel (visible above the text); and some ply the distaff while others attend the shining loom to expose the perverted twisting and muddled weaving of Albion's daughters. Though Los's daughters are mocked and their work maligned, in sorrow and without pity they labour incessantly. So that the artist may "live, & breathe & love" and divinely inspired art survive, these daughters carry on their work "in the Interior Worlds," weaving the "veil of Goats-hair" and "fine twined Linen" of the system that now hides the Divine Vision from the eyes of men.

Plate 60 recounts the proliferation of naturalism. "The clouds of Albion's Druid Temples rage in the eastern heaven" amid Urizen's "Starry Wheels," obscuring the Divine Vision and spreading murderous war over two continents. Terrified, Los sees Luvah become Albion's Urizenic Spectre as his sons separate the artist from his imagination, assimilating art into the system of abstract philosophy; he sees darkness over the earth; but still he sees within his living furnaces the Son of Man walking among Albion's druidic temples and protecting Jerusalem's children. Los also hears an exquisite, sad song of the Lamb sung by Albion's captives. Their complaint styled on the Psalms, with abundant allusions to biblical events intertwined with references to other ancient histories and connected by a fine thread to art, descants on Jerusalem.[9] God gave her "liberty and life"; but by misplaced commiseration on Albion's account, she has "bound" perception "down upon the Stems of Vegetation" growing round Albion's tree. God gave her Troy, the Greek Isles, and the "Counties of Albion"; he gave her also "Hand & Scofield," who originally "stood in innocence." In other words, every nation, every phenomenon, and every human being is a unique creation of spirit, whose immortal beauty is objectified in works of art. Why then does Jerusalem deface her beauty to serve "Idols in the pretended chastities of Uncircumcision?" Because Albion's sons have by false arguments driven Jerusalem to self-effacing acts, "their end shall come." Meanwhile, disparaged Jerusalem sits distracted at the "Mill"; daily "her reason grows like/ The Wheel of Hand" as spiritual powers are turned into mechanical motions and perceived particulars pressed into abstract ideas. "Satanic Holiness" has "triumph'd in Vala"; abstract reasoning and materialism have become a religion enclosing thought, desire, and creativity: "the Head & Heart & Loins." These recurrent anatomical metaphors embody three areas of human activity central to the subject of Blake's epic.

Because a vital, creative eternal spirit underlies Blake's system of art, the existence and nature of God are related issues. Jerusalem, "clos'd" in modern "Dungeons of Babylon," asks the Lord: "have the Gods of the Heathen pierced thee,/ Or hast thou been pierced in the House of thy Friends?/ Art thou alive, & livest thou for evermore? or art thou/ Not but a delusive shadow, a thought that liveth not?" Criticism of Reynolds is distinctly visible: is divine inspiration a phantom? "Babel mocks, saying there is no God nor Son of God,/ That thou, O Human Imagination, O Divine Body, art all/ A delusion."

The innuendos of Jerusalem's questions may be fully appreciated by referring to *Siris.* 321-323, where Berkeley confronts the issue of abstraction in religion. There he unequivocally states his position: God "truly acts or creates"; he is "not an abstract idea compounded of inconsistencies, and prescinded from all real things, as some moderns understand abstraction; but a really existing Spirit, distinct

---

[9] Cf. the plight of the woman in Rev.12:6 and the song in Rev.14:3 and 15:3.

or separate from all sensible and corporeal beings."[10] It is not the pagans but some Christians who have reduced God to an abstract idea. Philosophers such as Locke and clergy such as Clarke[11] have demolished the whole fabric of revealed religion and inflated abstraction to immense proportions. Not unlike some mathematicians deluded by the specious show of abstracted verities and some physicists seeking simplicity in nature, Deists, seeking purity, cry up a religion founded on abstraction. Blake is making similar points about Reynolds: it is not a non-Christian, nor a layman, who has reduced art to abstraction. But as the actual world of experience cannot be settled by a set of mathematical equations, nor God determined by an aggregate of abstractions, the creative imagination cannot be bound to rules of reason, nor the complexity of reality reduced to general forms.

Jerusalem penitently confesses she is "deluded by the turning mills" because she pities Albion. The Lord does not abandon her; he comforts her; though she has sinned against God's holy name, he forgives her. As Savior, he will demonstrate love and pity and raise Albion from death. To confirm this promise, the Lord presents Jerusalem with a vision dramatically relating the story of Joseph and Mary [plate 61].[12] It exemplifies universal pity and love embodied in forgiveness of sin and in sacrifice, designated by the creatural symbol of Chapter 3; it increases pathos; it accentuates the uniqueness of every work of art; and it functions dynamically in the plot. By drawing a parallel between Mary's and Jerusalem's experience, Blake advances the action towards the fulfillment of the epic's purpose. He places the two women side by side: like himself, both are outcasts of

---

[10] Because Deism lays emphasis on reason, it may more properly be called rational religion; but neither Berkeley nor Blake seems to distinguish it from natural religion. *Alciphron* is Berkeley's extended criticism of Deism, which he calls "free thinking" after Anthony Collins' *Discourse on Free Thinking* (1713).

[11] Locke argues we arrive at the concept of god by reflecting upon ourselves, abstracting certain attributes, and enlarging "these with our idea of infinity," II.xxiii.33. The continuous method of argument is mathematical in Samuel Clarke's *A Demonstration of the Being and Attributes of God* (1705). Others Berkeley has in mind are Wollston and Tindall. Jessop's "Introduction" to Vol.III, *Alciphron*, pp.4-7, outlines the deistic movement.

[12] Incidents in the vision recall those of *Paradise Lost*, Bk.XI, but the implied parallel to Adam and Eve is not exact; Blake never forgets he is dealing with a problem of his time.

their society because it does not recognize the Holy Spirit's power. Those who insist upon compliance with rigid Judiac general laws call Mary an adultress; and those who demand conformity to iron rules and abstract forms in art regard Jerusalem an adultress. If Joseph rejects Mary, he murders her; similarly, if critics reject spiritual perception, they murder both artist and nation. Judgments should not be passed without considering the attendant circumstances in particular cases. Mary's sentiments express this truth; if she were pure, she could never experience the power of spirit and beauty of human love. Morality is based on love in "the Continual Forgiveness of Sins" and "Perpetual Mutual Sacrifice," not on "Virtues of the/ Heathen," who devise laws by abstract reasoning and enforce them by harsh punishment in complete disregard of divine purposes. Joseph forgives and sacrifices by taking Mary for his wife; she in turn forgives and sacrifices in becoming the mother of God; Los forgives and sacrifices for Albion's sake.

This episode is another example of the language of vision as direct communication between the eternal spirit and finite spirits. What has Jerusalem learned from the vision? She is not Babylon drunk with "Sacrifice of Idols," not intoxicated with worship of natural powers; she is not a lost adultress; she is called that by naturalists because she pities Albion. But she is not mother nature; rather, she is the mother of Albion's spiritual children. Though she has been distracted by the turning mills of abstraction, she is sympathetically received by a merciful God. He is her protector as he was Mary's. Blake perfects the analogy between the two figures: "Mary leaned her side against Jerusalem: Jerusalem received/ The Infant into her hands." Like Mary, who was the Lord's instrument in the salvation of man, Jerusalem's restoration is the means to Albion's regeneration. While Albion lies in limbo's den, Jerusalem suffers; Los labors on; time passes.

At plate 62 Blake fills out the action by describing Jerusalem's anguish and displays the cause. There we see a tortured Albion in darkness, victim of his giant sons, their full-blown pride of selfhood symbolized by a peacock-plumed crown and their satanic holy reasonings represented by a coiled serpent formed into a halo. These sons have titanic pride in their reasoning power and arrogance of judgment; they lack belief in the efficacy of spirit and in humanity; the depth of Albion's fall matches the height of their pride. Jerusalem bewails the cruelty she and Albion endure at their hands. She is "an outcast," ignored in philosophy, spurned in religion, and trampled in art. That's why "Albion is dead." Naturalists have replaced her with Vala, planted the seed of life in the "Body of death," denying immortality by denying the artist his inspirations. Troubled Jerusalem asks, "Shall Albion arise?" She has faith, "but Emanations/ Are Weak" in his land of dead souls. In extreme economy of speech to suit the occasion, Jesus replies: "I am the Resurrection & the Life"; resurrection passes the limits of possibility according to sensory appearances; it transcends natural law of bodies; as body he dies, but as spirit he arises. Hence for Albion to rise again, Luvah and Vala must be infused with spirit; they "must be Created" in a divinely inspired work.

Even while the Lamb of God promises renewed life and peace, the war rages as Albion's sons extend their conquest over nature and order human life on their principles. Love diverted from its human channels is turned into hate; vegetated, Luvah's passions of hate explode throughout Albion's land; cruelty and punishment prevail at Albion's courts of art. The war is long and painful. Like Jerusalem, Los is often discouraged; but like her, he is heartened by the divine presence. Yet again like her, he suffers when his creativity is denied. Though Albion's Spectres have obscured the visions of God, like Jerusalem "Los beheld the Divine Vision"; therefore in hope he returns to his anvil, but also in terror because Albion's Spectres like wild beasts are ready to spring upon him at every blow of his hammer and tear apart him and his works.

The war is boundless [plate 63]. Strife in religion and in art is great since Albion brought Luvah to justice, denying resurrection. Vala's forces contend with those of Jehovah. As naturalism gains ascendancy, superstitions of the past return: the giants, witches, and ghosts of former ages join the "dance of death" in the valley of life and humanity. Divisions, accusations, vengeance, and murder multiply as friends, families, and tribes battle among each other. The Living Creatures no longer govern Albion's land; his "Druid Sons" are in control. Because these sons assume bodies exist independent of human perception, Albion's land has become "Rock & Sand Unhumanized" and "the Heavens a Void around, unfathomable;/ No Human Form but Sexual" is cast by Vala's clouds and reflected from Albion's cliffs, forcing the Cherubim to hide their heads and

13. *Jerusalem* 63

succumb to "deep slumbers": generating bodies in motion are the all in all; spiritual perception is shut out.

This disaster results primarily from Locke's opinion, represented by Gwendolen's derisive "laughter" [63:32], that if spirit exists it must be known in the manner of a simple idea; and since it is not experienced as such, it must be dismissed as a cause of existence. But as Berkeley explains, it is "absolutely impossible" there should be any such sensory impression because "*spirit* or that which acts" or perceives ideas "cannot be of itself perceived, but only by the effects which it produceth."[13] Spirit is not something to be seen like color; as metaphysical principle, it does not belong to the world but is the cause of it; nor is it something in man, but the human form itself. He characterizes naturalists as "a sort of sect which diminish all the most valuable things, the thoughts, views, and hopes of men; all the knowledge, notions, and theories of the mind they reduce to sense; human nature they contract and degrade to the narrow low standard of animal life, and assign us only a small pittance of time instead of immortality." He compares a person who has "not much meditated upon God" or "the human mind" to "a thriving earthworm."[14] Paradoxically, through the dexterity of human reasoning, naturalists have made man into a mere procreative creature, and an ignoble one at that, bound to earth.

Blake applies this arresting comparison to naturalists in art, for indeed the earthworm is hermaphroditic. Like the net and chain, the worm is a recurrent image in *Jerusalem*. At mid-plate this aspect of naturalism appears in visual form: the moon symbolizes a female goddess of nature; the triglyphs of a druidic temple project natural religion; and the thriving worm thrice coiled round Vala's body represents man as her product.[15] Below this disquieting visual form we have in Los's reaction another reminder that this lowly state of the artist's creativity is not merely a morbid fancy of a distempered brain, and another allusion to Blake's experience stemming from Reynolds' ridicule of "inspiration from heaven" along with his depreciation of

---

[13] Berkeley, *Principles*.27; *Alciphron,* Dialogue I.10.

[14] Berkeley, *Siris*.350. The comparison recalls Job, who losing faith in immortality, sees himself as merely corruptible body, a worm (17:13-14).

[15] Whether the woman is identified as Vala or Jerusalem, the meaning is the same: spiritual power denied; nature controls.

"native power."[16] At first Los thought "the Murder" of spirit and individuals was an illusion; but when he "saw in Vala's hand the Druid Knife of Revenge & the Poison Cup/ Of Jealousy," he knew these cruelties were not a "Poetic Vision of the Atmospheres"; he knew they were actualities.

Fittingly, plate 64 describes how Albion's daughters manipulate the threads of human existence to enlarge Vala's veil. They "Weave the Web/ Of Ages & Generations," of creation and life, arbitrarily "folding & unfolding it like a Veil of Cherubim" to give their reticulated world of abstractions an appearance of holiness. Sometimes this ensnaring net "touches the Earth's summits & sometimes spreads/ Abroad into the Indefinite Spectre." Under the aegis of reason all becomes "One" with Vala. She is made the all encompassing divinity, male and female, combining the functions of a Zeus, of an Athena, and the muses: she is the shaker of earth, the distributor of justice, the companion of armies (critics) in battle, the inspiring goddess of the arts, the destroyer of individuals. While the ground runs with their blood, Vala cries: "The Human is but a Worm, & thou, O Male! Thou art," as Vala's product, "Thyself Female, a Male, a breeder of Seed, a Son & Husband." In an obvious allusion to Reynolds' view of divine inspiration as a phantom, a view based on Locke's claim that we have no knowledge of spirit, either in memory or fancy, other than an abstract idea compounded wholly out of ourselves,[17] we hear Vala loudly proclaim, "The Human Divine is Woman's Shadow, a Vapor in the summer's heat." She commands her overseer: "Go assume Papal dignity, thou Spectre, thou Male Harlot!" Why male harlot? Because the Spectre by an adulterine method flatters and misleads concerning the source of creativity. Here is another indirect reference to Reynolds' papal-like decree carried out by sycophants who judge bare and naked forms as immoral while they praise the moral purity of abstract forms.

Los questions the validity of Vala's assertions. If man is (in contemporary idiom) a clone of Vala, he too must possess within himself the source of life. Even logically Vala cannot claim creative powers and at the same time deny them to man. In fact Vala owes her life to man, not vice-versa, because physical objects have their

---

[16] Reynolds, Disc. Six, p.87,86.
[17] For Locke's argument see IV.xi.12.

existence only in the mind. This cause-effect relation is irreversible. Isn't "Vala the Wife of Albion," his natural complement rather than harlot and mother of all? Isn't Vala the "Daughter of Luvah," the creation of an eternal spirit rather than the spurious progeny of the Spectre? Blake again challenges Reynolds' doctrines and attributes the present aesthetic difficulties to abstract reasoning. Los confronts Vala with a reproof: Albion's quarrels, violence, and murderous wars "arise from Reasoning." But like a protective parent shielding its daughter from attack, "the Spectre drew Vala into his bosom, magnificent, terrific,/ Glittering with precious stones & gold,.../ ...dazling with Love/ And Jealousy immingled..../ A dark Hermaphrodite they stood," combining diverse elements. In this composite picture resembling a collage, Blake conveys the folly of aligning art with science, fixing its principles as the basis not only of artistic but also of moral integrity. Together the Spectre and Vala control the destiny of nations and men; while the Spectre's plow ruthlessly furrows the land of nations, Vala's ominous spindle turns "fierce with the Lives of Men." Albion's peaceful valleys resound with the tumult of iron war to decide between "Two Worlds, ...a World of Mercy and/ A World of Justice," a world of love and a world of vengeance.

To reinforce the tyranny and cruelty that enemies of spirit inflict upon their victims, Blake, who surely was one of these, again utilizes the naturalists' chain (depicted along the margin at the right), here inserting links of Christian myth and druidic practices [plate 65]. While Los and Erin labour to reconcile the "Two Contraries of Humanity," body and spiritual powers, Urizen's intractable sons continue their corporeal war and inhumanities against Jerusalem's sons. "They sound the clarions strong; they chain the howling Captives" to earth (visible at the bottom of plate 67); they give the oath of death. As they have done to Albion, so to Luvah: "they nail'd him to Albion's tree" and "stain'd him with poisonous blue," signifying a return to druidism. In this crucifixion scene Blake gives a vivid picture of natural philosophy transformed into a religion. Urizen has removed spirit from every domain; his authority is absolute. His sons exert their utmost power in politics, religion and art, binding Albion's people to the grinding wheels of mechanical science; they forge intruments of torture and war; they change "all the Arts of Life... into the Arts of Death"; they leave their peaceful occupations to fight in Vala's holy war. "In ignorance" they "view a small portion & think that All,/ And call is Demonstration." These lines telescope the many complaints in *Siris*—specifically §264, 294, 295 and 303—about those who consider only sensory effects, reason about them, reduce them to a mechanical system, and ignore their true cause, which is God, who is *All*.

Blake is unsparing in his criticism of this philosophizing in art. Here he sets his remonstration to the harsh sounds of a war-song sung by "the Spectre Sons of Albion"; the melancholic words kindling the cruel war are accompanied by the lyre of Urizen, who has harnessed nature to humanity and beauty, for these come together in art.

> Now, now the battle rages round thy tender limbs, O Vala!
> Now smile among thy bitter tears, now put on all thy beauty.
> Is not the wound of the sword sweet & the broken bone
>   delightful?
> . . .
> Gird on thy flaming zone [breastplate], descend into the
>   sepulcher of Canterbury.
> . . .
> Arise, O Vala, bring the bow of Urizen, bring the swift arrows
>   of light.
> How rag'd the golden horses of Urizen, compell'd to the chariot
>   of love!

Again contrasting Albion's irenic past with his grisly present, the poet tells us this is no shepherd's song of happy cheer sung near a limpid brook beneath Jerusalem's "mirtle tree"; it is a warrior's song of "blood and wounds and dismal cries" sung in the "shadows of the oak"; it is a song Vala's conquering heroes sing at the trial of Luvah, whom they mock and deride as they drink "his Emanation," for spirit is the vital flame of all existents. Albion's daughters join his sons in these rituals, forcing men to surrender their souls to Vala. "Howling the Victims on the Druid Altars yield their souls/ To the stern Warriors; lovely sport the Daughters round their Victims,/ Drinking their lives in sweet intoxication." Blake then creates another compelling image conveying obeisance to Reynolds' system: as the daughters perform their ceremonies, smoke from the burning incense rises in spiral volutions (illustrated on the next plate), simultaneously symbolizing the intricate windings of abstract reasoning and the elusive character of material substance serving religion. The warriors laud this "feminine indefinite cruel delusion" ascending from druidic altars; they do not recognize it is "their beloved Mother Vala." Spellbound, they undergo the startling experience of conversion: "Sudden they become like what they behold," thoroughly corporeal.

Blake dialates upon the subject of natural religion, morality and art, presenting a complete picture of their origin and characteristics, which he connects explicitly to the philosophies of *"Bacon, Newton & Locke"* [plate 66]. Albion's sons arrogantly attack and audaciously pull down an institution that for centuries has embodied humane values and replace it with a new structure founded on doctrines of science, another sanctuary for Vala. They construct "a stupendous Building on the Plain of Salisbury, with chains/ Of rocks round London Stone, of Reasonings, of unhewn Demonstrations/ In Labyrinthine arches"; its designer is Urizen; its rough materials are formed by the hard rock of reason, unshaped by human imagination. Blake here connects the rock to Deism, relating it to Druidism (Part Six). The plain located near Stonehenge perfectly situates the Deists' shrine of natural religion, for they belittle divine inspiration and revive Druidism, offering "a wondrous rocky World of cruel destiny," a world of "eternal death," hence a life of despair. Blake then alludes to Voltaire's and Rousseau's views on spiritual religion and love: "Luvah is France." Statues of these rationalist and naturalist literary figures in France, which like England is a "Victim of the Spectres of Albion," adorn the edifice. And at the center of the altar stands Vala, invisible like abstract matter, "turning the iron Spindle of destruction"; natural philosophy has become dogma.

The reader is brought before the sacrificial altar to witness in gruesome detail the separation of spirit from the human form. This ceremony involves the abstracting process, which Berkeley characterizes as "cutting off all those circumstances and differences" that determine "any particular existence."[18] He was especially infuriated when Locke cut away the "inner garment" of the human body to form an abstract idea of man.[19] With a fury far surpassing Berkeley's, Blake conveys the painful and deadly effects of this operation by the knife, particularly by the "Knife of flint," thereby sharpening the likeness between beliefs of naturalists and druidic

---

[18] Berkeley, *Principles*, Introd.9.
[19] Berkeley, *Siris*.86; in §171 he refers to spirit as "interior clothing."

practises by critics. Albion's daughters pass the "Knife of flint...
over the howling Victim," dismembering his human form; they inflict
upon the son of spirit all the tortures suffered by the Saviour; mockingly they bind his "forehead with thorns of iron" and "put in his
hand a reed," symbols of a mechanical and vegetative world. Then
"they cut asunder his inner garment" and search with "cruel fingers
for his heart," the seat of love. Having constricted his mind, stripped
him of spirit, and in hate entered his heart, these daughters proceed
with the task of turning their victim into a complete Lockean man
incapable of initiating ideas. They "pour cold water on his brain,"
freezing and solidifying the artist's creative powers into hard particles.
Concomitantly, they feed him from "dishes of painted clay," the
artful abstract works moulded from earth's own substance to signify
his total subjugation to forces of nature and necessary compliance
with Reynolds' iron rules.

Spectators at this ritual are transfigured; they become like the
victim. As confirmed naturalists, their sensory organs shrink; because
they have cut away the cause of existence, they do not perceive reality;
they experience only secondary qualities of material powers acting
upon the senses. As their senses "shrunk, the heavens shrunk away."
The "Divine Vision" became "a globe of blood wandering distant in
an unknown night"[20] because Albion's Spectre-Sons murdered the
source of perception. The "Human Form" is altered to conform to
their theories; particularized qualities perceived by the imagination are
"dissipated into the Indefinite" of generalized forms. All is placed in
the cloudy shadows of Albion's tree, grown into a "mighty Polypus"
that not only interposes insurmountable difficulties in the way of
knowledge but also nurtures a parasitic art: "As the mistletoe grows
on the Oak, so Albion's tree on Eternity. Lo!/ He who will not mingle
in Love must be adjoin'd by Hate" to further naturalist doctrines,
carrying them with a vengeance into art.[21]

In this long plate Blake gives another concrete image patently
showing that the hateful war arises from the controlling philosophy of

---

[20] An oblique allusion to Locke's discussion on the weakness of human senses to discern realities: "Blood, to the naked eye, appears all red; but by a good microscope ... shows only some few globules of red" (II.xxiii.11).

[21] Pliny the Elder relates that Druids venerated the mistletoe when they found it growing upon the oak, which they held sacred (*Natural History,* §77).

Locke, for "Gwendolen cast the shuttle of war, as Cambel return'd the beam." The ferocity of Albion's warriors cannot be stayed: his streams run red with the blood of Jerusalem's sons "because of the griding Knife." In vain her sons attempt to bring peace by restoring spirit to Albion's land: "They send the Dove & Raven" and "the Eagle & Lion over the four-fold wilderness;/ They return not, but generate in rocky places desolate," separated from human perceptions. The conflict expands, involving all parts of the universe: the earth, sun, moon, and stars are caught up in Albion's war.

The enemy cuts, weaves, circumscribes and binds as it manipulates abstract reasoning and thrusts the new science on all sides [plate 67]. While Albion's sons take in captives, his "Twelve Daughters," counterparts of male disciples, carry out the covenant of death at the altar of art. These daughters, who possess the monstrosity of a Rahab and the beauty of a Tirzah, like vampires feed on human blood; they enflame their passions and advance their seductive prostitute arts by drinking the blood of Jerusalem's sons. Some daughters pass the knife of flint over the victims; others work at the loom drawing out fibers of life from rocks of inanimate matter. As they cut their opaque materials into "various divisions," they weave a tapestry depicting a story of creation, "Calling the Rocks Atomic Origins of Existence, denying Eternity/ By the Atheistical Epicurean Philosophy of Albion's tree." This picture of Reynolds' system parallels Berkeley's criticism of Locke's material substance: it is ever the pedestal of *"atheists"* and "Epicureans," who regard atoms the "root and origin of all beings."[22] Modern philosophers support this view, leaving no place for a substantial God in the universe; they exert such immense influence that people are ashamed to admit belief in spiritual powers because that is unscientific. Blake records a similar situation in art: Albion's daughters disdain Jerusalem's sons; instead, they "feed with their Souls the Spectres of Albion,/ Ashamed to give Love openly to the piteous & merciful Man." They eagerly seize and twist Vala's dark fibers and Jerusalem's golden threads to form a great consortium of Vala's powers. Under her consecrated banners the warriors fight with blood weaving "a Tabernacle/ For Rahab &

---

[22] Berkeley, *Principles.*92-93. According to Epicurus, there is neither divine purpose nor divine power in the world; all that happens in it is explained by atoms and their own laws.

Tirzah, till the Great Polypus of Generation," which began with Bacon in "Verulam" and wound around the South of England from East to West, insidiously spread its poisonous tentacles through the entire world.

False religion has produced a false moralistic system of art. Acting in accord with its laws, Rahab and Tirzah together righteously chain the artist to earth: they "circumscrib'd the Brain" and "bound down with a hot iron" the senses (visualized at the bottom of the plate). Tirzah explains she cannot but be cruel because Hand and Hyle have deprived her of humanity. The irony of the situation is great, for Tirzah means *delight*.

Blake continues in plate 68 to draw out still more ill consequences resulting from reasoned naturalist values, interweaving the narrative with his own experiences. The "ever-expanding cruelty" sanctioned by the autocratic system of art spreads also into politics, graphically portrayed in fastening Skofield to the accursed rock, a biblical symbol of irreverence, which Blake connects to spirit debased by naturalists. "Bind him down, Sisters, bind him down on Ebal, Mount of cursing./ ... Come circumscribe this tongue of sweets, & with a screw of iron/ Fasten this ear into the rock." Tirzah urges her sisters to their task because their "life depends on this." Unless the beloved "is bound upon the Stems of Vegetation," the war against "mercy & truth" is lost.

Therefore Tirzah, who combines beauty of body and worship of natural powers, inspires the warrior's song:

> Look! the beautiful Daughter of Albion sits naked upon the Stone,
> Her panting Victim beside her; her heart is drunk with blood
> Tho' her brain is not drunk with wine.

She is dominated by cruel passions and exhilarated by the blood of others because her brain is not suffused with spirit. "In pride of beauty, in cruelty of holiness," Tirzah zealously performs the violent ceremonial rites, delighting "the eyes of the Kings."

In this series of long plates decrying the nation's apparent inhumanity and bitter wars across Europe, Blake does not spare the reader's sensibilities. With an overwhelming precision of detail, again and again he shows Albion's daughters almost sadistically carrying out their tortures, piercing a victim's limbs, cutting his flesh, and manacling his body with red-hot brass. Under Tirzah's direction, these pitiless daughters enact barbarities reminiscent of bacchic orgies. Naked they dance round their victim on the stone of human sacrifice; gleefully "they sport before the Kings/ Clothed in the skin of the Victim!" The dancers act out the naturalists' intoxication with their own theories; they gladden the hearts of Kings because "human blood" of the victim is the "delightful food of the Warrior." Albion's daughters sacrifice at the altar of nature to strengthen his sons in the field. Blood of slain spiritual sons feeds the warrior, filling the fertile valleys with "Breeding Women" committed to generation. "With pleasure, without pain" they supply the warrior with new food. Consequently, "Jerusalem's Pillars fall in the rendings of fierce War," which overspreads the Continent.

The verbal description of cruelties is made more vivid in visual form on the next plate [69]. There under the auspices of Vala's revered objects, the moon and stars, and in front of an altar near a phallic stone the daughters perpetuate abstraction and sexual organization in politics and art. Like maenads possessed by wild passions, two daughters dance before a sacrificial victim whom they lay out in cruciform position, symbolizing murder of spirit, and shackle to Albion's accursed rock. They cut out the victim's brain, which one daughter flaunts while the other balances a chalice-like cup containing his blood, which they drink. It is not reason that gains proselytes to the extravagant doctrines; rather, it is the stupefying madness of the dancers.

As if these acts were not horrid enough to behold, Blake adds an element of savagery, undoubtedly to reflect the brutality of attacks upon his political beliefs and his art. The beautiful daughter of Albion has been taught "to cut the flesh from the Victim/ To roast the flesh in fire, to examine the Infant's limbs/ In cruelties of holiness, to refuse the joys of love." Devoid of spirit, Tirzah cannot express human love. Deprived of love, denied the opportunity to satisfy their desires in constructive and peaceful ways, Albion's sons are passionate for battle. So the warrior sings, "I am drunk with unsatiated love,/ I must rush again to war." Regretfully he adds, "my Soul is harrow'd with grief & fear & love & desire/ And now I hate & now I love, & Intellect is no more": these are effects of repressing impulses of love and creativity. In Albion's land there is neither human affection, nor intellectual pleasure, nor individual creativity; there is only torment, war, and death; Vala holds all in her fatal embrace.

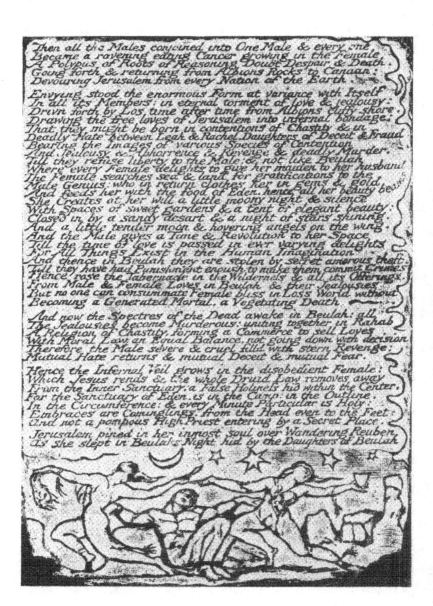

14. *Jerusalem* 69

After making a general statement about the proliferation of natural philosophy, Blake continues to particularize disasters that have developed from its doctrines [plate 69]. The vegetative universe like a noxious plant has produced a polypus of roots, going forth from England, destroying belief in spiritual power, spreading despair of salvation, and death of humanity. Time and again Los exposes visual "Images of various Species of Contention." Jealousy, revenge, and murder abound as naturalists militantly force every aspect of human life into "the enormous Form" of Coban, Hand and Hyle, drawing the free spirit into an "infernal bondage" of their machinery.

Against this philosophical background and without break, Blake passes to the creative process in art, personifying it as an act of love between the sexes, an intimate relation between female and male, between the artist's free spirit and his deep desires. The female "Creates at her will" the conditions for expressing beauty; thus inspired, "the Male gives a Time & Revolution to her Space"; he gives body to his inspiration by particularizing it in space-time as an art object. As Berkeley insisted that human consciousness cannot be explained by mechanical motions of particles, nor natural phenomena represented by abstract ideas, and that all things have their existence in the mind, so with equal insistence Blake holds that the artist's inspiration cannot be bound to forces in nature, nor perfect forms reduced to abstract ideas as Reynolds purports, "For All Things Exist in the Human Imagination," in "Minute Particular."

The harmonious relation between the artist's imagination and his works, between female and male loves, exists in Beulah. There spiritually perceived particulars are created into sweet garden of beauty and delight. But "Spectres of the Dead" united in a "Religion of Chastity," which lies in "Equal Balance" with "Moral Law," awaken to punish those in Beulah for their free loves, for perpetrating 'crimes' of spirit, thus encouraging stealthy love and prostitution, which in turn leads to deceit. At plate 71 Blake adapts the Zeus-Leda myth to express these sentiments in visual form. Literally, in terms of art, naturalist critics authoritatively enforce abstraction as if it were a moral law, driving the artist of imagination to prostitute himself for sheer survival. Hence Vala's "Infernal Veil" of "False Holiness" grows. In 69:39-42 Blake alludes to the Israelites' march from Egypt, comparing their four grand divisions to Golgonooza's four gates, and extrapolates into the present Jesus' tearing of the Temple's veil, comparing it to his epical act: in the "Camp" is the divinely inspired artist and his detailed company, "in the Outline,/ In the Circumference & every Minute Particular," which will bear away "the whole Druid Law" from art and uncover the Divine Vision to the eyes of all men. Then he answers his critics: "Embraces are cominglings from the Head even to the Feet":[23] embraces are human expressions of love dictated by the heart, not by Reynolds' rules preached by a "pompous High Priest." Very likely these lines allude to Hunt's censure of Blake's drawing entitled "The Meeting of a family in Heaven" (plate I). Hunt criticizes the embrace of man and wife as too fleshy: an inappropriate "display of the chastity of celestial rapture.... libidiousness intrudes itself upon the holiness of our thoughts."[24] As naturalist, Hunt would have spirits represented by some abstract idea since to him, as to Locke and Reynolds, spirit is not experienced as a measurable quantity and therefore not known. Indeed Hunt praises whatever is "simply natural," and condemns "all the allegory" as "absurd." For Blake, however, human beings are spirits; and since spirit is the principle of love and eternal life, human love radiates in heaven as on earth.

But natural philosophy wields its enormous power. An almighty form of "Three strong sinewy Necks & Three awful & terrible Heads,/ Three Brains" incessantly quarreling among themselves, sits on Albion's cliffs. This mighty form rejects spiritual man and his perceptions "as nothing"; it holds "all Wisdom/ To consist in the agreements & disagreements of Ideas." Comparison of ideas, as Berkeley pointed out, discovers relations; reasoning is a logic of meaning. Blake's notion of wisdom is fundamentally biblical: a prophetic perception of particular events concerning the future of humanity. Albion's twelve sons have taken on a grand form that combines the "Three Forms named Bacon & Newton & Locke." Their philosophies have revived a religion that threatens humanity and is certain death to Albion. Thus along with the blotted sun setting over the land, the stone monument spanning plate 70 is at once a trilithon of a druidic temple, an unhewn dolmen, and a visible symbol of the three natural philosophies fanatically worshiped. The new

---

[23] Cf. *Paradise Lost,* VIII.626-627: "if Spirits embrace,/ Total they mix."
[24] Bentley, *Blake Records,* p.197.

religion issues from "a hideous orifice" of a form devoid of divine love, precluding inspiration and hence destructive to "Imagination the Divine Humanity." Within the threefold form of Hand sits the threefold wonder of Rahab. Outwardly she is attractive, but her heart is enclosed in hard matter, "bonified"; her "threefold kiss" is deadly to god and man. Nature as a glorious creation of the eternal spirit is called *Vala;* but when it is adjudged by men to be the universal power, Vala becomes an abomination; hence "in Time her name is Rahab."

Although Albion's sons have divided among themselves the nation's districts and all therein, they cannot appropriate these as their own because the whole of creation belongs to the eternal spirit [plate 71]. Over Albion's land and above his sons is "the Heavenly Canaan" seen by Jerusalem's ungenerated sons. Heavenly Canaan is to Albion's land as, in traditional terminology, substance is to shadow, or in Berkeley's language as spirit is to natural phenomena, but in Reynolds' system as "invariable ideas of nature" are to particulars.[25] "As the Soul is to the Body, so Jerusalem's Sons/ Are to the Sons of Albion," or more explicitly as "that which moves and acts" is to what is moved and acted upon.[26] Albion's sons are acted upon by external objects, whereas Jerusalem's sons create their objects of perception. In the present context Blake parenthetically restates this causal principle in slightly different form from that expressed earlier [36:46-50]. "What is above is Within, for every-thing in Eternity is translucent." Reality is clearly perceived by the human spirit, where things have their existence: "Rivers, Mountains, Cities, Villages; /All are Human." Since everything is a creation of the eternal spirit, as a spiritual being you walk in "Heavens & Earths." Though what you behold appears to have a subsistence of its own, "it is Within/ In your Imagination," of which the external world is a "Shadow," an effect.

For reasons unknown the catalog of Albion's sons who are Vala's disciples lists only eleven, leaving out Kwantok. Because these formidable sons led by Coban, Hand and Hyle mercilessly pursue their war against spiritual perception, "Albion is darkened, Jerusalem lies in ruins," and the anguished hero in desperation shouts to heaven for divine aid.

---

[25] Reynolds, Disc. One, p.20.
[26] Berkeley, *Siris*.171; his discussion of the soul extends through §178.

The action is interrupted for yet another epic catalog. Whereas in the previous plate Blake associates leaders of Albion's armies primarily with districts in England, where natural philosophy reigns supreme, at plate 72 he names Jerusalem's defenders by counties in "the Land of Erin" and subsumes them under the tribes of Judea. Here also is another coupling of Blake's fourfold poem and Los's exertions: Jerusalem's majestic task force centers "in London & in Golgonooza," where Los "in fury Fourfold" defends spiritual perception, from which all nations are created and to which they owe their survival. The poet impassionately pleads with them to recognize their foundations; he calls upon Albion to awaken, to avow spiritual power: "O Come ye Nations! Come ye People! Come up to Jerusalem!/ ... Reuben wanders." These biblical intonations and references to Israelish history add urgency and depth to Blake's complaint: as natural philosophy has sent man wandering after second causes, so Reynolds' rules send the artist wandering after forms of existence; like Reuben dispossessed of his homeland, the artist deprived of his own powers searches nature in vain for true forms. But the armies of Golgonooza "surround the Universe Within and/ Without," for spirit is the source of eternal forms. To preserve "the wondrous Creation" of imagination, metaphorically "the great Winepress of Love," spiritual sons join Beulah's inspiring daughters guarding Albion's tomb.

Within Golgonooza, Los's furnaces roar, "living, self-moving," not moved by outer forces [plate 73]. Like the Gospels that kindle men to life in every region of humanity, the furnaces "stretch from South to North," from spirit to generation, from inspiration to visible particulars through "all the Four Points" of the universe. Countless courageous labourers work unweariedly to deliver dead souls. How these "came forth from the Furnaces, & how long/ Vast & severe the anguish e'er they knew their Father, were/ Long to tell." Through this epic formula Blake underscores the immense struggle against the strong hold of mechanical philosophy upon men's minds: the "mill of many innumerable wheels resistless" closed the gates to immortality and opened wide the gates to death.

Albion's sons attempt to create the whole world—men, animals, seasons, planets, stars, and "Vegetative Nature"—out of "their hard restricting condensations." Where spiritual perception ended and rational power assumed control, reality passed into "a Rocky hardness without form & void," and art forced into abstraction. That is why Los, messenger of the eternal spirit, opens the furnaces and fixes "the Sexual into an ever-prolific Generation," removing the limits of opaqueness and contraction (cf. plate 42, Part Six).

As he frequently does, Blake interjects fact into allegory: Voltaire mocks the remover of limits; but Los aided by divine strength with his thunderous hammer time after time demolishes limits (demonstrated at mid plate). He labors to destroy a system that applauds "Satan, Cain.../ Arthur, Alfred.../ *Edward, Henry... Charles, William, George,*" and all adversaries of spirit or worldly conquerors. These he creates into states of evil, pride, selfishness, and earthly glory "to be in Time Reveal'd & Demolish'd." By removing the limits of fixed rules and creating an expansive system of spiritual perceptions, Los secures a place for "Adam, Noah, Abraham, Moses, Samuel, David, Ezekiel, */Pythagoras, Socrates, Euripides, Virgil, Dante, Milton,*" and all divinely inspired religion leaders, kings, prophets, philosophers, dramatists and epic poets. Spiritual perceptions reveal recurrent states of human nature: "Men pass on, but States remain permanent."

While Los crushes the "rocky forms of Death," their adherents like wild beasts howl round Golgonooza hoping to devour Albion's body. Los's sons "clothe them & feed, & provide houses & gardens,/ And every Human Vegetated Form in its inward recesses" is "a garden of delight" created in the fiery belly of Los's furnaces, "in Bowlahoola" and on Enitharmon's looms "in Cathedron." Literally, in the fire of inspiration the spiritually moved craftsman through his imagination and genius creates a work of art, giving eternal habitation to events and aesthetic pleasure to mankind: such is *Jerusalem*.

Plate 74 makes explicit the poet's main concern is to defend imagination. Reynolds has blocked this fountain of energy by confining creativity to nature; he proudly proclaims he has brought art "down from her visionary situation" and placed her in a "solid mansion upon the earth."[27] Albion's sons fiercely enforce this proclamation. The Four Zoa of Albion in deadly opposition with each other turn their heavy wheels empowered by natural philosophy against Jerusalem's sons. "Entering into the Reasoning Power,

---

[27] Reynolds, Disc. Seven, p.106.

forsaking Imagination," the Zoa become spectres; their bodies separate from spirit; they enclose themselves "in a Ratio/ Of the Things of Memory." Within this Lockean system, spectres frame "Laws & Moralities" governing inspiration, subject and execution in art to "destroy Imagination," the dynamic force of creativity.

At this critical point the poet calls upon the "Holy Spirit" for inspiration, elaborating upon the epic theme: to tell how Los drove from "their ancient mountains" Albion's sons and daughters worshiping natural powers and opposing the Divine Vision of the eternal spirit; to tell how in art Albion's sons by rules of "Lights & Shades" opposed "Outline" and "by Abstraction" opposed "Visions of Imagination";[28] to tell how Albion's sons, committed to material forces and "opposed to Thought," to active powers of the mind, strove "to draw Jerusalem's Sons/ Into the Vortex of his [Hand's] Wheels";[29] to tell how Albion's sons abstracted a "Rational Morality" of art; and, finally, to tell how Reuben took root "in the Land of Hand & Hyle," how Albion's daughters in love with natural man divided Reuben and sent him over Europe, how his fibers enrooted beneath the shining looms of art activated by spirit "to dissipate into Non Entity" the tribes of Judea. Hence the poet's theme of the passage through death and awakening to life, telling how Los exposes a system that enslaves the artist and why he must create a system to liberate him.

The poet sees "a Feminine Form" struggling to free itself from vegetative fibers that bind it to earth (visible at the bottom of the plate). We are told this form is "Dinah, the youthful form of Erin." As Cambel and Gwendolen are the emanations of Newton and Locke, Dinah may be the emanation of Berkeley, though Blake does not make this connection explicit. In any case, Dinah symbolizes creative spirit. Why is Dinah oddly apposite to the subject? This daughter of Jacob, from whom descended the tribes of Judea, was violated by a male of a tribe who did not observe rites of circumcision.[30] *Dinah* therefore suggests natural philosophy's rape of spirit and forms part

---

[28] For Reynolds' rules respecting light and shadow, see Disc. Eight, pp.137-139.

[29] Newton's system of the world based on mathematical principles governing particles in vortical motion is in contrast to a world of particularized objects perceived by spirit; the vortex cannot, therefore, be interpreted a positive element in Blake's system.

[30] Gen.34 relates this incident.

of Blake's mosaic depicting sexual organization of Reynolds' system.

"Rahab, Babylon the Great, hath destroyed Jerusalem" [plate 75].[31] Blake weaves another biblical strand into the aesthetic conflict. Through pride of reasoning Albion's sons have overthrown Jerusalem; not unlike powerful Babylonian rulers, they have brazenly set an idol on the throne of God. By affinity to Locke's material substance, *mystery* is another of Vala's characteristics: "all her Twenty-seven Heavens, now hid & now reveal'd,/Appear in strong delusive light in Time & Space."[32] Like Rahab, she has become the proud virgin-harlot and mother of all. As in the past, so in the present, unbelief in spirit ever leads to idolatry.

Very like the poet-prophets who recorded the destruction of Jerusalem and their visions of her restoration, Los similarly inspired walks up and down the ramparts of Golgonooza, surveys "Six Thousand Years" of biblical history, and makes permanent through art the present ruin of Jerusalem and her rebuilding. Whenever men or nations hide the cause of existence within body, they worship a hermaphroditic deity, either male hid within a female or a female hid within a male,[33] a deceit based on mystery that ends in "the Abomination of Desolation."[34] At such times, in mercy a prophet of eternity breaks through the zones of death to avert this disaster, for spirit is free, not limited to laws of nature. The "Eternal Prophet" is an agent of God's intervention in the transformation of human history, giving it an apocalyptic dimension: Jesus by his acts opened "Eternity in Time & Space"; Los by his art builds "Heavens" to bring Albion back to life and immortality.

Diaphonous emblems of heaven stretch across the upper plate of 75. Below these Blake completes the picture with a visualization of natural religion and art conjoined; Rahab and Tirzah, first seen at plate 25, here embrace the seven-headed and ten-horned beast,[35] which

---

[31] The allusions are probably to the harlot of Jericho (Jos.2) and the Babylonian king who destroyed the temple of Jerusalem (Ezra.5).

[32] the meaning is obscure; does it refer to the naturalists' interpretation of the twenty-seven books comprising the New Testament?

[33] Perhaps a vague allusion to 1 Cor.11:11-12: "neither is the man without the woman, neither the woman without the man, in the Lord."

[34] Cf.Lk.21:20.

[35] Traditionally, its head represents the seven deadly sins and its horns offenses of the ten commandments.

15. *Jerusalem* 75

hungers to devour Albion by destroying revelation in religion and divine inspiration in art. This beast receives its strength from natural philosophy, but its end is near. The full page vision that follows, showing Albion with outstretched arms in a gesture of atonement before the icon of redemption, marks another important point in the narrative and anticipates the climatic events in the final chapter.

16. *Jerusalem* 76

PART EIGHT

JERUSALEM RESTORED

Consistent with the general pattern of the Gospels, Chapter 4 is a long epiphany addressed to Christians. The quotation from Acts 9.4 adds poignancy to the repeated attacks upon Blake's art. The "golden string" of the narrative provides a clew to the way out of the labyrinth of abstract reasonings and leads readers to "Heaven's gate" revealed by Saint John. This is not a surrender to abstruse mystical experience; the visible and verbal forms Blake creates in earlier chapters here coalesce and find their consummation in a new system of art within empiricism, analogous to Berkeley's philosophic reflections culminating in a new empirical system of knowledge.

Upon completing the construction of his system, Berkeley tells us it was the main drift and design of his labours to inspire readers "with a pious sense of the presence of God" in the minds of men.[1] Having untangled and laid bare the "falseness or vanity of those barren speculations" by abstract reasoners, and having proved that spirit is the cause of all ideas and sensations, Berkeley hoped he would dispose men to "embrace the salutary truths of the Gospel, which to know and to practise is the highest perfection of human nature." These truths, he reminds us, are no late invention. The writings of Greek philosophers, Egyptian cosmologists, and Chaldean sages contain a remarkable confirmation of the doctrine stated in "Saint John's Gospel... that Christ is the Wisdom of God by which all things were made." And "the notion of a Trinity" appears in many world-systems of old heathen philosophers, who logically connect "Authority, Light, and Life," thereby implying their reciprocal relation. For "indeed, how could

---

[1] Berkeley, *Principles.*156; *Siris.*359. 361-362.

power or authority avail or subsist without knowledge? Or either without life and action?" The three categories in ancient philosophical schemes have a certain analogy to the three persons of the Christian Trinity designated "Father, Son, and Spirit."

Yet Berkeley guards against readers interpreting such analogues as exact identities between pagan systems and his own philosophy. He is ever alert to the dangers in appealing to antiquity for support because one can find there support also for doctrines associated with natural philosophy. In his reflective journey he must steer clear of the two fearful tenets that regard God as nature itself or as far above nature, the very notions he is opposing. Therefore, to distinguish his view, on the one hand, from pantheism and the abstract idea of God in ancient heathen doctrines, and, on the other hand, from natural religion and Deism of modern naturalists and rationalists, Berkeley constantly interjects his own first principle, explicitly connecting it to Newton's term but re-defining it. He explains that in conception "vis, or spirit, might be distinguished from mind"; he, however, does not do so.[2] Spirit is "closely connected to intellect"; specifically, it is "that power or force" humans possess, which experiment and reflection make evident. To act, to know, "to create" is "to manifest" this infinite power eternally inhering in the Holy Trinity and belonging to mankind. Why admit the speculations of those lured by abstractionism, so limiting to man and ruinous to a nation's well-being? "Liberty is the greatest human blessing that a virtuous man can possess, and is very consistent with the duties of a good subject and a good Christian."

To reestablish these sublime truths and at the same time authenticate the true metaphysical principle of art is, Blake tells us in the fourth address, his design. Since he has defined this principle as spiritual power, imagination is essentially related to Christian doctrine. Christians have abandoned God and entangled themselves "with incoherent roots" of natural philosophy, leaving the fruits of spirit to the enemy. "God [is] a Spirit who must be worshipped in Spirit," not in some unknowable corporeal substance. The poet calls upon Christians to admit that inviolate right secured by the Gospel: "the liberty both of body & mind to exercise the Divine Arts of Imagination," which imparts immortality to things.

---

[2] Berkeley, *Siris.* 322,325, "Preventing the Ruin of Great Britian" (cited in Pt. Three, n.7), p.70.

Through a series of rhetorical questions, Blake translates the trinitarian doctrine into the fundamental principle of his system. As Father, Son and Holy Ghost co-exist, so power, intellect and life are identical. He does not distinguish spirit from mind or imagination; it is the source of all living things as well as the "Intellectual Fountain.... Spirit [is] Every-thing to Man," his divine gift of life, creativity and knowledge. "What is the Life of Man but Art & Science?" Both are expressions of the divine body. Whereas Reynolds held that "art is not a divine gift" and subsumed it under principles of science,[3] Blake places both art and science upon the efficacy of spirit. He defines heaven and hell in terms of this first principle: joys of heaven he equates with "improvement in the things of the Spirit"; pains of hell he associates with the devouring monsters of natural religion and Deism. Advancement of knowledge depends on the exercise of spirit; ignorance results from contempt of this power: "to labour in Knowledge is to Build up Jerusalem, and to Despise Knowledge is to Despise Jerusalem." The poet urges Christians to reclaim their divine heritage and restore the uniquely human power: bodies die; spirit lives eternally. Men have an obligation to acknowledge God's generous gift by engaging "in some Mental pursuit for the Building up of Jerusalem."

The metrical verses following the prose introduction recount in visionary language why and how the poet builds up Jerusalem. As he stood in the region of spirit (south), he saw the wheel of mechanical philosophy turn from east to west against the free flow of human creativity, compelling the artist to obey Reynolds' imperatives. He saw the artist compressed into a shoot of Albion's tree, reduced to a quantitative object, a root measuring six feet, a mind powerless. He saw life and ideas made into effects of a material substance bearing a deadly disease: like a wheel of fire revolving from earth to heaven, it devours all things. Los, like Jesus, comes to heal the spiritually sick, whom the poet compares to Pharisees. Like them, Albion's sons worship a tyrannical and punishing deity; they crucify those who believe in spiritual power. The closing lines of the lyric end in a burst of hope promising Albion's joyous awakening and provide a harmonious bridge for the poet to resume his narrative. "And now the time

---

[3] See Pt. Two; for Reynolds, as for Locke, God's gift to man is reason.

returns again:/ Our souls exult, & London's towers/ Receive the Lamb of God."

Appropriately, the fourth apocalyptic animal in the likeness of a man with the face of an eagle heads plate 78.[4] Suffused by light, this living creature with its clarity of vision and physical vantage point sits on a white cliff above Albion's land, otherwise enveloped in darkness, and looks towards a great globe of light reascending on the horizon in expectation of Albion's redemption, specifically, to use a phrase from *Siris*.358, "waking out of his body into himself." The proximity of this event moves the action to Albion's tomb, where his sons rage, determined to devour sleeping humanity. But Los, mighty in words and deeds coextensive with his sacred tools, issues loud threats. Courageously he confronts Albion's sons and dashes to pieces their "rocky Spectres"; he divides these into "Male & Female forms," which have been fused in an abstract idea culled out of particulars. Lest the false doctrine which conflates cause and effect destroy visible forms of existence and their true cause, Los breaks up the hermaphroditic forms, hurls the pieces into his furnaces to purify them from the corruption of material substances, and thereby set free at once the real agent of creativity and his perceptions.

While Los heroically fends off the enemy from the tomb, another contingent of Albion's armies surrounds the "Gates of Erin." Having attacked, captured, and laid Jerusalem in ruins, Albion's sons now furiously fight "to destroy the Lamb of God," whom they have impiously replaced with nature itself and set over the artist. Thus we have Vala in another pose:

> They took their Mother Vala and they crown'd her with gold;
> They nam'd her Rahab & gave her power over the Earth,
> The Concave Earth round Golgonooza in Entuthon Benython,
> Even to the stars exalting her Throne, to build beyond the Throne
> Of God and the Lamb.

Naturalists have limited perception to appearances, absurdly abbreviated reality, and created a hollow world of abstract ideas: they have curved the earth inward by placing causes of existence in its interior, posited a generalized material substance, superimposed divinity on this substance, and directed the artist to abstract his forms from it.

---

[4] Erdman, quoting Mitchell, identifies the figure as Hand.

JERUSALEM RESTORED

17. *Jerusalem* 78

Exactly how veneration of nature came about Berkeley explains in *Siris*.270. Upon the mathematical notions of absolute space and motion, natural scientists postulated external existences independent of mind, assigning power on earth to particles. Subsequently, some modern philosophers identified God with absolute space, which truly is but a void; they dissipated spiritual powers into "nothing" and extended material powers beyond God himself.[5]

The tragical consequences of this presumptuousness in art, Blake elaborates in prolonged outpourings by women sounded in the next four plates, increasing the pathos and building up the emotional intensity preliminary to Albion's waking. Since Jerusalem is causally related to Albion as his emanation, she too suffers: both are victims of his sons. As an enemy strips its captives of their armor, so Albion's sons strip Jerusalem of her power: "Naked" she lies before the gates of her ruined nation and pitifully moans:

> My brother & my father are no more! God hath forsaken me!
> The arrows of the Almighty pour upon me & my children!
> I have sinned and am an outcast from the Divine Presence!
> My tents are fall'n! my pillars are in ruins! my children dash'd
> Upon Egypt's iron floors & the marble pavements of Assyria!
> [78:31-33]

Her psalm of grief, continuing for another eighty-five lines [79:1-80:5], recapitulates her history: the attack upon Israel, the capture of Jerusalem, and the oppression of its people by Hesbons and others. As always, Blake pairs biblical with contemporary events: attacks upon spirit and seizure of power by naturalists remain the poem's center, the point from which epic actions arise and towards which biblical parallels constantly converge. Berkeley moved between philosophy and religion; Blake moves between philosophy and art. Once the inspiration of all the arts, once beheld everywhere and worshiped by everyone, Jerusalem now is fiercely attacked and despised by all, as if she were not "their Mother," their source of nourishment. Her reminiscence of past glories and complaints of present woes echoes Albion's [24:4-60]; her story is his story. Gone

---

[5] For a fuller account see Pt. Five.

are the days when Albion gave her "the whole Earth" to walk upon; then, all nations rejoiced in harmony, peace and love. "Once a continual cloud of salvation rose" from her altars; now she is shut out from "the Four-fold World" and forced into "narrow passages" of a Lockean world, an altogether dark and destructive world. She is separated from Albion and from the "four-fold wonders of God"; at her altars in deference to science, naturalists carry out their Druidism, rationalists their Deism, and art critics their cruelties. [79:21,57-62]

Jerusalem reminds Vala: "Humanity is far above/ Sexual Organization," far above laws governing gross masses [79:73]. Blake metaphorically expresses the contention that, as Berkeley put it, "there is a principle of the soul higher than nature" which exempts man from headlong forces of unintelligible matter.[6] Humane acts are initiated by spirit; they depend on affections freely given by thinking beings; similarly, works of art are unconstrained acts of love inspired by the divine body. Though nature appears to be the source of creativity, and though the structure of the world appears to be the function of corporeal bodies, all things exist in the interactional imagination. Forms of existence have two genders, the masculine and feminine. Jerusalem asks Vala why she has put these apart and assumed creativity unto herself alone? A self-subsistent nature is "the frozen Net" woven by abstract reasonings from the roots of Albion's tree, a delusion which depresses mankind into low animal form. Already in earlier plates we have heard Vala call man a worm, heard Albion compare himself to a worm, and seen Hyle take on this lowly shape; now, passing to art, we hear Jerusalem complain: "I am a worm and no living soul!/ . . . rais'd up in a night/ To an eternal night of pain." In darkness, in ignorance of the true cause of existence and through wrong judgments, naturalists have reduced human souls to a situation bordering on mere animal life. Blake's convoluted design along the right margin of plate 80 pictures this transmogrification, increasing our revulsion at the Lockean man. [79:73,80:3-5]

Under current scientific doctrines, spiritual power is called a vain fiction; man, like a piteous earthworm, is confined to "narrow places in a little and dark land"; knowledge of reality is made impossible; humanity is changed into an insensate rock; revealed religion is turned into a curse; morality is harnessed to abstract forms; the living beauty

---

[6] Berkeley, *Siris*. 272.

of thought and art is reduced to fixed rules; divine inspiration is made an object of contempt; the man of imagination is dragged into eternal torment of deepest hell. Utterly cast away, Jerusalem wanders like a lost sheep. Deprived of her vivifying powers, "Albion is himself shrunk to a narrow rock in the midst of the sea!"—an entire nation lost in a boundless sea of abstract reasonings. [79:14,17]

Hidden in a thick cloud of opaque matter is Jerusalem's shadow Vala, howling upon the winds of natural philosophy [plate 80]. Why does this beautiful goddess crowned in gold wail? Though she shines in pride of beauty, she knows the "Delusion" that she is the ultimate power of the universe will in time be discovered. As Jerusalem's dolorous songs chronicle her history, so Vala's lamentations relate her story. Briefly, Luvah, a personification of universal love, participates in the Holy Trinity; as father, he is the source of Vala's origin: he gave her to Albion; as beloved, he bestows tender affections. But when Albion came under control of his giant sons, he smote Luvah and tyrannically forced him into the system of natural philosophy: Luvah became a Spectre of Albion, and art a limb of his dread tree. Consequently, Luvah motivated by hate and revenge, ordered Vala to murder Albion: he put the knife in Vala's hand, heretofore an unheard of act. This is the way of human reason gone mad; this is the way of natural virtue: it turns love into hate, forgiveness into revenge.

Vala keeps Albion "embalmed in moral laws" of art, laws for which natural philosophy provided the theoretical machinery, and critics its preserving spices. She prays that Albion will remain forever in death because, if he awakens to eternal life, she loses her power over both him and Luvah. Moreover, Albion's waking restores not only the nation to its renowned humanity and Luvah to his proper metaphysical status but also Jerusalem to her rightful place in Albion's life, and hence art to its true foundations. Indeed these events are simultaneous. So Vala furiously turns her iron spindle to weave Jerusalem a body out of material substance while she prays for Albion's eternal death and, incongruous with her own doctrine, implores pity for herself: "Pity me then, O Lamb of God, O Jesus pity me!/ Come into Luvah's Tents and seek not to revive the Dead!/ So sang she," twisting, drawing out, or cutting off the thread of life as she pleases.

Since Vala's spindle operates according to the principles of Newton's and Locke's philosophy, the emanations of Hand and Hyle complement her efforts to keep themselves in power—spinning, weaving, dancing, enticing, procreating, begetting. While Vala spins, Cambel and Gwendolen sing and dance before the soldiers to charm them into fighting for their goddess. And bewitched they are: deadly war against Jerusalem rages throughout Europe; natural religion gains ascendancy. Possessing the same characteristics as Vala, to whom she is directly related, "Rahab, like a dismal indefinite hovering Cloud,/ Refus'd to take a definite form"; like Locke's generalized material substance, she stretched out and spread over the whole earth animating "Serpent Temples." Typical of Blake's images, *serpent* encases manifold meanings; it refers at once to the architectural style of druidic temples and the physical shape simulated by Satan; to worship of powers in nature; to intellectual pride; and to art of deception in abstract reasoning. Blake then unfolds these meanings in terms of action [80:56-82:71], giving yet another allegorical description of how Newtonian physics grew into a metaphysics, how Locke gave birth to natural religion and morality, and how these branched into art, making the definite forms of spiritual perception a sin.

To establish and extend their newly-found power, Cambel and Gwendolen must keep their hold on Hand and Hyle, which, as their counterparts, entails interpreting reality and behaving in strict compliance with laws formulated by these mighty sons. Albion's tree and Locke's looms, like Los's furnaces and Cathedron's looms, function as complementary images. Fortified by fruit of Albion's tree and shaded by Vala's cloud, Cambel surreptitiously uses her beauty to delude and adulation to dominate Hand, sending him fiber by fiber across the continent to "weave Jerusalem a Body repugnant to the Lamb," replacing spiritual powers by natural forces. And Gwendolen? Because Locke patterned his system on Newton's principles he unreservedly praised and specifically beamed his epistemology at religion, Blake describes Gwendolen glowingly gazing on Albion's tree to give Hyle a form abstracted out of nature's proliferous fibres. She hides his heart and tongue, the organs for expressing human love and speaking the truth;[7] she removes, deforms, then transplants his

---

[7] For a biblical account concerning the gift of tongues and the uses to which man should put this divine gift, see 1Cor.12,14.

kidneys to his loins, which generate a pernicious substance. Out of it, Gwendolen abstracts fibers to weave "in the thunderous Loom" changes that Locke introduced into philosophy and Reynolds transferred to art, opposing the law of spirit and mercy with the law of abstraction, turning the wine of love into a law of cruelty: figuratively filling the sacred chalice with human groans. Blake caps the performance with an allusion to Locke's mingling Newtonian science with religion and morality, conferring upon this act a glittering visual property: Gwendolen consulted Cambel "as their long beaming light/ Mingled above the Mountain" and imparted an aura of sacredness.

Gwendolen obeys Hyle's moral law of "selfish natural virtue"; she refuses love to the compassionate man but admires the cruel warrior [plate 81]. Moreover, since her long beaming light of particles permeates art as well, she also rejects "in chastity" the "Images" of "Love." By implication and express words her utterances refer to Blake's art, his ornaments of love: his images are not gathered from nature; his forms do not exemplify the purism and generality of abstract science. According to Gwendolen's principles, art that purports to be divinely inspired and runs into sensory particulars of all sorts is promiscuous, fit only for the amusement and revilement of the austere critic. Such impure works are unworthy of respect and should be treated like "Harlots," who are turned out into the streets for entertainment and abuse of the "stern Warrior." *Chastity, Cruelty, Inhumanity* are emblazoned in sparkling gems across Gwendolen's breastplate and plainly inscribed on her beloved's shield.

These ideals derive from Locke's dual substances. He placed material substance solidly in the world; he then relegated immaterial substance to a remote space of unembodied spirits. Plate 81 shows Gwendolen beclouding truth as she points to the difference between natural or earthly and spiritual or heavenly way of life: cruelty and punishment govern human relations on earth; whereas love and forgiveness belong to heaven alone. The plaque below this scene carries Gwendolen's motto: "In Heaven Love begets Love, but Fear is the Parent of Earthly Love,/ And he who will not bend to Love must be subdu'd by Fear."

Since Reynolds constructed his system on Locke's principles, not surprisingly, the action for several more plates centers on Gwendolen. She forewarns Cambel they will perish unless they solidify their

JERUSALEM RESTORED

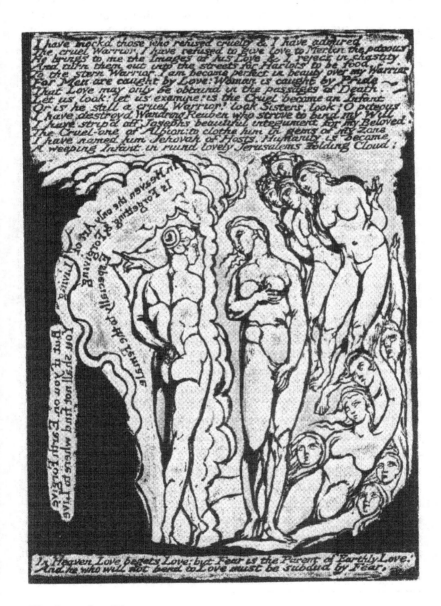

18. *Jerusalem* 81

power. What is the most efficacious way? Make philosophy into a religion: mingle the doctrines of science with Christian theology and control man's spiritual life. This is what Blake, using symbols associated with the Advent, elaborates at plate 82, beginning with Reynolds' Lockean dictate that inspiration not conformable to rules of reason must pass for delusion.[8] Gwendolen informs Cambel she has already laid the foundations:

> Look! I have wrought without delusion. Look! I have wept,
> And given soft milk mingled together with the spirits of flocks
> Of lambs and doves, mingled together in cups and dishes
> Of painted clay; the mighty Hyle is becoming a weeping infant.

Twelve daughters of Albion listen attentively; in response, one partially covers her nakedness (visible on the previous plate)—another reference to reprimanding critics. Gwendolen seizes this opportunity to build a band of faithful followers. Perversely twisting the New Testament's account of Christ's coming and his apostles' ministrations, she utters a series of falsehoods and instructs the daughters of art in their duties. "I heard Enitharmon say to Los: 'Let the Daughters of Albion/ Be scatter'd abroad and let the name of Albion be forgotten./ ... And let the Looms of Enitharmon & the Furnaces of Los/ Create Jerusalem & Babylon'"; therefore, Sisters, let's lead the stems of Albion's Tree to Jerusalem's gate. Go! Preach selfish natural virtues; let "the fury of Man exhaust in War, Woman permanent remain": let the powers of mother nature rule supreme. Locke as a 'son' of Newton imaginatively projected as son of Hand appears as deliverer of the human race: "Look, Hyle is become an infant Love!" Look! we have a natural object of worship; behold the new messiah. On drawing aside her veil, however, she discovers "*Hyle was become a winding Worm & not a weeping Infant*"; the androgynous nature of material substance engenders an earthworm. Gwendolen does not realize she is the Lord's instrument for exposing falsehood. Blake here develops another startling picture of Locke's derogation of revealed religion and Reynolds' denial of divine inspiration to reveal mankind's cheerless end. The elongated worm, illustrated at the right margin, in analogy with the winding sheet represents death and corruption of corporeal bodies.

---

[8] The exposition is given in Pt. Two.

JERUSALEM RESTORED

As Reuben served Los to particularize Locke's restrictions upon the senses, and Gwendolen to display his erroneous concept of man based on Newtonian principles, so Cambel serves to lay bare the determination of others, notably Reynolds in art, to build a system on these same principles. Beneath Albion's tree, Los pumps his bellows, draws Cambel before him, and shows her the fibers with which her beloved framed the system of the world. Cambel fiercely envious of Gwendolen's ingenuity, or more accurately her boldness, is only too eager to emulate her sister's achievements. After many days of consuming labor in Los's furnaces to shape "the mighty form of Hand according to her will," she bears an infant in her "iron arms of love," which like the chain of reasonings binds his soul to earth. Blake then complicates the epic action by adding some rivalry between the two women.[9] Not to be outdone, drawn in by winds running contrary to spiritual powers purposefully created by Los's bellows, Gwendolen begins to shape her offspring "into a form of love," hoping thereby to expunge Jerusalem forever. The infant ascending in a cloud to heaven and the blindfolded man chained to the cloud of unknown substance engraved along the right border of plate 83 caricatures Locke's conversion of Newton's natural causes into universal powers.

Los is grieved by the daughters' afflictions in his furnaces; yet he is encouraged because these events hasten the prophetic day of deliverance. Despite the travail, Los vows not to rest until Albion is awakened; the extremity of Albion's condition justifies Los's suffering and sacrifices. This and much more is contained in his long apostrophe to the nation and to art [plate 83]. Agonizingly he cries out: "O Albion, my brother/ Jerusalem hungers in the desert." Mysterious material forces control not only natural phenomena but also human life and values; abstraction has given Vala and Luvah, nature and humanity, a "Form of Vegetation; .../ O when shall the Lamb of God descend?" The offenders of divine law "listen not to my cry... O Land/ Forsaken!" The situation in art is intolerable:

---

[9] Though Newton was eager for recognition of his contributions to mathematics and physics, I have seen no evidence of competition for fame between himself and Locke, nor between the latter and Reynolds, nor, more pointedly, between Reynolds and Burke, though it is a fact that the latter's contribution to the *Discourses* is not acknowledged by Reynolds (see Pt. Two).

spiritual powers denied; Reynolds' triple edict imposed: study nature, abstract, generalize; the divinely inspired particularizing artist is forced to conceal his perceptions. Los will build a secluded couch for Enitharmon to repose until Jerusalem's restoration. Meantime he dare not own his inspirations or display his particularized creations. Therefore Los asks, "Where hides my child? in Oxford hidest thou with Antamon?/ In graceful hidings of error, in merciful deceit/ ... In chaste appearances" of abstracted qualities?

He then expatiates upon naturalist principles. Blake builds this segment of the narrative [83:33-80] around cardinal points of Reynolds' system. A philosophic thread to guide us through Blake's concatenated images can be found in *Siris*. Berkeley complains that natural philosophers "explain the formation of this world and its phenomena" by simple mechanical laws; they attribute the steady motions of masses in the "mundane system" to universal qualities of bodies; they ascribe the "unfolding" of minute parts in nature to particles; from the hypothesis of universal gravitation they infer inner powers in matter; from its unperceivable qualities they limit the capacity of human senses and then argue "reciprocally" to an unknown material substance from which they "deduce the phenomena"; they satisfy themselves with a "shadowy scene" of reasonings upon appearances and do not penetrate into the true causes of existence.[10]

Appropriately, Los addresses his philosophical remarks to the daughters of Beulah, who walk in the spaces of Erin. Albion's spaces are deformed by false principles, but not for much longer. "Let Cambel and her Sisters sit within the Mundane Shell" of Hand's world; let them form "the fluctuating Globe according to their will." Busily they weave human perceptions into "labyrinthine intricacy" after Hyle's designs, which conceal the real world. These women arbitrarily "fold the World," sometimes assimilating the earth with particulars and sometimes rolling it apart into the abyss of unfathomable space; they "fold and unfold" the earth according to their abstractions, a "shadowy Surface superadded to the real Surface" directly perceived by human spirits, the unchangeable cause of ideas as well as illustrious art. Because this truth is not recognized

---

[10] Berkeley, *Siris*. 232,261,267,228,294.

by Albion's sons and daughters, his art is degraded, his land desolated, his mountains covered with blood of war, and Albion originally marked for greatness is headed for oblivion: "The night falls thick."[11] The watchman of eternity urges Beulah's daughters not to sleep before the furnaces: "Eternal Death stands at the door" of Albion's tomb. Responding to Los's appeal, they swiftly turn their silver and golden spindles, harmoniously weaving the "Web of life," uniting spirit with visible particulars to animate the deadly voids of Entuthon and return the earth to its "Center" of energy, art to its source of creativity, and the nation to its place in eternity. Los directs their myriad labors; his golden sandals and iron mace indicate he is given powers of heaven and earth to accomplish this great task. On seeing the mace, the Spectre submits: forging, shaping, and watching alternately with Los.

Making his rounds, Los hears Albion's daughters wistfully singing of their nation's past glory, bewailing its current pitable state, and yearning for its return to greatness [plate 84]. Like previous laments, this one summarizes the causes and consequences of Albion's downfall: Hand and Hyle have separated themselves and Albion from spirit. Thus he lies in darkness; Jerusalem is in ruins; and Reuben with senses turned downward wanders homeless. The daughters complain they are compelled to build Babylon, worship mysterious powers in nature; they "see London, blind & age-bent, begging thro' the Streets/ Of Babylon, led by a child." Blake here personifies and scrupulously engraves below the text a philosophically oriented natural man, whom Berkeley describes as a soul "depressed by the heaviness of animal nature," unable to perceive the light of truth.[12] Through his choice of imagery, Blake continually builds on the historical events so that the poetic function does not become crushed under philosophical and aesthetic issues. London's sufferings resulting from Albion's naturalist sons recall Gloucester's fate brought about through the instrumentality of his natural son, thus

---

[11] These evocative words (repeated at 84:20) are perhaps a subtle allusion to Lady Macbeth's words preliminary to Duncan's murder, plunging the nation into chaos, darkness and more death (*Macbeth,* I.v.50); or to Gloucester's remark, "Alack, the night comes on," when Lear is turned out by his daughters to content with the cruel forces of nature (*King Lear,* II.iv.303); or, not improbably, to both plays.

[12] Berkeley, *Siris.*340.

adding drama to the tragic sense of Albion's plight. Because London is blinded to its source of power and weighted down by matter, it is near death and in darkness begs for life: in short, this great city suffers spiritual deprivation. The guiding child symbolizes innocence in the New Testament's use: spirit incarnate in the Christ child.[13]

Now Albion's daughters sing Los's song: "The night falls thick." At last they perceive that darkness soon will descend upon the entire earth if Hand's march is not checked; for the first time they express fear of his magnification. The combined sway of Newton's and Locke's philosophy is likened to a powerful natural deity whom Canaanites worshiped with the most inhumane rites: Hand "combines into a Mighty-one, the Double Molech & Chemosh." For the first time these daughters question the soundness of applying principles of physical science to mental phenomena and individual creativity, contriving an inhumane world and demanding both an abstract and imitative art; they are terrified at seeing Hand's armies sweep through nations; even those who never practised humanity "pale at his course." For the first time the daughters call upon Los for help, entreating him to bring light of truth to their dark land and subdue the conquering armies: "O Los come forth..../ Arise upon thy Watches, let us see thy Globe of fire/ On Albion's Rocks & let thy voice be heard upon the Euphrates," where Babylon stands.[14] Their song is a prelude to Los's forthcoming triumph.

Albion's daughters join Los and voluntarily direct their energies towards exposing the false foundations of art. Uniting with Rahab at her "iron Spindle of destruction," they "took the Falsehood which/ Gwendolen hid in her left hand: it grew & grew till it/ Became a Space & an Allegory around the Winding Worm." Specifically, they took the thread of material substance Locke had spun out of matter, drew it out, and showed how first he and then Reynolds wound it around man. The daughters named the space *Canaan* and thus prepared the way for revealing the true source of ideas and artists' inspirations.

Los is elated [plate 85]. It is the first practical sign of victory for Jerusalem's defenders and defeat for her attackers. At this point in

---

[13] Cf. Los's remark, "I have innocence to defend and ignorance to instruct" [46:26].

[14] The Euphrates is linked with the most important events in biblical history; it is first mentioned in Gen.2:14 as the fourth river in Eden.

the narrative Blake again reaches far back into biblical history, connecting it to the principles of his art. Inspired, Los led Reuben into the Canaanite space of the vegetal world to plant there seeds that in process of time will redeem Albion (visible at the bottom of the plate); he "gave a Time & Revolution to the Space, Six Thousand Years" and "call'd it Divine Analogy." As on plate 69 (Part Seven) Blake explains the creative act allegorically and as always draws existences into space-time: "the Feminine/ Emanations Create Space, the Masculine Create Time & plant/ The Seeds of beauty in the Space." The impulse to create emanates from within the artist; the divine power of imagination perceives tangible objects in visionary form, presenting to the poet-artist ideas which he shapes according to his genius and artistic purpose into a work of art. The daughters here function as muses, providing Los with sensuous material for embodying eternity in space-time, a new revelation of spirit necessary to Albion's salvation conveyed by a work of linguistic and visual forms. Thus once more Blake exemplifies his view of the creative process in the very act of creating his system.

Los replies to the inspiring daughters; and the whole world listens. He invokes the eternal spirit to aid him in his formidable enterprise. In joyous anticipation and in contradistinction to the sexual threefold, he envisions Jerusalem's return [plate 86]: "I see thy Form, O lovely mild Jerusalem, Wing'd with Six Wings/ In the opacous [opaque] Bosom of the Sleeper, lovely Three-fold/ In Head & Heart & Reins," intellect, affection and desires, "three Universes of love & beauty" blending together in art. Since spirit is also the source of all existence, Albion's landscape and cities come to life in Los's vision of Jerusalem. Blake describes it in minutiae, as if he were depicting on canvas the radiant qualities of a lovely woman: "Thy bosom white, translucent, cover'd with immortal gems/ A sublime ornament not obscuring the outlines of beauty." Los beholds the New Jerusalem descending bejewelled and in flames of holiness out of heaven bringing life to Albion. Like Israel's watchmen Ezekiel and Isaiah, like John the Evangelist,[15] Albion's watchman experiences a vision of divine glory signalling good tidings for the nation. As he sings the praises of wandering Jerusalem and in the act of creation

---

[15] Cf. Rev.21:1.

moves shudderingly among his furnaces, his children respond. Viewing the nation's inhumanity and Los's suffering, his sons are spurred on in their labors at the flaming furnaces; his daughters are inspired anew in their work at the golden looms; they concenter their energies "in the majestic form of Erin." Even nature stands ready to obey Los.

In the long section that follows [86:49-93:16] explaining why Los labours so furiously for Jerusalem, Blake turns again to autobiography, giving the conflict a personal dimension throughout. The sterility of academical abstract art, the rejection of his spiritually inspired works along with his particularized ideas and the pressures put upon him to comply with Reynolds' principles he here personifies in Enitharmon's separation from Los, her contentions, and the Spectre's mockery, fitting these incidents into the allegorical scheme of the female will (forces of nature), the powerful selfhood (abstract reasoning), and the male-female functions (distinctive characteristics of body and spirit). The necessity of union between male and female for creativity is the dominant motif in these several plates; everywhere *separation* and *division* resound like a death toll: death to man, to art, to nation.

The separation of Enitharmon from Los is portrayed as a parturition of a tremulous "Globe of blood." The artist's life-giving substance, his faculty of creativity, is severed (as in childbirth) from Los; he "fed it with his tears" and for a time successfully hid his Spectre from it. Inevitably, however, exposed to natural forces it became an opaque mass, "a separated cloud of beauty" in darkness; and Los's creative power was blocked: "Even Enitharmon separated outside; & his Loins closed." Her separation, like Jerusalem's, is a consequence of Hand's law, which Blake depicts mythologically at plate 87: in the upper left quarter we see the indefinite form of Tharmas, one of Albion's four zoa, namely body, separated from his emanation Enion; directly below she is shown weeping, driven into Albion's dark deserts, here signifying absence both of life and of particulars as well as ignorance concerning the cause of forms; at the right, forced to take their way in this darkness are Los and Enitharmon "like two infants wand'ring."[16] Blake's graphic

---

[16] Cf. the final lines of *Paradise Lost* describing the removal of Adam and Eve from Paradise: "They hand in hand with wand'ring steps and slow./ Through *Eden*

representation may be amplified by sentiments Berkeley expresses about naturalists wandering after hidden causes; the will of a governing *spirit* constitutes the settled laws of nature, without which mankind must always be at a loss: "a grown man no more know how to manage himself in the affairs of life than an infant."[17] Blake's simile expresses a parallel situation in art brought about by Lockean principles: reversing Reynolds (see Part Three, note 20), Blake contends that Reynolds' rules send the artist wandering after forms; hence, like Reuben, Enitharmon and Los separated from spirit wander.

Cut off from his inspirations and subjected to the entangling roots of Albion's tree, Los is anguished [plate 87]. He pleads with Enitharmon to grasp the fibers shooting around him and draw them out in pity so he may resume his creative life. But she has been won over by the Spectre's reasonings: in "scorn & jealousy" she retorts: "No! I will sieze [seize] thy Fibres & weave/ Them, not as thou wilt, but as I will." Natural philosophy has had its cumulative effect on her. She has joined Albion's daughters in their conceit arising from Vala's elevation to supremacy: "Let Man's delight be Love, but Woman's delight be Pride." Like Albion's daughters also, she has accepted Gwendolen's falsehood as a fact about earthly love: "In Eden our loves were the same; here they are opposite." Henceforth, she will weave Los's perceptions "in Albion's Spectre." Smugly, she tells Los he is "Albion's Victim," helpless: Vala has been set in his path. Reynolds' theory controls.

Los reacts [plate 88]: "I care not! the swing of my Hammer shall measure the starry round," shall include spiritual perception, going beyond Euclidean space and Newton's law. In the lines that immediately follow, undoubtedly directed to critics, Blake touches on another aspect of art, the aesthetic response, interpreting it in accord with his metaphysics. Art cannot be bound to the external machinery of science. Through works of art, in "mutual interchange" men enter

---

took their solitary way." Also the altercation between Los and Enitharmon recalls the strife between Adam and Eve. But the resemblances here as elsewhere are formal (literary) rather than substantial (philosophical): failure to use reason separates Adam and Eve from each other and from Paradise, whereas reasoning is precisely what separates Los from Enitharmon and hence from the spiritual world.

[17] Berkeley, *Principles*.31.

each other's worlds of imagination, those "Universes of delight." In this act of empathy and discovery, viewers experience the exciting forces through which an artist's "Human Four-fold Forms" have originated; they participate in the universal spirit of creativity, the quality that gives works their dynamic and communicative power. When men meet as spiritual beings, there is respect for individual creativity and sympathy between them. But when they encounter each other only as corporeal objects, "they roll apart," discord ensues.

> For Man cannot unite with Man but by their Emanations
> Which stand both Male & Female at the Gates of each Humanity.
> How then can I ever again be united as Man with Man
> While thou, my Emanation, refusest my Fibres of dominion?

Blake is not implying male superiority;[18] within the sphere of art he is marking out the distinction between the Lockean nominal view of "corporeal being" with reason in control and the Berkeleian essential definition stating that we are created spirits, who communicate with "other spirits by means of our own."[19] He is proclaiming inspired or imaginative art; he is opposing Reynolds, who decries spiritual powers, minimizes individual genius, and teaches that art forms are discovered by rules of reason: "We are very sure that the beauty of form, the expression of the passions, the art of composition, even the power of giving a general air of grandeur to a work, is at present very much under the dominion of rules."[20] Blake insists upon full sovereignty; he contends that the individual spirit excites those ideas which an artist's genius effects into a work, and further that invention is under the governance of an artist's own powers. This is what Los tells Enitharmon, who now sympathizes with Reynolds' view. Blake continues to develop along narrational lines the metaphorical description of creativity he introduced at plate 69 and activated in the scene with Albion's daughters: sexual relations convey at once the intimate conjunction of inspiration and invention in the creative act and the depth of Blake's personal involvement in his resistance to Reynolds' theory. The issue between Los and Enitharmon concerns power of the artist, not power of the sexes.

---

[18] See Pt. Five, n.15.
[19] Locke, III.vi.4 and Berkeley, *Principles*.140.
[20] Reynolds, Disc. Six, p.88.

As a disciple of Vala, Enitharmon rebuffs Los. She vows to build on the emanations of Coban, Hand and Hyle a "triple Female Tabernacle," making even God obey nature, actually making natural power into a god.[21] But in sending the "fibres of Los," the very nerves of his being, to Albion's daughters for weaving on their loom, she unknowingly acts contrary to her own purposes; she is in fact contributing to the exposition of falsity and revelation of truth because the "lovely Allegoric Night of Albion's Daughters" extends through "all the World of Erin & of Los & all their Children": through the world of Blake's poem.

Contentions between Los and Enitharmon gratify the Spectre, "author of their division"; abstract reasoning has come between the artist's inspirations and his works, labeling them immoral, licentious, unscientific. Diabolically, the Spectre anticipates complete success in subjugating Los to corporeal powers:

...I will make their places of joy & love excrementitious,
Continually building, continually destroying in Family feuds.
While you are under the dominion of a jealous Female,
Unpermanent for ever because of love & jealousy,
You shall want all the Minute Particulars of Life.

Blake applies to naturalist art the term *excrementitious,* an adjective Berkeley uses in describing processes of vegetable bodies (*Siris*.33); he compares abstracting qualities from perceived particulars to breathing out waste matter in the vegetative world. Under naturalist doctrines the artist is forbidden to particularize his spiritual perceptions, forbidden to express the eternal emanation of richly varied creations that are a pleasure to behold. The spiteful scene is another criticism of Reynolds, who conceives of the artist as continually breaking down particularized qualities in nature to build abstract forms, a system critics cherish and guard with fierce jealousy, thereby destroying the Divine Vision. Blake emblematically impresses the deplorable situation at plate 72.

---

[21] Although Bacon held that science and religion travel the same road through nature, and although Newton explained the world's motions by universal qualities in bodies, there is no implication here that either one joined religious beliefs to the "natural way of knowledge," as did Locke.

The division between Los and Enitharmon is great and deep. Los will not submit. Patiently but boldly in his workshop, with "brazen Compasses" he fixes, measures and divides the spaces (as does Blake for the visual and verbal forms of this poem), hammering out his perceptions against the perishable, against the indefinite, and therewith against the critics' cruelties, which they perform with ritualistic holiness, to bring Urizen's world under the law of Love, which dispenses mercy and forgiveness. Nonetheless, under Vala's influence, Enitharmon begins weaving Jerusalem a body out of deadly fibres. As the climactic redemption approaches, the conflict between opposing forces heightens. In a striking move, Jerusalem wrests from Vala's hand "the Cup which foam'd," indicative of the ferment flowing from the prolific womb of abstract reasoning.

It has spawned an "indefinite Hermaphroditic form," a duplicitous harlot in religion and art, hence "double Hermaphroditic" [plate 89]. This gigantic image of "Selfhood," which covers "the eastern heaven" of the eternal spirit, is now made visible as "a Human Dragon terrible." The beast embodies features of naturalist doctrines; but, as usual, Blake enriches his presentation with literary allusions and parallels from biblical and secular history, citing nations that worshiped natural powers. The dragon's head, made up of impenetrable particles, is "dark, deadly"; its brain "incloses a reflexion/ Of Eden all perverted," decreeing that external powers rule over man and destroy his freedom. Naturalists' perversions result from their confused, "many tongued" theories of reality; they disorganize the organically structured visible world and represent this living system by lifeless abstractions. The dragon's bosom reflects "Moab & Ammon," gross idolaters of nature. Jerusalem is hid far "within the Covering Cherub." The many eyes in its black wings keeps Albion's people subservient to the "Generalizing Gods," Coban, Hand and Hyle. The dragon's loins "inclose Babylon" in intimate relation with Vala. Altogether, the dragon represents "the World of Generation & Death," another concrete equivalent for Reynolds' system. Its "devouring Stomach" is like a tabernacle finely crafted on principles of natural philosophy. Within thrives a "Double Female," Tirzah and Rahab (in action along the right border), cruelty in holiness: "a Dragon red & hidden Harlot/ Each within other":[22] Reynolds' system

---

[22] An obvious allusion to Rev.17 adapted to repressions in art.

made into a religion by critics who judge and mete out punishment by his scientific laws. Atop the mountain from which the law is given sits mighty Hand.

Plate 90 describes how Albion's "warlike sons" carry this law into art and supplement the work of his twelve daughters described at plate 67. "The Feminine separates from the Masculine & both from Man" while the sons "circumscribe his Brain," his "Heart" and "Loins," covering them with a "Veil" of fibrous roots and "Net" of abstraction to constrict his ideas, his desires and creative powers. Blake then refers back to plate 1: "the Sublime is shut out from the Pathos"; there is no compassion for the spiritual.

The details. On Hand's mountain, Albion's twelve sons cut the fibres that sustain the land, absorbing unto themselves "the Life & eternal Form of Luvah" manifested in spiritual art. They turn living thought "into Bones of chalk & Rock." Hand cut apart the enlivening human fibers from the visible mass and abstracted from the hard rock of reason a world of self-contained forces in bodies. Upon these foundations his disciples constructed a system of knowledge separating existence from perception and a system of art separating male from female, resulting in deadly consequences because "the Male is a Furnace of beryll, the Female is a golden Loom." These metaphors conjoined with spiritual perception convey the fire of imagination (for beryll has a transparent fiery brilliance) and the artist's genius, his execution, which gives art form to his inspiration. Again through figurative language Blake counters Reynolds, who regards divine inspiration and native genius as "prejudices" and "errors."[23]

As elsewhere, Blake emphasizes the centrality of Newton's law and Locke's material substance in Reynolds' system occasioning the present conflict between abstract reasoning and human imagination. Hence, "in the Spirit of Prophecy." analogous to John's prophetic narrative symbolized by the far-sighted eagle, Los exclaims: "No individual ought to appropriate to Himself/ Or to his Emanation any of the Universal Characteristics." Perceived particulars are the only universal characteristics. Hand and Hyle have become like Gods: Hand orders the universe by his law; Hyle makes the son of man a product of Vala, a "Vegetated Christ & a Virgin Eve," another

---

[23] Reynolds, Disc. Six, p.85.

variation on worship of nature's powers and denial of an active spiritual agent, another aberration of naturalists. These blasphemous hermaphroditic products of abstract reasoning must be overcome lest man be engulfed completely by a dark and destructive world of material forces. Alluding to Reynolds' fundamental principle, the poet tells us Albion's sons seek to "Vegetate the Divine Vision/ In a corporeal & ever dying Vegetation & Corruption." Impugning the reality of spiritual power, "they become One Great Satan," for they seek to pervert mankind and consign it to eternal death.

While Hand and Hyle pass all objects through the mill of abstract reasoning, condensing spiritual perception into rocks of generalized shapes to erect a temple to Vala, Los exposes its unsound foundations so that humanity may not be wiped out. Pounding away at the undifferentiated forms, he muses upon naturalist systems: if one removes spirit from existence, he worships natural powers and natural law; lacking humanity, he cruelly enforces these, ironically compelling his victims to turn to a merciful god: "These are the Demonstrations of Los." This pronouncement parallels Berkeley's contention that his philosophical arguments, both empirical and logical, against material substance are "equal to demonstration," Locke's criterion of truth.[24] Blake makes a similar claim for his aesthetic argument and Los's exertions against Reynolds' scientific discourses on art.

The sublime character of Los's demonstrations is now apparent; his thunderous and highly burdened "Words" are earthshaking. They terrify Albion's sons and presage a resolution of the conflict: the apocalypse draws near. Los becomes more assertive [plate 91]. He sends an envoy to his enemies charging them with pretended holiness and orders them to obey their humanities. His message plainly reflects cruelty of attacks upon Blake's art and reiterates his principles. In denying an artist's native powers, Reynolds and his followers "are murderers" of God because "Genius" is an individual's spirit; conversely, the source of creativity is the eternal spirit: "there is no other/ God than that God who is the intellectual fountain of Humanity." Los commands his Spectre to deliver this categorical imperative: "Go, to these Fiends of Righteousness,/ ...tell them this, & overthrow" their rituals grounded on abstractions. Blake here associates

---

[24] Berkeley, *Principles*. 96.

disciples of Reynolds with Deists and implicitly compares them to fanatical Pharisees, who based their religion and morality on strict observance of rules. Worship of God is not conformity to rules nor to abstract laws. These, like all abstractions, are "Disorganized" contrivances having no real existence; the extravagantly venerated Spectre is like a cruel pagan deity, a "brooder of tempests & destructive War." As sublime art resides in "Minute Particulars, Organized," so virtue consists in acts of "benevolence": both are concretions of spirit.

Los's communique is a scathing criticism of Reynolds' governing principle, baldly stated in Discourse Four:

> perfect form is produced by leaving out particularities, and retaining only general ideas; ... this principle, which I have proved to be metaphysically just, extends itself to every part of the Art;... there is but one presiding principle which regulates, and gives stability to every art. The works, whether of poets, painters, moralists, or historians, which are built upon general nature, live for ever (page 55, 68).

The above passages are additional instances showing how closely the *Discourses* adhere to Locke's *Essay*. Reynolds restates the theory of general ideas and its justification put forth by Locke primarily to "break in upon the sanctuary of vanity and ignorance" of those who claimed direct perception of divine truth.[25] All knowledge, divine as well as secular, is about general ideas, which "the mind makes... from particular objects" by abstracting their separate qualities; truth consists in "reasoning" about abstract ideas: "it is called demonstration." Such truths "are eternal."

Part Two of the present study explains why on empirical grounds all this is disclaimed by Berkeley. In brief, he holds "that the qualities or modes of things do never really exist each of them apart by itself."[26] A particular "becomes general by being made to represent or stand for all other particular ideas of the same sort." Since every general idea taken absolutely is a particular, knowledge is about

---

[25] Locke, Epistle, p.14; II.xi.9; IV.ii.2-3; IV.iii.31. For an exposition of his system, refer to Pt. Two.

[26] Berkeley, *Principles,* Introd.7,12; his theory of general ideas is set forth in Pt. Six in connection with *J* 43:19,53-54.

existent things. This is Blake's view of forms in art, made explicit in Los's rebuke to Albion's sons, who would have a demonstrative science of art by compounding a large number of abstract qualities from existent objects into general forms with moral connotations:

> You accumulate Particulars & murder by analyzing, that you
> May take the aggregate, & you call the aggregate Moral Law,
> And you call that swell'd & bloated Form a Minute Particular;
> But General Forms have their vitality in Particulars.

Reynolds calls particularities of every kind *defects* and consistently refers to general ideas as expressions of "perfect form" and "real simplicity of nature."[27] The Newtonian rule of simplicity adopted by Locke is repeatedly invoked by Reynolds (for example, see Discourse Four). In his opinion art must keep pace with science: it is "the application of science, which alone gives dignity and compass to any art"; hence, the most respected arts "are not addressed to the gross senses"; rather, they embody "what never existed."[28] When an artist "has reduced the variety of nature to the abstract idea," he has attained a "distinct idea of beauty and symmetry."[29] According to Blake, however, Reynolds' system advances science, not art; delighting in the rich variety of existents, he firmly believes that beauty of art resides in particulars; he regards abstract ideas as turgid and swollen constructions reflecting inflated reasonings, not the living forms of unmediated perceptions. So Los adamantly states: "every/ Particular is a Man, a Divine Member," because every object has its existence in the mind of a spiritual being.

But Albion's sons ignore Los's demand to put on spirit; they yield not. While the Spectre keeps on building in the grand style of abstract designs, Los "reads the Stars" foretelling the Spectre's ruin. With one stroke of his mighty hammer he brings down the stupendous works of abstraction, demolishing the amorphous forms; then with many blows on his anvil he removes the covers from the Spectre's eyes and unbinds his ears. Earlier, Los binds Reuben's senses [plate 36, Part Six] to expose the principle of abstraction; now, with the apocalypse imminent, he opens up the senses by attacking the source

---

[27] Reynolds, Disc. Three, pp.49-50.
[28] Reynolds, Disc. Thirteen, p.203,214.
[29] Reynolds, Disc. Three, p.48.

of their closure. Blow after blow he alters the Spectre's senses and "every Ratio of his Reason," the mathematical method Newton used to formulate his general law and Reynolds applies to the "proportions" of his general figures.[30] To preserve the distinct beauty of particularized qualities, Los repeatedly smites the Spectre until he overcomes him.

This action signals a visible turning point in the war. Los beholds Albion's tribes amalgamate "into one Nation, the English," foretokening his resurrection, the end of warfare, and a state of concord [plate 92]. As Los's labors near completion, we hear Enitharmon's complaint, a reminder that inventions in a work of art are determined by its creator for a particular purpose: "The Poet's Song draws to its period, & Enitharmon is no more." Except for the philosophical summary on plate 98, visual language preponderates in the concluding plates. The design on 92 fittingly in the background bares the outlines of a druidic temple on the left and the city of Jerusalem on the right, adumbrating the Spectre's annihilation and Jerusalem's restoration; in the forefront Enitharmon disconsolate sits upon the ground amidst the fallen mighty warrior Urizen and Albion's three giant sons. But it is not a sad farewell we bid her. As Los's "vegetated wife," Enitharmon necessarily will be nullified along with corporeal generation; as spirit, however, she persists. So Los explains: "Sexes must vanish & cease/ To be when Albion arises from his dread repose." Then an artist's inspiration, his work and his audience will be spiritually united; then cruelties resulting from laws ruthlessly imposed with moral fervor upon an artist will exist "only in the Outward Spheres of Visionary Space and Time," in a work of art that captures these events, and in the "shadows of Possibility," no longer in actuality.

Though Reynolds, it will be recalled, labels visionary art misty and falsely magnified (Part Two), Blake points to its immensurable value and didactic function: *Jerusalem* will serve to inform future generations what can happen when man denies spiritual perception. In a kind of epilogue, we hear Los tell Enitharmon that through vision and prophecy "we may Foresee & Avoid" the errors and terrors displayed "in the Emanative Visions of Canaan" and "in the Chaos of the Spectre" that now besiege mankind and now visible "in

---

[30] *Ibid.*

Length, Bredth & Highth." The human spirit has in past, from the Canaanites to the Druids, triumphed over worshipers of idols; it must and shall again prevail.

Figures at the top of the next plate remind us that false charges were brought against Socrates and Jesus, divinely inspired men accused of publicizing ideas that threatened the religious, moral and political status quo. By implication Blake includes himself in this category, represented in the work and sufferings of Los. Vegetated Enitharmon wishes to perpetuate her present authoritative position and force him to obey current doctrines. In self-pity she appeals to his sons Rintrah and Palamabron. But Los, invested with divine power and obliged to vindicate the imagination addresses his sons, provoking them to join him in vigorous action:

> Fear not, my Sons, this Waking Death; he is become One with me.
> Behold him here! We shall not Die! we shall be united in Jesus.
> Will you suffer this Satan, this Body of Doubt that Seems but Is Not,
> To occupy the very threshold of Eternal Life? if Bacon, Newton, Locke
> Deny a Conscience in Man & the Communion of Saints & Angels,
> Contemning the Divine Vision & Fruition, Worshiping the Deus
> Of the Heathen, The God of This World, & the Goddess Nature,
> Mystery, Babylon the Great, The Druid Dragon & hidden Harlot,
> Is it not that Signal of the Morning which was told us in the Beginning? [93:18-26]

Blake casts this strong reproof against Reynolds' system into apocalyptic language commensurate with a redemptive act. The implied answer to Los's last question, therefore, is *yes*.

The bird of heaven unfolds its powerful, wide wings and fights for the sons of spirit, vanquishing Albion's three giant sons, who have assumed universality unto themselves. At the top of plate 94 we see the three-headed indefinite human form of Coban, Hand and Hyle toppled to the ground. "Albion cold" still lies on his rock; howling winds and raging seas of nature beat against him; "weeds of Death inwrap" his body. Below, we see him totally bound to England's rocky shore, Britannia underneath him, and upon his bosom the "Female Shadow" of England tempest tossed, threatening the nation with extinction. Eternal death seems certain. But over them is Los furiously laboring at his furnaces, indicated by brilliant flames from his globe of fire visible on the horizon. And "sitting at the Tomb" is Erin watching night and day to protect Albion from destructive forces set in motion by his militant sons. Since Berkeley was the most penetrating philosophical critic of abstraction and most tenacious defender of the soul, holding it to be "incorporeal," not liable to dissolution by physical forces (*Siris*.171), it is not surprising that Blake nominates Erin to guard the "immortal Tomb" waiting for Albion to shed the "wormy Garments" of corporeal substance with which naturalists have clothed him. Into this tense scene Blake injects irony: Albion attacked Erin; now Erin watches over Albion that he may not be destroyed by his own forces.

Suddenly, "Time was Finished!"[31] Not that time is abolished; not that the world is ended; rather, the time anticipated by Los [7:54-56] to perform a series of acts to awaken the nation has arrived. Erin's watch is over; Los's work is done: the divine plan is fulfilled. Britannia awakens "from Death on Albion's bosom," symbolic of pity; seven times she faints but in strength rises up again.[32] Penitently, she confesses that in "Dreams of Chastity & Moral Law" she slew Albion. Here as elsewhere in the poem, dreams carry Berkeley's philosophical meaning: naturalists "dream, as it were," when they think abstract ideas of material substance explain experience (*Siris*.318); there is no intermediate cause between man's active spirit and his ideas. Conversely, art forms are the artist's direct perceptions, particularized; through abstraction Britannia killed Albion. Present at her murderous act were adversaries of spiritual power, the enemies of human life and individual creativity: the famished eagle (bird of prey); the wolf (killer of lambs, of innocence); the monkey (mimic animal); the owl (bird of night); the king (autocratic ruler); and the priest (mediatory agent between God and man). These attendants represent death, cruelty, imitation in art, intellectual blindness, political tyr-

---

[31] This statement should discourage critics from arguing a non-narrative work (Pt. Three, n.1); *time* means *before* and *after*, an interval between events, between Albion's sleep and awakening.

[32] Cf. Proverb 24.10,16.

anny, and authoritarianism, undoubtedly a reference to critics who carried out with a religious zeal Reynolds' principles as if they were sacred rites, and perhaps a reference to Reynolds himself, natural philosophy's high priest in art. In druidic fashion through art Britannia with an abstracting knife had sacrificed Albion to the powers of nature.

"Albion mov'd/ Upon the Rock, he open'd his eyelids in pain, in pain he mov'd/ His stony members," [plate 95]. Blake dramatically conveys the extraordinary effort Albion must exert to rise from the abysmal darkness of nothingness into the region of light. In this third attempt, he succeeds in shaking off sleep and intrepidly springing upwards, boldly set above the text and sharing equal space with it. He beholds the way to eternal life: "into the Heavens he walked, clothed in flames,/ Loud thund'ring... & pillars/ Of fire, speaking the Words of Eternity in Human Forms," the immortal words of the poet. Thus awakened, Albion unreluctantly takes his wide bow and arrows of flaming gold, symbolizing divine power; he lets fly the long-winged arrows of thought through space from heaven to earth, compelling his four zoa to resume their peaceful and productive functions, but not without recognizing Los's unwearied labours. Despite allurements, despite cruelties, Los did not abandon Albion during the long and difficult ordeal. Therefore the sons of spirit praise Los: "he kept the Divine Vision in time of trouble"; he did not succumb to naturalist art.

Lamentations give way to communal celebration [plate 96]. The commonwealth rejoices at Albion's awakening from his heavy sleep of death. "Then Jesus appeared standing by Albion"; and "Albion knew that it/ Was the Lord, the Universal Humanity, & Albion saw his Form/ A Man..../ And the Divine Appearance was the likeness & similitude of Los." In this vision Albion perceives the causal connection between the eternal spirit and humanity, between eternal life and art: humanity and art have a common source. Previously Blake has emphasized Los's qualities as a divinely inspired artist; now he fills out the ideal character: Los is Albion's friend and redeemer, a type of Christ. Blake thus demonstrates the poem's introductory statement that the fate of the human race and of nations depends on the arts. Blake's hero, it should be remembered, is not a supernatural agent, not a god remote from man; he does not appear upon a cloud or chariot of fire; instead, as a son of man, he is, like all men, a spiritual being free to exercise his uniquely human gift. The persona of the artist coincides with his identity as man.

Jesus' appearance makes explicit Blake's belief that we know God as spirit incarnate in human form; he is not an abstract idea, not something unknown. The Lord converses with Albion "as Man with Man" and confirms the causal and ethical principle Erin and Los defend, namely the law of Love and forgiveness of sin in "Friendship & Brotherhood": sacrifice through an act of love. Again, one cannot fail to see the background of humiliation Blake bore from malicious critics. Jesus, the exemplar of love explains that the relation between God and man is reciprocal: "For Man is Love/ As God is Love"; as God eternally gives himself to man, so man in kindness gives himself to another. Morality is an act that involves giving up of self in "the Divine Image." This is what Los has done for Albion. The clearly defined image of Britannia in the Lord's embrace demonstrates divine mercy, without which neither man nor nation can exist. Love in its metaphysical import is the source of humanity in all its dimensions, great and small. Upon revelation of this divine truth, Albion recognizes that matter regarded as the universal power and abstract ideas as reality are a "Dream," an illusion; he throws himself into the furnaces of affliction. Simultaneously, his land, cities, sons and daughters spring into life. Regenerated, Albion stands "Fourfold among the Visions of God."

Plate 97 opens a great and eventful scene stretching to the end of the epic. Having shaken off "that slumber" and recovered "the lost region of light" (Berkeley's phrases, *Siris.*314), Albion promptly restores his source of creativity to secure a place in eternity. He rouses exiled Jerusalem, who lay reposing among the spaces of Erin while Albion himself had lain dead among the roots of his fatal tree.

> Awake, Awake, Jerusalem! O lovely Emanation of Albion,
> Awake and overspread all Nations as in Ancient Time:
> For lo! the Night of Death is past and the Eternal Day
> Appears upon our Hills. Awake, Jerusalem, and come away!

This climactic moment is in full view: surrounded by radiating light of eternity, Albion with Los's globe of fire in hand fearlessly strides along the white cliffs, looks out into profound darkness where his giant sons have cast Jerusalem, and summons her return.

IMAGINATION UNBOUND

19. *Jerusalem* 97

After restoring his emanation, Albion gathers his full strength, then reaches "into Infinitude" for the universal bow. The lines that follow evoke a charming picture of him and his zoa shooting spiritual arrows of love, bringing heaven, literally the divine principle and hence life, to his people. But Blake's detailed symbolism of spiritual causality in relation to art is extremely complex. Albion's "breathing" bow is fourfold and, like the apocalyptic animals of Golgonooza's north gate facing Beulah and Eden, is of gold, silver, brass and iron. We are told further that his bow is "Male & Female," contraries with no separation between them: no separation between body and spirit, between the artist's forms and his imagination. The vision is fourfold because Albion's zoa (Tharmas, Urthona, Urizen and Luvah), taking on qualities of the living creatures that have their course upon earth, lay their hands on the bow, thereby acknowledging that generation, man, reason and affection have their being in spirit. The arrows are "of Love" propelled by spiritual power; and the quiver are "the Children" created by the artist. In sum, spirit both sustains life and inspires the artist. The bow symbolizes a new covenant of mercy, peace and creativity. The corporeal war of cruelty and death has turned into a war of love and life.

Into heaven's wide and horned bow the four eternal zoa, embodied in the Gospel, carefully fit "Arrows of Intellect"; they draw the vibrant "unreprovable String" and send the poet's "flaming Arrow fourfold" into dark Ulro, annihilating the "Druid Spectre" [plate 98]: Blake's epic way of saying spirit is the unrefutable principle of energy and all things exist in the imagination. The combined forces of these living creatures implemented by Los loosen the chain binding the imagination to the hard rock of reason. Concurrently, "innumerable Chariots of the Almighty appear'd in Heaven,/ And Bacon & Newton & Locke & Milton & Shakespear & Chaucer,/ ... & each Chariot was Sexual Threefold," manifesting the Baconian three states of nature as well as the three natural philosophies (see page 90, note 22). "And every man stood Fourfold." The galactic display signifies victory for imagination and its particularized forms; Albion's three natural philosophers acknowledge the efficacy of human spirit to perceive realities; they join the company of his three great poets whose detailed descriptions of human nature live forever; Coban, Hand and Hyle lay aside their iron arrows, and correspondingly critics their killing barbs. In accord with a merciful god, the Almighty does not inflict punishment. The judgment is *forgiveness*.

Upon cessation of hostilities and inauguration of peace the highest strains of the poet's song are heard as the system of Los, whose actions have been progressively directed towards this objective, is revealed. Each man stands on earth fourfold facing four directions: humanity (west), harmony (south), generation (north), and eternity (east), all upheld by spiritual power. The "Horses," the carriers of this knowledge, are the four chapters of *Jerusalem,* whose author, like the four evangelists, was inspired by the divine body. Similarly inspired, Los reunites man to this sublime cause. Immediately, "the dim Chaos" of abstraction brightens and the world assumes a clear order of particularized qualities because "the Human Nerves of Sensation" are the source of experience, and the actual world consists "in the Outline, the Circumference & Form" of perceivable objects. As a first principle, imagination awakens man to his visible world and eternal life. Through his exertions Los has removed the covers abstract reasoning placed upon objects of experience and has created a system causally uniting imagination to perception, "revealing the lineaments of Man" because in imagination man finds himself reflected. The new system of art concomitantly opens the senses to forms of eternity. There is an implied parallel here between Los's accomplishments and Christ's miracles: expanding the nostrils, opening the eyes, freeing the ear and tongue is comparable to raising the dead, healing the blind, and curing the deaf and dumb.

The fact of man's fourfold nature is confirmed by the four living creatures, who appear at earth's "Four Cardinal Points." These conveyors of "Humanity Divine" manifest themselves in the four parts of *Jerusalem,* conversing "together in Visionary forms dramatic" and "in Visions": epical and prophetic events communicated in object language of sound and sight consonant with "the wonders Divine/ Of Human Imagination." This creative power has ranged "through all the Three Regions immense/ Of Childhood, Manhood & Old Age," all the circumstances of a false system of art, specifying its origin, maturity and death, varying the forms to accord with "the subject of discourse; & every Word & Every Character/ Was Human," a particularized perception of the human imagination.

It has been a commonplace of Blake criticism to regard *visionary* in its general meaning as utopian or relating to non-existent things, such as supernatural and imaginary phenomena. In Blake's system, however, visionary forms are not fictitious ideas, nor individual distortions of reality as Reynolds held. Rather, as visible objects, the universal language of humanity, visions of the imagination are forms of reality, sensuous images having an existential content (see page 124). Blake not only philosophically justifies this concept of language but also aesthetically demonstrates it. He thus concretely reinstates divine inspiration and visionary forms, which Reynolds brought down from heaven and submerged in abstractions from nature. As Locke censured divine revelation and insisted on rules of reason in knowledge, so in art Reynolds chained the artist to earth and fettered genius to rules established by science. These limits placed upon experience and knowledge in Locke's philosophy set too small a measure for Berkeley's comprehensiveness of mind, so in Reynolds' system they fixed too narrow a compass for Blake's far-reaching visions. Los liberates the artist by unbinding "Imagination, the real & eternal World" [77:prose], thereby validating particular ideas as forms of beauty and visionary art as the perfection of human nature. This is the *good news*[33] according to Blake.

He casts the restoration of Jerusalem and the fall of Ulro into an *ubi sunt* lyrical form composed around the philosophical tree. The system of art constructed on natural powers and abstract reasoning has produced the dessicated "Fruit of Albion's Poverty Tree." Upon revelation of the true principles, the City of Golgonooza and the whole earth resound with the cry of living creatures rejoicing to see natural art, natural religion, natural morality, and warrior values of the Trojans (from whom Britons claimed descent), cruelty, and eternal death deprived of their grand support. By implication, the exultant shout is in praise of perceived particulars, revelation, forgiveness of sin, peace, love and eternal life issuing from imagination. Inspired by this divine power, the poet-artist has exposed in particularized forms the disastrous consequences resulting from abstract reasoning, annihilated its Druid Spectre, and supplanted the moralizing critics' "Tree of Good and Evil" with the Tree of Life, for "Art is the Tree of Life."[34]

Berkeley conceived of his philosophical criticism and system of knowledge in similar imagery. He undertook the "deliverance" of mankind from the deception of abstract ideas. After he dissolved the

---

[33] *Gospel* means *good news*.
[34] Blake, The Laocoon, p.777.

erroneous connection between abstract ideas and actual things, he drew "the curtain of words, to behold the fairest tree of knowledge; whose fruit is excellent and within reach of our hand."[35] This tree springs from a universal spirit, which "keeps up the perpetual round of generations and corruptions, pregnant with forms which it constantly sends forth and resorbs" in "an eternal necessary emanation" producing in succession visible, knowable objects perceived by the human mind or spirit. In early life Berkeley discerned this to be the principle of existence and constructed his system upon it; in age, after long poring on it, he ended his philosophical reflections with a confirmation of it.

Blake assumed in all his art that perception is an act of the human spirit, which he alternatively calls *imagination,* and forms embodied in art are the source of immortality. The bard voices this truth in the concluding notes of his song [plate 99]. As Erin has supported Los in the construction of his system, Berkeley has philosophically accompanied Blake to the end of his heroic fourfold argument:

> All Human Forms identified, even Tree, Metal, Earth & Stone: all Human Forms identified, living, going forth & returning wearied Into the Planetary lives of Years, Months, Days & Hours;
> reposing,
> And then Awaking into his Bosom in the Life of Immortality.

The five-line pendant recapitulates the principles of the new system: all things, even natural phenomena, are effects of spirit, eternally creating, sustaining, and perfecting in perpetual cycle the whole system of generated beings and visible forms perceived and known by the imagination. Identity connects the immediate perceptions of visible objects by the senses or imagination and the particularized qualities of art. Albion's continued existence depends on admitting the efficacy of imagination. Below the text, paralleling the legend of the Lord delivering Adam's spirit from the nether world, Blake allegorically represents the recovery of Albion's spirit from the Spectre's demonic world. Amidst consuming flames of Ulro, Jehovah and

---

[35] Berkeley, *Principles*. Introd.23-24; *Siris*.152,362 (he presents a similar theory of generation in §344).

JERUSALEM RESTORED

20. *Jerusalem* 99

Jerusalem with outstretched arms of love are shown in total embrace, commingling from head to toe, reuniting body and spirit, art and imagination. In this perfect image of divine love, Blake executes a final thrust at Reynolds' obligatory concealment of the body and at misguided critics' imperatives of decency (Part Two).

The last plate brings into full view Blake's new machinery, epitomizing his theory of art and the artist's social function. Bacon provided a new logic in his tables of abstract substances for interpreting nature; Newton abstracted qualities from physical objects to frame mathematically the system of the world; Locke instituted abstract reasoning along with agreement and disagreement of simple ideas for determining truth; Reynolds fixed this apparatus as the means for attaining perfect art form; Berkeley introduced the active human spirit for perceiving the world; Blake demonstrates that imagination is that creative spiritual power and its visions are the socially responsible artist's work. The redeemer comes through a new medium. At the center and in the foreground on Mount Golgonooza is Los pictured as a youth in bare and naked form, symbolizing vigorous creativity of the inspired artist, fitted with appropriate attributes: a divine smith who shapes the stubborn structure of reality in the language of vision, in sensuous particulars fixing error and disclosing truth.[36] On the left is Albion moving upwards, stepping over a druidic temple, and ascending into the region of light and immortality; the sun he shoulders symbolizes the luminous energy of the imagination diffusing its radiant light over the darkness that has enveloped the nation. At the right stands liberated Jerusalem, drawing out milky fibers from the upper region, passing them through the moony spaces of Beulah to indicate divine inspiration through unity of heaven and earth, and sending the fibers of love into the rocky circles of druidic worship revived by naturalists. Through his extraordinary labors, the visionary artist has overcome the satanic Spectre, awakened Albion, and restored Jerusalem, the Emanation of the Giant Albion.

---

[36] Blake's epic machinery differs not only from Homer's *Iliad* and Milton's *Paradise Lost* but also from the enchanted armors, giants, marvelous gardens, wizards, magic rings, titanic duels, etc., of Tasso's *Jerusaleme Liberata*.

JERUSALEM RESTORED

21. *Jerusalem* 100

PART NINE

EPILOGUE

The foregoing critical narrative analyzing Blake's annotations to Reynolds' *Discourses* and *Jerusalem's* component parts conspicuously discloses striking similarities to Berkeley's criticisms of natural philosophy, to the principles of his system, and to his defense of it, throwing light on the philosophical meaning and internal structure of Blake's convoluted poem. Materials synthetically displaying these similarities come primarily from *Siris* and supplementally from the *Principles* along with some of Berkeley's other works. The extensive parallels strongly suggest that besides *Siris* Blake may have owned other of Berkeley's works, now lost. If Blake's copy of *Siris* were not extant, we would have no proof in the sense of historical evidence that he even read this work, let alone annotated it. However that may be, pointing to sources is not identical to explicating a poem. Even if some day other of Berkeley's writings annotated by Blake or a document indicating he consulted copies of these, in Hayley's library for instance, were discovered, the argument here would not be strengthened because it stands, as any interpretation must, on facts of the poem. In composing *Jerusalem* whether or not Blake used Berkeley as a quarry, the philosophical similarities are there, though the poetic inspiration, literary form and tone are entirely Blake's own. The same cannot be said of Reynolds' *Discourses,* which have a genetic affinity to Locke's *Essay,* closely connected to it, as has been shown, not only in principles but also in form and diction. By contrast, whereas Berkeley relies chiefly on discourse, speculation and dialogue to disseminate his ideas, Blake conveys his ideas through epic and illustrations. Still, *Jerusalem* is not merely an illustrated poem expressing opposed philosophies. Through the creative processes of his imagination Blake unites select philosophical points and related imagery to his own purposes, varying the points according to his subject of art, to his perceptions, to his experiences as artist, and to epical demands.

Reynolds' system founded on Locke's popular doctrine of nature and abstract reasoning was exerting a powerful control over art. Reynolds rejected inspiration and replaced genius with rules fixed by science, defining art as invention dependent upon gathering and putting together simple impressions from observation into abstract ideas analogous to the simplicity of nature's forms. These rules, enunciated by him at the influential Royal Academy, embodied in his *Discourses,* venerated and uniformly carried out by most critics, were inimical to Blake. Though Reynolds saw his rules as artist's guides to eminence and as avenues to the advancement of art, Blake saw them as obstacles to both artist and art; he saw that the exigencies of science are not those of art; what is fruitful for science is not necessarily fruitful for art. Though physicists aim for the simplicity of an ultimate unified theory based on natural forces, Blake insisted art is an individual free expression of the imagination, which cannot be legislated.[1] The artist is slave neither to nature nor to another's system; he is his own master. It seemed to Blake that Reynolds did not think sufficiently into the depth of the creative process; he disagreed with Reynolds on both metaphysical and methodological grounds. Blake believed the human imagination is both a revelatory and a creative faculty. Moreover, he held that excellence in art depends on an individual's genius to particularize his visions, not on any abstraction of external objects. He stoutly resisted the current of natural philosophy, which had overflown into art. Predictably, the public, with minor exceptions, enamoured of Reynolds' scientific system not only rejected but ridiculed Blake's non-conforming art.

Out of this conflict Blake created a critical philosophical narrative opposing Reynolds' system. He put his criticism of it into deep perspective through biblical and druidic parallels, expanding the

---

[1] Cf. Samuel Taylor Coleridge's great dictum: "Could a rule be given from without, poetry would cease to be poetry, and sink into a mechanical art. It would be μόρφωσις [shaping], not ποίησις [creating]. The rules of the IMAGINATION are themselves the very powers of growth and production," *The Portable Coleridge,* ed. I.A. Richards (Viking Press, 1969), *Biographia Litteraria,* Ch. XVIII, p.573.

dimensions in space-time. Merely to point to these allusions, however, is not enough: Blake's main purpose is not to interpret the Bible or examine Druidism; he uses biblical along with other historical and literary elements as scaffolding and reinforcements for *Jerusalem*. It is necessary to explain how the various analogies and allusions function in the continuum and contribute to the contexture of the epic's narrative. The particular problem Blake faces belongs to a new space and time, requiring a new solution. It depends on combating the Lockean principles of Reynolds' system and constructing a new system on new principles.

Berkeley throws a clarifying perspective on this task, for in philosophy he had opposed Locke's principles. In his opinion these principles not only introduced doubt into knowledge but also undermined revealed religion. He challenged the supremacy of reason's absolute power, which through abstractions tragically propelled humanity into a region of darkness inhabited by phantoms and ultimately into interminable disputes; he dared to trust the power of the human senses and mind to perceive directly the real qualities of things; he labored mightily to unbind the ligaments struck from the hard rock of reason that chained humankind to earth and to lift it from this lapsed state. He replaced Locke's doctrines by a theory of particular ideas and spiritual causality, a metaphysical principle he faithfully defends at great length in *Siris*.

Berkeley hoped his principles would be conducive to peace since those of natural philosophy were fruitful of controversies but barren of all else. Nevertheless, Locke's philosophy prevailed and found its aesthetic incarnation in Reynolds' system. But Blake, like his cognate spirit, refused to join the dead souls of an abstract world based on reasonings, and like him possessed the mental rigor to contest the empire of natural philosophy, whose machinery was blocking the fountain of human creativity. Blake writes as an artist; he conceives the task of liberating art from the Lockean confines of Reynolds' system, from the moral laws of critics, and at the same time publicly formalizing his principles as awaking the nation from a deadly sleep: the crisis in art becomes a crisis for the nation because its immortality derives from the arts. He carries out this theme in the structure of the narrative. Through various literary devices appropriate to epical action, Blake creates a system on the efficacy of the divine body of human imagination and its visions particularized to ensure the nation's greatness and lasting fame. He thus not only gives epical stature to the conflict in art but also points to the pragmatic value of visionary art.

Besides the external similarity of philosophical principles, Berkeley's criticism of naturalist principles enables us to see how nature-worship by Druids and rejection of spirit recorded in biblical history parallel the doctrines of natural philosophy. The philosophical materials are not simply of general interest as background; they are significant from a literary standpoint. They help to trace a sequence of events through Blake's involuted imagery: Los's labors consist largely of exposing false principles of art based on natural philosophy and their consequences for the nation; denouncing the fallacy of confusing morality with abstract science; liberating human creativity from material forces; unravelling nets of abstract reasonings; opening up the narrowed senses; and, not least, bringing to light the true principles of art based on the sensuous imagination. The artist here performs philosophic functions to undermine the foundations of Reynolds' system.

In addition, numerous actions of characters who adhere to false doctrines are eluciated: for example, folding and unfolding the world through abstract reasonings; severing sense impressions from the active spirit; dismembering the human form; deceptively mingling natural science and divine inspiration; confounding natural religion and imaginative art; infolding art in moral law; diabolically separating the artist from his source of inspirations and his genius, and hence the significance of the motifs cutting, separating, hiding, mingling, wandering. Contingent upon these acts is the meaning of Blake's curious metaphors *female will* and *knife of flint* along with such recurrent images as *non-entity, barrenness, the rock, the void, the veil, the labyrinth.*

The controlling image of the tree branching throughout *Jerusalem* is grounded in natural philosophy: its sapling planted by Bacon, nourished by Newton, cultivated by Locke, and though opposed by Berkeley with his fair tree of knowledge, was brought to full maturity by Reynolds, made into a tree of good and evil by art critics, and subsequently replaced by Blake with his tree of life. As a conflict of systems, the epic is semantically related to concepts of empirical philosophies, without which not only the text must remain vague but also the illustrations continue to be written off either as capricious, in line with opinions of critics in Blake's time, or as arbitrary, essentially independent of the verses, which some present-day critics suggest.[2]

In this epical battle defending himself against charges of absurdity leveled at his works and of madness directed at his character, understandably Blake does not explicitly name Berkeley, who was called a madman and whose works were ridiculed.[3] Difficulties in understanding his philosophy are related directly to his theory of vision, which holds that immediate perception of visible objects is the language of reality. Having rejected externalizations of abstract reasoning, Berkeley kept his expositions close to naked forms. In relying at bottom on the language of vision and minimal discourse, he assured himself he would not be misled by abstract ideas, by words appended to things actually occurring in the mind, which now pass for existents while they obscure particulars. Too much reliance on object language without sufficient explanatory context, however, resulted in density of objects, in vague formulation of thought, and hence in misunderstood meanings.

For similar reasons *Jerusalem* has suffered a similar fate. The poetic argument proceeds almost exclusively by bare and naked ideas perceived by the imagination. This visual quality, as has been shown, is not merely an artistic flourish; it reflects the language of determinate objects and directs the variable meanings of words. The immediacy of perceived forms also accounts for the originality of Blake's works. By dialectical juxtaposition of metaphysical principles Blake presents through visible particulars the principles and social

---

[2] For example, W.J.T. Mitchell considers Blake's illumination "as a picture in a world of pictures," *Blake's Composite Art: A study of the illuminated Poetry* (Princeton University Press, 1978), p.5. From the fact that words and illustrations are "independent modes of expression," p.4), it does not follow they are unrelated in meaning; if they are unrelated, it is difficult to see how a study of the illustrations can be a *guide* to Blake's poetry.

[3] Berkeley's friend Sir John Percival wrote: "I did but name the subject-matter of your book of Principles to some ingenuous friends of mine and they immediately treated it with ridicule, at the same time refusing to read it.... A physician of my acquaintance undertook to describe your person, and argued you must needs be mad, and that you ought to take remedies," *The Works of George Berkeley,* ed. Alexander Campbell Fraser (Oxford, 1801), vol.1, p.xxiii. Additional references: A.A. Luce, *The Life of George Berkeley* (London, 1949), pp.228-229; and Geoffrey Keynes, *A Bibliography of George Berkeley* (Oxford, 1976), pp.vi-vii.

consequences of conflicting systems of art. To avoid the deception of abstract ideas as well as to overpower them, he, like Berkeley, not only indicated the way but in the process himself entered it. Both men, seeking to transmit their visions directly and objectively through naked forms, became too subjective and remote, and in Blake's case, according to critics, immoral. So while they disentangled themselves from the net of abstract ideas, at the same time they entangled their readers in another kind of net, one of exacting style and obscure meanings. It is a critical irony that readers found incoherent those very works in which the authors implementing a theory of direct communication based on a universal principle labored to disencumber men from the deception of words.

Berkeley's theory of vision gave a daring interpretation to knowledge and concomitantly provided new philosophical foundations for revealed religion together with a humane morality within *empiricism*. He reformulated its principles, making perceived particulars the effects of human spirit, which alone can act. Blake in his unique way complements this philosophy by extending spiritual perception into art, equating spirit and imagination, thus bestowing a new and vital quality on the imagination, making it at once divine, universal, creative, visionary, individual, eternal. He also introduces a new kind of epic into English literature; he moulds his perceptions into a free-verse poem patterned on the fourfold gospel. This form conveys the profundity and scope of his subject, demonstrates his theory of divine inspiration, and suggests an analogue to attacks upon his art. Blake refused to emulate "either Greek or Roman Models" of epic,[4] or submit to Reynolds' naturalist system. Intensely sensitive to the social significance and timeless character of art to express eternal human values, Blake places art upon spiritual foundations, intrinsically relating artist, works, and society. He continues the gospel tradition; yet he never forgets that his visions belong intimately to his own time. He gives a new historical dimension to the law of spirit, identifying it with the human imagination and subsuming art under its power in the context of empirical philosophies. Though he and Berkeley were committed to traditional Christian values, neither was conventional in his view of the world. The same radical empiricism, the same human orientation, the same expansiveness of

---

[4] Blake, *Milton*, "Preface," p.480.

EPILOGUE

vision characterizes their outlook. Both men perceived the metaphysical complexities of reality; to them the world is more humanly profound than any materialist theory or any abstract system can explain.

By incremental stages in the light of Berkeley's principles *Jerusalem* reveals what Blake means by "Imagination, the Divine Body" and acquires coherence and unity consistent with the whole poem. Blake's "Tree of Life" unites kindly with Berkeley's philosophical tree, variously disclosing itself in words and helping to articulate a number of visual forms, notwithstanding the maddening, that is, the inspired degree to which Blake's creative imagination allegorizes, personifies, synthesizes, and combines ideas of others with his own both in his verbal and visionary forms to enrich the theme by contrasts as well as by similarities.[5] As an epic narrating a war in art, *Jerusalem* is independent of other works, either philosophical or literary. Blake is doing something new and difficult: making creative use of Old Testament history, of prophetic, apocalyptic and Gospel traditions, of Christian myth, and of empirical philosophy, all united in his imagination. His spiritual authority derives from the Bible, his philosophical support comes from Berkeley, and his aesthetic authority emanates from himself. Despite the immense accumulation of diverse ideas, despite the rush and sweep of incidents and episodes, despite the seemingly confused narrative, there is an inner structure progressing from the destruction of Reynolds' system to the creation of a new system based on reality of particulars perceived by the imagination. All that we see in *Jerusalem* ultimately is owing to this metaphysical principle, which allows us to enter into Blake's visions and perceive the depth of this representations.

The results of this historical and philosophical study it is hoped may not only contribute to understanding Blake's last and longest work, enhancing the reader's aesthetic experience of it, but also open up access to his other works, for poets and artists embody their

---

[5] This is not to say that Berkeley's philosophy is the *cause* of *Jerusalem;* rather, his system of knowledge is related to Blake's system of art logically by similarity of principles. This fact does not subtract from either Blake's genius or the poem's artful structure. A poet who transforms into an epic a philosophical system, giving it a new dimension, creates the highest species of poetry: Dante is no less a poet for incorporating in the *Divina Commedia* the philosophy of Aquinas' *Summa Theologiae,* nor Lucretius for poeticizing Epicurean philosophy in *De Natura Rerum.*

metaphysics in many different ways depending on subject matter and purpose. The detailed examination of *Jerusalem* makes clear that Blake does not reject either nature, or reason, or bodies, as is often supposed; he replaces corporeal powers with spiritual or imaginative powers; abstract reasoning with perceived particulars; and abstract ideas with particular ideas. In its most significant aspect, however, the present study reveals that Blake was the first to associate the human imagination with the modern philosophical concept of cause, an association that has proved singularly fruitful. He created an epic not merely to justify his own practices in art but to present a system based on imagination. This fundamental principle has retained its eminent place in all creativity: Blake's causal principle is also ours.

INDEX

Abomination of Desolation, 44, 62, 173
Abstract forms/ideas, 5, 9, 18, 20, 26, 29, 42, 46, 81, 86, 110, 122-3, 127, 150, 158, 201-2
────── generalization, 63-6 *passim*, 127
────── reasoning, 28, 43-6, 52-3, 64, 74-5, 91-2, 110-1, 116, 134, 159, 163, 177, 184, 198, 210; *see also* Reason
Abstraction, 8, 17-8, 31, 38, 44, 50, 61-6 *passim*, 71, 103, 107, 111, 129, 142, 152-3, 165-7, 171, 185, 200-2, 205
Adam, 91, 117-8; and Eve, 50
Adams, Hazard, 35n
Adulterine method, 73
Agreement or disagreement of ideas, 18, 29, 168
Albion and art, 37, 39
Albion's role in the epic: his armies, 52, 180; beauty and perfection, 50; children (creations), 52, 66; crucifixion, 55; daughters, 41, 46, 95, 113, 147, 158, 160-5 *passim*, 191-2; delusions, 110-12; disease, 39, 108-9, 130; Emanation, 39; fall, 40, 50, 56, 63, 117-8, 142, 154, 182-3, 191; mountains, 39, 41, 75; sacrifice, 53-4, 56; sin and shame, 50, 54, 56; skirts, 108, 110, 125; Spectre, 80, 82, 100, 103, 110, 119; sons, 41, 86, 91, 102-3, 126, 129, 134, 142, 147, 169, 182, 199; struggle to uplift himself, 54-6, 143; tents, 45; tomb, 94, 170, 205; tree, 53, 63, 83, 102, 140, 159, 162-3, 179, 185, 211; universities, 41; waking and regeneration, 206-9; war, 35, 40-1, 59, 74, 98, 100, 110, 132, 159; war-song, 160; zoa, 171-2, 209
All, the, 119-20, 160
Apollyon, 87
Aristotle, 6, 45n, 60n, 73
Armstrong, Paul B., 24n
Art: and metaphysics, 1, 3, 24, 223-4; and science, 22-3, 38, 116, 145, 159, 179, 192, 195, 202; systems in opposition, 35-214
Ascending and descending, 129, 135
Aschenbrenner, Karl, 84n
Atheism, 31, 40, 59, 72-3, 103

Babel, 66, 75
Babylon, 75-6, 112
Bacon, Francis, 23, 46, 59-64, 71, 74, 92, 129, 214, 220
────── *The Advancement of Learning*, 60; *Novum Organum*, 60
"Bacon & Newton & Locke," 23, 143, 161, 168, 204, 209
Bare and naked forms/ideas, 52, 106, 116, 123-4, 146, 158; *see also* Particulars
Bath, 130

225

INDEX

Beauty, 21, 26, 29, 38, 42, 53, 116, 128, 202, 211; and perfection, 45, 88, 95
Became what they beheld, 115, 161
Bentley, G.E., Jr., 2n, 13n, 17n, 117n
Berkeley, George, 2-13, 27-9, 31-2, 36-47 *passim*, 52, 54, 64, 67, 72-7 *passim*, 80-5 *passim*, 90-2, 96-7, 102, 105, 110-1, 116-24 *passim*, 129, 133, 140, 142, 149, 161, 163, 169, 172, 177-8, 191, 197, 200-1, 211-2, 217-223
────── *Alciphron*, 44n; *Essay on the Ruin of Great Britain*, 37; *On Eternal Life*, 12n; *A New Theory of Vision*, 52, 122; *The Principles of Human Knowledge*, 3, 27-8, 73, 149, 217; *Propagation of the Gospel*, 12, 81n; *Siris*, 2-13, 27-9, 31-2, 36-7, 54, 64, 67, 73, 86, 90, 120, 123, 140, 142, 149, 160, 180, 182, 190, 197, 205, 207, 217-220 *passim; Three Dialogues between Hylas and Philonous*, 73
Berkeley and Blake vs Plato, 4-13
Beulah, 85, 89, 98, 133, 167; daughters of, 86, 133, 135, 151, 170, 190
Biblical analogy, 36-7, 99-100, 193
Binding, 45, 152-3, 163-5, 189, 195
Blake, William: *Annotations to Berkeley*, 1-12; *Annotations to Reynolds*, 23-6; *Epitome of Hervey's Meditations*, 68n; *Grave Illustrations*, 32; *Island in the Moon*, 14; *Jerusalem*, 14-224; *Leonora designs*, 30; *Marriage of Heaven and Hell*, 1, 117n; *Milton*, 32, 67n; *Night Thoughts drawings*, 30; *Song of Los*, 8
Bodies, 96-7, 134, 143
Bowlahoola, 171
Brain, heart and bowels, 92
Burke, Edmund, 23 and n14

Cambel, 163, 185-9
Cathedron, 151, 171
Causality, 9, 66-70 *passim*, 75, 82, 86-7, 100, 112, 122, 133, 169, 180, 209, 224; a metaphysical issue, 3, 24-5, 28, 48, 96, 120; *see also*, Material forces; Spirit
Chain, the, 159, 161, 211
Chastity, 81, 144, 152, 186, 205
Cherub, the, 91
Childhood, Manhood & Age, 93, 210
Children, 66
Christianity, 14n, 54
Christian myth, 36, 146, 159
Christians, 177; and Jews, 99-100
Circumcision, 145
Circumscribing, 164, 199
Clouds, 91
Coban, 62, 73
Coban, Hand and Hyle, 59, 73-5, 80-5 *passim*, 90-1, 98, 107, 115, 121-2, 134-5, 143, 167, 204, 209; Emanations of, 146-7, 197
Constable, John, 26
Contracting and expanding, 119-20, 125, 144
Contraries, 97, 134, 159, 209
Corporeal bodies, *see* Material forces
Couch of repose, 132-3
Covers, 54, 202, 210
Creation of a system, 84-215
Creation, Redemption & Judgment, 115
Creativity, 106-7, 112-3, 118, 125, 142, 146, 157, 165, 167, 172, 178-9, 193-6, 200, 224; *see also* Spirit
Critics, 17, 30, 50, 56, 83, 90, 95, 104-7 *passim*, 154, 162, 167, 183-4, 188, 197-9, 205
Curran, Stuart, 35n
Curtain, 146, 212
Cutting, 161-5 *passim*, 184, 199

Damon, Foster S., 62n, 98n
Darkness, 40, 43, 55-6, 68, 72, 76-7, 98, 119, 134-5, 159, 192, 194, 206
Dead, the, 84
Deism/Deists, 139, 149, 161, 183
DeLuca, V.A., 103n
Demonstration, 22, 61, 63, 74, 76, 100, 102, 108, 145, 147, 160-1, 200-1
Despair, 76, 82-3, 107-8, 125, 128, 161
Dinah, 85, 172
Discourses on Art, *see* Reynolds

226

INDEX

Disputes, 40, 72, 84
Divine inspiration, 35, 48, 80, 83, 88, 98, 134, 211; Reynolds' view, 20, 22, 128, 144, 199, 211
Divine Vision, 50, 75, 83, 89, 92, 111-2, 121, 124, 142, 151, 206
Doskow, Minna, 35n
Doubt, 30, 56, 76, 83, 102, 115, 128
Dreams, 40, 126, 143, 205, 207
Druidism, 54-6, 159, 161, 183

Eaves, Morris, 1n, 96n
Eden, 41, 50, 89, 102
Elohim, 70, 111
Emanation, 40
Embraces, 168, 214
Empathy, 195
Empiricism, 2-4, 7, 13, 177, 222
Energy, 118, 127-8
Enitharmon, 82, 92, 104-5, 290, 194-8
Enthusiasm, 19-20, 25, 83
Entuthon-Benython, 76
Epicureans, 163
Erdman, David V., 2n, 33n, 56n, 85n, 147n
Erin, 85, 94, 133-5, 159, 170. 172, 180, 194, 197, 205, 207, 212
Error, 72- 102-3, 118, 121, 125, 130, 199
Eternal: death, 9, 77, 90, 103, 128, 161, 191, 205; life, 39, 143, 206; prophet, 173; zoa, 209; *see also* Immortality
Eternity, 90, 121, 144, 193, 206-7, 210
Existence, 5-6, 27, 93, 118, 120-1, 127, 163, 167, 183
Ezekiel, 68, 89

Fall of nations, 37-8
Female will, 113, 146, 194
Fetters, 33, 37-8, 211
Fleshy tabernacle, 146
Folding and unfolding the earth, 158, 190
Forgiveness, 128, 135, 139, 154, 107, 207
Fourfold, 36, 89, 207-12 *passim*
Fraser, Alexander, 4
Freedom/free power, 41, 68, 127-8, 142, 178
Frosh, Thomas, xii
Frye, Northrop, 1n, 89n

Gainsborough, Thomas, 21, 25-6
General: forms, 29, 93, 100, 107, 127-8, 153, 201-2; names, 117-8, 122-3; nature, 201; truth, 38
Generation, 80, 89-90, 106, 150, 164-5, 198
Genius, 20-2, 24, 35, 37, 83, 92, 193, 196, 199-200
Gibbon, Edward, 140
Gilchrist, Alexander, 65
Globe of blood, 162, 194
God, 10-11, 39, 113, 118, 120, 126, 152-3, 160, 178, 182, 200, 207; driver in a chariot, 121; eyes of, 87; finger of, 87, 124; hand of, 64-5, 87; *see also* Jesus
Golgonooza, 88-91, 140, 167, 170
Good and evil, 45, 145
Gospel, the, 12, 35-6, 39, 55, 89, 94, 170, 209, 222; the First, 37, 48; Second, 99, 106; Third, 139; Fourth, 177
Grain of sand, 121
Gravitation, 63, 68
Gwendolen, 163, 185-9

Hand, 65-8, 73-4, 83, 98, 113-4, 150, 164, 169, 199; *see also* "Coban, Hand and Hyle"
Hand of God, 64-5, 87
Hard rock, the, 59, 75, 84, 106, 161, 199, 209
Harmony, 41, 82, 85
Harper, George Mills, 2n, 12n, 14n
Hayley, William, 31, 95
Head & heart & loins, 152, 159
Heaven and hell, 134-5, 179
Heavenly Canaan, 168
Hermaphroditic, the, 111-2, 149-50, 157, 173, 180, 198, 200
Hoopner, John, 30
Human dragon, the, 198
—— forms, 50, 93-4, 112; *see also* Bare and Naked forms; Particulars
Humanity vs inhumanity, 40, 47-9, 53-4, 80, 89, 103, 106-7, 126, 130, 150, 183, 186; 206
Human senses, 71-2, 89

227

INDEX

Hume, David, 140
Hunt, Leigh, 168
Hyle, 73-4, 87, 135, 150, 164, 185, 188, 199; *see also* "Coban, Hand and Hyle"

Ideas, theory of: Berkeley, 5-6, 27, 97, 120-1, 143; Locke, 18, 71; Plato, 4-5
Identity, 128, 212
The Iliad, 33, 35, 144n
Imagination, 7, 12, 23, 26-7, 30, 33, 43, 49, 55, 82-3, 88, 90, 93-4, 100, 106, 115, 120-1, 125, 128, 133, 142, 147, 152, 167, 178, 193, 199, 209-12, 214, 224
Imitation, 17, 21, 49-50
Immortality, 12, 80, 150, 173, 178, 212, 214; *see also* Eternal life
Indefinite, the, 102, 145, 162, 198
Infant, 66
Infant loves, 50, 53, 66; *see also* Children
Innate ideas, 18, 21, 29
Inner garment, 161-2
Invention, 20
Isis, 140, 149

Jackson, M., 56n, 96n
Jehovah, 99, 132, 212
Jerusalem: epic, 33, 35; structure, 35, 36, 124, 132; theme, 39, 172; visual and verbal forms in minute particulars, 88, 98, 132-3, 193, 198, 210
Jerusalem (character), 39, 46, 74, 80, 94, 130, 132, 152, 182, 207; and Albion, 99, 104, 108; and humanity, 49, 53-4; and Mary, 153-4; and Vala, 48-50, 100, 108, 130, 183-4, 198; as art, 53, 56; as harlot daughter, 74, 108; as liberty, 68, 142; restored, 211, 214
Jersualem's daughters, 39; sons, 163, 169
Jerusalem Delivered, 94n
Jessop, T. E., 2n, 4n
Jesus, 12, 43, 146, 173, 204, 206-7; the Christ, 119, 199; God of fire and Lord of Love, 36-7, 67-8; Lamb of God, 99
Job, 50

Keynes, Sir Geoffrey, 2n
King Lear, 191n
Kiralis, Karl, 93n
Knife, the, 161-3, 184
Knowledge, 8-10, 18-9, 25, 29, 60-1, 63-5, 70-2, 87, 179, 201
Know not what, 71; and why, 96-7

Labyrinth, 19n, 102-3, 110, 161, 177
Language of vision, *see* Bare and naked forms; Particulars; Vision
Lapsed state of humankind, 31
Length, breadth and height, 93, 124, 204
Liberty, *see* Freedom
Life, 11-2, 83, 179, 209
Light, 77, 192, 206-7, 214
Limits, 117-8, 125-6, 171
Living, the, 80-1, 84
Locke, John, 18, 29, 42, 47, 70-4, 87, 92, 97, 100, 103, 107, 113, 139, 163, 188, 192, 217, 220; *see also* Newton and Locke
—— *Essay Concerning Human Understanding,* 18, 70-4, 217
London, 191-2
Looms: of Enitharmon, 151, 171; of Locke, 41, 185-6
Los: creator of a system, 84, 88-9, 171; defender of imagination, 77, 206; demon of the furnaces, 83-4, 151; divine smith, 83, 214; son of man, 206; spirit of prophecy, 125, 129
Los's role in the epic: anticipation of Jerusalem's return, 193; apostrophe to art, 189; army, 88, 94; buildings, 80, 92; children (creations), 83, 93, 95, 197; counter-attacks, 119, 126, 200-1; daughters, 92, 151, 194; demonstrations, 200; Emanation, 82; fighting addresses to his sons, 126-9, 204; forge, 142; furnaces, 126, 151; gate, 121; globe of fire, 77, 106, 192, 207; human perfection, 80; sons, 89, 92, 194; Spectre, 77-8, 80-4, 95, 191; victory, 210, 212
Love: false and generating, 95, 119, 155, 162, 165, 184, 197; spiritual, 48, 52, 128, 186, 198, 207

INDEX

Luvah, 52, 135, 150-1, 159-61, 184; and Albion, 105, 184; *see also* Vala and Luvah

Macbeth, 191n
Machinery, 33, 60, 63, 84, 103, 147, 195, 214
Malone, Edmond, 23n, 68
Man, 12, 47-9, 82, 93, 95-7, 105-6, 110, 113, 116, 130, 142, 146, 157-8, 161, 196, 207, 210
Material forces/powers/substance, 18, 28, 39-46, 53, 61, 63, 71-5, 81-2, 84, 91, 95-7, 102, 105, 107, 110, 113-6, 125, 134, 152, 188, 205, 207; *see also* Causality
Mates, Benson, 27n
Matter, *see* Material forces
Mellor, Anne K., 85n
Memory, 18, 20, 110
Merlin, 114-5
Metaphysical principles: Berkeley and Blake, 29, 120, 123; Berkeley vs Locke, 25-6, 28; Blake vs Reynolds, 24, 29, 107, 116, 146, 196; Locke and Reynolds, 18-20, 110, 147
Milton, John, 41
Mind, 5-7, 18, 20, 72, 110, 120-1, 127, 147, 159; *see also* Spirit
Mingling art, demonstrative science, natural philosophy and religion, 140, 149-51, 160, 185-8
Minute particulars, 88, 100, 106-8, 127-8, 167; *see also* Particulars
Morality, 154, 207; vs art, 108, 164, 186
Murder, 44, 74, 107, 154, 158, 165, 184, 200-2, 205

Natural morality/virtue, 20, 56, 139, 161, 167, 186, 205
_____ philosophy, 32, 37-8, 40, 52, 59-66 *passim,* 74, 103, 107, 113-5, 167, 184, 220
_____ religion, 56, 106, 132, 140, 147, 149, 160-1, 169, 185; vs spiritual religion, 128
Nature, 8, 20, 22, 60-1, 70, 113, 143, 169; deified, 52, 56

Negation/negatives, 42-44, 73, 97-8, 144
Net, the, 124-6, 130, 134, 158, 183, 199
New Testament, 36, 49, 52, 94, 99, 133
Newton, Sir Isaac, 8n, 18, 29, 36, 42, 63-74 *passim,* 87, 92, 100, 113-4, 192, 203, 220; and Locke, 8-9, 11, 23, 113; *see also* "Bacon & Newton & Locke"
_____ *Principia,* 42, 63-4, 70
Nineveh, 66, 74
Non-entity, 42-3, 97-8, 108, 146

Old Testament, 36, 94, 99, 133
One, the, 10, 82, 119
Orc, 91
Orlando Furioso, 92
Ostriker, Alicia, 85n, 96n
Oxford, 130, 132

Paley, Morton, 35n, 39n, 89n, 117n, 118n
Paradise Lost, 33, 35, 50n, 82, 90, 91n, 153n, 168n
Particulars, 26, 28-9, 88, 94, 123-4, 128, 142, 145, 191, 199, 209, 211; Reynolds' view, 21, 25, 116, 201-2; *see also* Minute particulars
Peace, 41, 84-5, 129, 210
Perception, *see* Existence; Spirit
Perceptive organs, 115-6
Phantom, 39-40, 113, 144
Plato, 4-14, 17, 24, 26n, 73
Platonism, 1, 4, 21n
Pride, 81, 90, 110-1, 154, 173
Principles: false, 23, 42, 72, 84, 92, 122, 125, 128, 192; true, 92, 210-2
Proclus, 4, 54
Prometheus Bound, 80n, 83n
Pythagoreans, 14-5

Rahab, 56, 139, 169, 173, 180, 185; and Tirzah, 163-4, 173-4
Raine, Kathleen, 2n
Reactor, the, 104
Reality, 5, 10, 14, 25, 107, 121-4 *passim,* 153
Reason/reasoning, 2-4, 8, 14, 17-9, 29, 38-9, 59, 63-6, 70-1, 76, 81-3, 97, 102, 110-1, 115, 130, 143, 147, 153, 171, 201; spurious, 43, 46, 73, 91, 132

229

INDEX

Redemption, 32
Regeneration, 77, 80
Resurrection, 155, 193
Reuben, 113-5, 170, 189
Revealed religion/revelation, 19, 72, 102-3, 140, 153
Reynolds, Sir Joshua, 19-33 *passim*, 37-9, 41-53 *passim*, 59-60, 66, 68, 73-7 *passim*, 84, 90-5 *passim*, 100, 103-7, 110, 113, 116, 127-8, 144, 152-3, 163, 179, 186, 190, 192, 196-206 *passim*, 211, 217-23 *passim*; and Locke, 19-23
———— *Discourses on Art*, 19-23, 68, 80, 201, 217-8
Robinson, Henry Crabb, 73n
Rousseau, Jean-Jacques, 139, 161
Royal Academy, 19, 32, 37, 41
Rules, 20-1, 37-8, 53, 61, 63, 68, 70, 77, 107, 144, 153, 162, 170, 196, 211

Satan, 117-8, 125
Scepticism, 32, 40, 73, 102
Selfhood/self-righteousness, 81, 91, 110, 125, 130, 198
Sensible appearances, 116-7
Separating, 50, 81, 105, 112, 151, 161, 172, 183, 194-5, 199
Serpent, 185
Setting free, 77, 180
Sexual: as epithet, 105; hermaphroditic, 111; love, 143; machine, 129-30; organization, 106, 116, 142, 165; religion, 105-6; threefold vs human fourfold, 193
Shadows, 9, 53, 104-5, 120, 169
Shakespeare, William, 41
Simplicity, 100, 202
Sin, 49, 54, 185; and jealousy, 103; and shame, 50, 74, 163; *see also* Albion's sin
Siris, *see* Berkeley
Skofield, 98, 150, 164
Socrates, 24n, 204
Spaces of Erin, 85-6, 88, 98, 190, 207
Space-time, 86, 133, 193; abstract, 42-3, 53, 86, 110

Spectre, the, 43-4 and n20, 46, 115, 143, 147, 158, 197, 209; and Vala, 159; *see also* Albion's Spectre; Los's Spectre
Spirit, 6-7, 27-8, 30, 35-7, 41, 43-4, 47-8, 50, 52, 55, 64, 72-3, 80-3, 85, 88-9, 96-7, 118, 121, 126, 132-5, 146, 157, 160, 167, 169, 178-9, 191-2, 200, 206, 209, 212; acts of, 32-3, 94, 133; Locke's view, 71, 157; separation from the human form, 47-8, 161
Spiritual fourfold, 35-6, 49, 89, 170; vs sexual threefold, 193
———— perception, 24, 26, 45, 50, 77, 80-2, 84, 93, 100, 142, 157, 170-1
———— power/substance, *see* Spirit
States, 117-8, 135, 171
Stubborn structure of the language, 122-5
Style, grand vs ornamental, 100, 193
Sublime, the, 25, 59, 73, 120-1, 201, 210; Reynolds' view, 100
Swedenborg, 1, 92n, 117
System: Berkeley's, 84-6, 125; Blake's, 84-6, 90, 124, 152; Locke's, 18-9, 110; Newton's 86, 111; Reynolds' 20-2, 59, 84, 90, 110, 127, 149, 169, 172-3, 198, 218

Thomson, James, 49n
Threefold, 90n, 209
Tirzah, *see* Rahab
Tree: of good and evil, 83, 211; knowledge, 60, 63, 70, 73-4, 83; life, 211; *see also* Albion's tree
Trinity: demonic, 62, 65, 74, 132; Holy, 59, 178-9
Trusler, Dr. John, 29

Ulro, 39, 41, 55-6, 62, 74-5, 84, 89, 91 104, 115, 125-6, 129-30, 144, 211-2
Uncircumcision, 81, 106, 129, 152
Universal language, *see* Vision
Universality of art, 43
Universals, 107, 127, 199
Urizen, 91, 121, 125, 150, 159, 161
Urthona, 104-5, 150

230

INDEX

Vala, 46, 56, 135, 149, 158-6, 180, 184; and Albion, 52, 104-5, 108, 112, 184; and Luvah, 80, 105, 155, 184; deified, 52-3, 75, 105, 112, 140, 173; *see also* Jerusalem and Vala

Vala's temple, 149; veil, 46-7, 53-5, 126, 144, 151, 158, 167, 199

Vegetative universe, the, 90, 140

Vengeance, 55

Virgin form, 129-30

Virtue, 139, 201; *see also* Natural virtue

Vis, 63, 178

Vision, 122-4, 210-1; single, 142

Visionary forms, 32, 92, 203, 210-1; Reynolds' view, 24, 171

Void, the, 43, 53, 91, 129, 150, 182

Voltaire, Francois Arouet de, 139, 161

Vortexes, 133

Wanderers: artists, 53; Enitharmon and Los, 194; Jerusalem, 53; Reuben, 170

Weaving, 158, 163, 185-6, 190-1

Wheels: of Albion's sons, 74, 86-7, 89, 135; Eden, 41; Newton, 41

Wilson, Richard, 21

Worm, 157-8, 183

Wuellner, Wilhelm, H., 54n